全国翻译专业本科系列教材

A COURSE IN CHINESE-ENGLISH PASSAGE TRANSLATION
汉英语篇翻译教程

蒋　林　丛书主编
印晓红　编著

清华大学出版社
北　京

内 容 简 介

本教材基于语篇翻译的概念，选取了具有代表性的各类文本素材，注重培养学生的翻译实战能力。本教材分上、中、下三篇，共12个单元。上篇从翻译标准、翻译过程、中英语言差异和文化差异入手，探讨翻译的相关概念；中篇侧重实用翻译，从商务广告、企业介绍、旅游文本和科技文本入手，探究实用类文本的语言特点和英译要点；下篇为非实用翻译，包括小说、散文、诗歌和英语专业八级考试中的汉译英真题，探究文学类文本的语言特点和英译要点。

本教材的目标读者为学习汉英翻译课程的普通高等院校翻译专业和英语专业学生，以及爱好翻译的非英语专业人士。

版权所有，侵权必究。举报：010-62782989，beiqinquan@tup.tsinghua.edu.cn。

图书在版编目（CIP）数据

汉英语篇翻译教程/印晓红编著. —北京：清华大学出版社，2017（2021.2重印）
（全国翻译专业本科系列教材/蒋林主编）
ISBN 978-7-302-46170-8

Ⅰ.①汉… Ⅱ.①印… Ⅲ.①英语-翻译-高等学校-教材 Ⅳ.①H315.9

中国版本图书馆CIP数据核字（2017）第007875号

责任编辑：刘　艳
封面设计：平　原
责任校对：王凤芝
责任印制：杨　艳

出版发行：清华大学出版社
网　　址：http:// www. tup. com. cn，http:// www. wqbook. com
地　　址：北京清华大学学研大厦A座　　邮　编：100084
社 总 机：010-62770175　　邮　购：010-62786544
投稿与读者服务：010-62776969，c-service@tup.tsinghua.edu.cn
质量反馈：010-62772015，zhiliang@tup.tsinghua.edu.cn

印 装 者：北京九州迅驰传媒文化有限公司
经　　销：全国新华书店
开　　本：170mm×230mm　　印　张：13.25　　字　数：200千字
版　　次：2017年3月第1版　　印　次：2021年2月第5次印刷
定　　价：59.00元

产品编号：065300-04

前　　言

随着翻译专业的设立,我国翻译人才的培养机制变得更加完善。与其他的外语专业不同,翻译专业更注重翻译人才的应用性、专门性和特殊性。但由于该专业设立时间不长,目前国内出版的专门针对本科翻译专业的教材数量较少。现有的学术研究型教材或大众类翻译考试用书又多适合研究生使用,难以满足本科翻译专业教材建设的需求。正是基于这样的背景,本教材应运而生。

在学习过程中学生会发现自己面对的翻译任务往往以语篇为主,小到一个段落,大到一篇文章,而且不同类型的文本在翻译时需要注意的内容也各不相同。在翻译过程中,除了要把握原文的文体和风格之外,还要厘清文章的脉络和层次、衔接关系、连贯关系及内在逻辑关系。"翻译的直接对象是原文语篇,翻译的最终产品是译文语篇"(王东风,1998)。语篇作为意义和结构的统一体,在意义上具有连贯性和完整性,在结构上具有衔接性。因此,在翻译过程中只有从语篇层面进行操作,以语篇为单位,才能把原文的信息更好地传达给译文读者,从而顺利达到交际的目的,并使译文结构严谨、行文流畅、语气贯通。本教材正是从语篇着手,结合最新的典型材料对不同类型的语篇文本进行讲解,让初次接触汉英翻译的学生在语篇翻译中提高汉译英的实战能力。

本教材分上、中、下三篇,共12个单元。上篇从翻译标准、翻译过程、中英语言差异和文化差异入手,讲解翻译的相关概念;中篇侧重实用翻译,从商务广告、企业介绍、旅游文本和科技文本入手,探讨它们的语言特点和翻译要点,并阐述其翻译手法;下篇为非实用翻译,包括小说、散文、诗歌和英语专业八级考试的汉译英真题,介绍此类文本的外译情况,并分析其翻译要点,从而让学生更好地掌握文学翻译的内容。各单元均以两个语篇为例,对不同类型的文本翻译进行具体阐释。每个语篇包含原文、译前提示、参考译文和译文注释四大部分。同时,每个单元均配有相应的课后练习，以帮助学生巩固已有的知识，不断提高其翻译能力。当然，本教材提供的参考译文不是唯一，也不一定是最好的。教师和学生可以以教材中的参考译文为基础，不断修改和润色。此外，为帮助学生更好地掌握翻译的基本知识，各单元的翻译加油站还有关于翻译策略、翻译方法和翻译技巧的讲解，例子以句子为主，供初次接触汉英翻译的学生参照学习。

本教材从语篇翻译的概念出发，收集具有代表性的不同文体的素材和最新的材料，讲解语篇翻译中的各个注意事项。目标读者为初次接触汉英翻译课程的普通高等院校翻译专业和英语专业本科生，以及爱好翻译的非英语专业人士。希望在学习本教材后，读者能够掌握常见文体的汉译英方法，切实提高自己的翻译能力。

在编写过程中，编者参阅了大量已有的科研成果，也参考了一些网站的信息，借此机会表示感谢。同时，感谢浙江师范大学外国语学院翻译系各位同人的鼓励和支持，感谢浙江师范大学对本教材的经费支持。另外，本书得到了清华大学出版社的大力支持，特别是责任编辑刘艳老师付出了大量的心血，在此一并深表感谢！

由于编写时间较短，编者水平有限，错误、缺点在所难免，敬请各位专家和广大读者批评指正。

印晓红
2016年9月

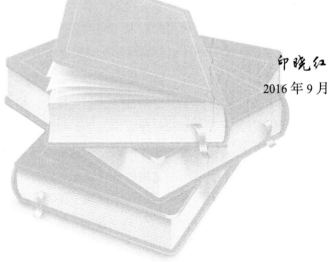

目　　录

上篇
译事探究

第一章　翻译的标准 2
　　名家名说 2
　　翻译语篇1　雨雪时候的星辰 5
　　翻译语篇2　二马（节选） 9
　　翻译加油站　语篇与翻译 12
　　课后练习 16

第二章　翻译的过程 17
　　名家名说 17
　　翻译语篇1　我们的女子教育（节选） 21
　　翻译语篇2　儒林外史（节选） 24
　　翻译加油站　翻译策略：归化与异化 28
　　课后练习 30

第三章　汉英语言差异 31
　　名家名说 31
　　翻译语篇1　竹马（节选） 33
　　翻译语篇2　母亲的微笑（节选） 36
　　翻译加油站　翻译方法：直译和意译 40
　　课后练习 42

第四章 中西文化差异 43
- 名家名说 44
- 翻译语篇1 祝福（节选） 47
- 翻译语篇2 我不愿做女孩儿（节选） 50
- 翻译加油站 翻译技巧（一）：选词 53
- 课后练习 57

中篇
实 用 翻 译

第五章 商务广告的翻译 60
- 翻译语篇1 63
- 翻译语篇2 65
- 翻译加油站 翻译技巧（二）：增词法 69
- 课后练习 73

第六章 企业介绍的翻译 74
- 翻译语篇1 78
- 翻译语篇2 中国北京同仁堂集团公司进出口公司 80
- 翻译加油站 翻译技巧（三）：减词法 84
- 课后练习 88

第七章 旅游文本的翻译 89
- 翻译语篇1 乌镇——中国最后的枕水人家 94
- 翻译语篇2 杭州——人间天堂 98
- 翻译加油站 翻译技巧（四）：词类转换 102
- 课后练习 105

第八章　科技文本的翻译 106
翻译语篇 1　磁悬浮列车：走什么样的道路（节选）................ 109
翻译语篇 2　宇宙中的生命 112
翻译加油站　翻译技巧（五）：语态转换 115
课后练习 118

下篇
非实用翻译

第九章　小说翻译 122
翻译语篇 1　三体·周文王·长夜（节选）................................ 128
翻译语篇 2　红楼梦（节选）... 133
翻译加油站　翻译技巧（六）：语序的调整 138
课后练习 141

第十章　散文翻译 143
翻译语篇 1　珍珠鸟（节选）... 147
翻译语篇 2　落花生 150
翻译加油站　翻译技巧（七）：区分主从 156
课后练习 158

第十一章　诗歌翻译 160
翻译语篇 1　黄鹤楼送孟浩然之广陵 164
翻译语篇 2　青青河畔草 167
翻译加油站　翻译技巧（八）：长句的翻译 170
课后练习 174

第十二章 专八汉译英 176

    翻译语篇 1 178

    翻译语篇 2 180

    翻译语篇 3 182

    翻译语篇 4 182

    翻译语篇 5 183

    翻译语篇 6 184

    翻译语篇 7 185

    翻译语篇 8 186

    翻译语篇 9 186

    翻译语篇 10 187

    翻译语篇 11 188

    翻译语篇 12 188

    翻译语篇 13 189

    翻译语篇 14 190

    课后练习 190

参考答案 192

参考文献 201

上篇

译事探究

第一章
翻译的标准

翻译过程中，翻译实践应遵循何种标准？品评译文时，应以何种标准衡量译文的得失？何种译文方为好的译文？这些恐怕是翻译界一再讨论的问题。的确，翻译标准历来是翻译工作者和翻译研究者讨论与关注的话题，是指导翻译实践的准则，也是衡量译文好坏的尺度。在这一核心问题上，中外名家众说纷纭，莫衷一是。早在1790年，英国翻译家泰特勒（A. F. Tytler）在《论翻译的原理》一书中，就提出了翻译的三原则：一、译文应完全复写出原文的思想；二、译文的风格和笔调应与原文的性质相同；三、译文应和原文同样流畅。此外，苏联翻译理论家费道罗夫的"等值翻译论"、美国著名翻译理论家尤金·奈达（Eugene A. Nida）的"动态对等"和"功能对等"以及英国著名翻译理论家彼得·纽马克（Peter Newmark）的"文本中心论"等在中国都引起了较多关注。就国内而言，诸多名家也提出了自己的翻译见解，较有影响力的包括严复、傅雷、朱生豪和钱锺书等人。

名家名说

∽ 严复的"信达雅"

说到翻译标准，自然会提到我国近代著名翻译家和翻译理论家严复。1898年，严复（1933）在《天演论》的《译例言》中提到："译事三难信达雅。"[1] 一般而言，"信"主要指译文应忠实准确；"达"是指译文的通顺流畅；"雅"指的是文字的古雅。严复的翻译标准对中国翻译界产生了重大影响，直到今天我们还在探讨他的"信达雅"标准。

这三大标准中，"雅"经常被人诟病，被认为没有遵循的必要。笔者以为，严复生活在文言文时代，认为译文必须古雅，自然无可厚非。但如今的"雅"，就不应再局限于"古雅"的原义，而应该从具体的语境着手分析，尽量让译文的语言风格与原文相似。这应该是译者在翻译过程中要努力达到的目标之一。

1　（英）赫胥黎.1933.天演论.严复，译.上海：商务印书馆.

◈ 傅雷的"神似"

傅雷（1951）在《高老头》重译本《序》的开篇就提出："以效果而论，翻译应当像临画一样，所求的不在形似而在神似。"² 同时，傅雷在此序中也提到，"而即使是最优秀的译文，其韵味较之原文仍不免过或不及。翻译时只能尽量缩短这个距离，过则求其勿太过，不及则求其勿过于不及"。"神似"，即"传神"，就是要传达原文的精神，透过字面，把字里行间的意蕴传达给译文读者。

傅雷一生致力于法国文学的译介，将众多法国著名作家，包括巴尔扎克、罗曼·罗兰等人的作品译介到中国。他的翻译态度严谨，译作丰富，译文流畅，文笔传神。他翻译的《约翰·克利斯朵夫》《贝姨》和《高老头》等作品，至今广为流传。

◈ 朱生豪的"神韵"

倾尽毕生精力翻译莎士比亚的朱生豪（2001）在《汉姆莱特》的《译者序》中提到："余译此书之宗旨，第一在求于最大可能之范围内，保持原作之神韵，必不得已而求其次，亦必以明白晓畅之字句，忠实传达原文之意趣，而于逐字逐句对照式之硬译，则未敢赞同。"³

朱生豪在丰富的翻译实践基础上，提出了保持原作神韵的标准，凸现了文学翻译的精髓。他翻译的莎士比亚戏剧文笔流畅，善于保留原作的神韵，传达了莎剧的气韵，问世以来一直拥有大量的读者。

◈ 钱锺书的"化境"

钱锺书以《围城》一书享誉内外，在翻译领域也颇有建树。在《林纾的翻译》一文开篇中他（1981）就提出："文学翻译的最高标准是'化'。把作品从一国文字转变成另一国文字，既能不因语文习惯的差异而露出生硬牵强的痕迹，又能完全保存原有的风味，那就算得入于'化境'。……换句话说，译本对原作应该忠实得以至于读起来不像译本，因为作品在原文里决不会读起来像经过翻译似的。"⁴

钱锺书的"化境"与傅雷的"神似"一说颇为相似，但就要求和难度而言，"化境"

---

2 （法）巴尔扎克.1951.高老头.傅雷,译.上海：平明出版社.
3 （英）莎士比亚.2001.汉姆莱特.朱生豪,译.北京：中国国际广播出版社, ii.
4 刘靖之.1981.翻译论集.北京：生活·读书·新知三联书店, 302.

比"神似"似乎更进一步、更深一层。一般而言，两种语言间都会存在一定的差异，甚至是很大的差异。经过翻译后既能忠实于原文，读起来又不像译文，的确难度较高。"传神云云，本谈何容易，入于化境，当然更难企及。'化境'……对提高文学翻译水平，要求译本精益求精，具有更多的鞭策和激励作用"[5]（罗新璋，1983）。需要指出的是，无论是"神似"，还是"神韵"和"化境"，恐怕都更适合指导文学翻译，对实用翻译而言并不完全适用。

除上述标准外，鲁迅的"宁信而不顺"及林语堂的"忠实、通顺、美"也曾一度引发热议。在翻译界，鲁迅的"宁信而不顺"多为人争议，他的部分译文也的确存在着过于生硬的问题。但需注意的是，鲁迅"宁信而不顺"的提出，与当时翻译界的"不信"风气有关。因此，这一标准的提出有其历史意义。但在翻译实践中，应当做到既"信"又"顺"，为了"信"而使译文佶屈聱牙的做法是不可取的。此外，林语堂的"忠实、通顺、美"与严复的"信达雅"似乎一脉相承，但他不再一味强调译文的"雅"，而是突出译语的文字之美。林语堂认为译文应再现原文之美，尽量保留原文的美感，因为在他看来翻译就是一种艺术，"忠实、通顺、美"不仅是翻译的标准，也是译者的责任。林语堂学贯中西，博古通今，一生著作和译作颇丰，给后人留下了宝贵的精神财富。

翻译标准是指导翻译实践的基本准则，也是评价译文质量孰优孰劣的重要尺度。到目前为止，虽然没有任何一个翻译标准被所有人接受，但严复的"信达雅"无疑是最知名也是影响最深的。对在校的学生来说，进行汉英翻译实践时，首先要保证译文的准确性，即忠实于原文；其次，在准确的基础上，使译文做到流畅、通顺；最后，在可能的范围内使译文的语体风格与原文基本一致。翻译一事，译无止境。

5　罗新璋.1983.我国自成体系的翻译理论（续）.翻译通讯，4：10.

翻译语篇 1

雨雪时候的星辰[6]

冰心

寒暑表降到冰点下十八度的时候，我们也是在廊下睡觉。每夜最熟识的就是天上的星辰了。也不过是点点闪烁的光明，而相看惯了，偶然不见，也有些想望与无聊。

连夜雨雪，一点星光都看不见。荷和我拥衾对坐，在廊子的两角，遥遥谈话。

荷指着说："你看，维纳斯（Venus）升起来了！"我抬头望时，却是山路转折处的路灯。我怡然一笑，也指着对山的一星灯火说："那边是丘比特（Jupiter）呢！"

愈指愈多。松林中射来零乱的风灯，都成了满天星宿。真的，雪花隙里，看不出来天空和森林的界限，将繁灯当作繁星，简直是抵得过。

一念至诚的将假作真，灯光似乎都从地上飘起。这幻成的星光，都不移动，不必半夜梦醒时，再去追寻他们的位置。

于是雨雪寂寞之夜，也有了慰安了！

译前提示

《雨雪时候的星辰》是冰心早期的抒情散文，语言表达与现在的表达方式稍有差别，但不影响理解。

1. 题目《雨雪时候的星辰》中的"雨雪"作"下雪"解，这里的"雨"是动词，读音为 yù。
2. "寒暑表"可译为 thermometer，即"温度计"的意思。
3. "荷和我……"可译为 My roommate and I...，用 My roommate 代替专有名词 He（荷），以免外国读者把 He 理解为男性第三人称代词。
4. "慰安"可理解为"安慰"，翻译成 consolation。

这一散文想象力丰富，文笔清新，充满了诗情画意。英译时应尽量保持这一风格。

---

[6] 张培基. 1999. 英译中国现代散文选：汉英对照. 上海：上海外语教育出版社，130.

参考译文

Stars on a Snowy Night[7]

The thermometer had dropped to 18 degrees below zero, but we still chose to sleep in the porch as usual. In the evening, the most familiar sight to me would be stars in the sky. Though they were a mere sprinkle of twinkling dots, yet I had become so accustomed to them that their occasional absence would bring me loneliness and ennui.

It had been snowing all night, not a single star in sight. My roommate and I, each wrapped in a quilt, were seated far apart in a different corner of the porch, facing each other and chatting away.

She exclaimed pointing to something afar, "Look, Venus is rising!" I looked up and saw nothing but a lamp round the bend in a mountain path. I beamed and said pointing to a tiny lamplight on the opposite mountain, "It's Jupiter over there!"

More and more lights came into sight as we kept pointing here and there. Lights from hurricane lamps flickering about in the pine forest created the scene of a star-studded sky. With the distinction between sky and forest obscured by snowflakes, the numerous lamplights now easily passed for as many stars.

Completely lost in a make-believe world, I seemed to see all the lamplights drifting from the ground. With the illusory stars hanging still overhead, I was spared the effort of tracing their positions when I woke up from my dreams in the dead of night.

Thus I found consolation even on a lonely snowy night!

译文注释

本译文选自张培基译注的《英译中国现代散文选：汉英对照》一书。张培基的译文保持了原文清新自然的笔调，将雪夜中的"星辰"美景真实地呈现在译文读者面前，是体现严复的"信达雅"和傅雷的"神似""传

---

7 张培基.1999.英译中国现代散文选：汉英对照.上海：上海外语教育出版社，131-132.

神"翻译标准的鲜活译例。另外，整个译文连贯流畅，衔接性好，做到了内容和风格的统一。

1. ……也有些想望与无聊。...would bring me loneliness and ennui.

    【注释】"想望"一词对现代读者来说，稍显生疏。此处根据上下文可理解成"孤独"之意，译为 loneliness。

    在翻译实践中难免会碰到一些不太熟悉，甚至从未见过的词语，如果时间允许，翻译过程中一定要勤查词典和文献资料，确定词义；倘若手头的资料中没有相关信息，应利用一切可能的渠道，如询问原文作者等方式，帮助确定词义。

    学生在完成老师布置的翻译作业时，也应在熟悉上下文和查找相关资料的前提下，合理揣测词语的含义，以便正确选词，使译文准确。

    "无聊"被译为 ennui，意即 a feeling of boredom caused by a lack of excitement or activity。该词是英语中文学翻译常用的单词，如"Since losing his job, he has often experienced a profound sense of ennui."（自失业以来，他常常觉得百无聊赖。）该词用于散文翻译较为合适，但日常口语中该词的使用频率较低。

2. 连夜雨雪，一点星光都看不见。It had been snowing all night, not a single star in sight.

    【注释】"一点星光都看不见"被译为 not a single star in sight，构成了句中的独立主格结构，与 not a single star being in sight 相同。

    译文用 s 押头韵，night 和 sight 压韵脚，富有音韵之美，体现了译者深厚的语言功底，使译文的文字之美超越了原文。

    学生在日常的文学翻译训练中，应在保证译文表达正确性和流畅性的基础上，通过押头韵或押尾韵等方法，使自己的英文表达更加优美。当然，日常的英语阅读和语言积累是汉译英的基础。汉译英水平的高低，英语的基本功是关键。因此，学生除了要完成老师布置的作业外，每天还需要阅读一定量的英文课外材料，以提高自己的英语水平。

3. 荷指着说："你看，维纳斯（Venus）升起来了！" She exclaimed pointing to something afar, "Look, Venus is rising!"

    【注释】译者为什么没有按照原文的表达顺序译成 She pointed and said, "Look, Venus is rising!"，而是采用了伴随状语？伴随状语说明"指"和"说"两个动作同时发生；结合本句内容，比较"指"和"说"两个动作后我们会发现，信息的重点是"说",因此译文中的谓语动词是"说",而"指"则转变成了伴随状语。

"荷指着说……"也不宜译为 She said pointing her finger at…,因为在英语中 to point one's finger at 有"指责"的含义。此处,译者省略了 her finger,以避免歧义的产生;同时又增译了 point 的方向——"远处"(something afar)。

另外,译者选用 exclaim 来表达"说",而没有用 say 的原因在于:exclaim 的英文释义是 to say sth. suddenly and loudly, especially because of strong emotion or pain。因此,exclaim 一词更能体现室友发现维纳斯升起来的喜悦之情。

4. 我抬头望时,却是山路转折处的路灯。I looked up and saw nothing but a lamp round the bend in a mountain path.

   【注释】"我抬头望时"不宜逐字死译为 I raised my head to take a look,译为 I looked up 即可,否则译文稍显冗余拖沓。另外,"我抬头望时"在原句中是时间状语,译者把它改成主谓结构,并用连词 and 后接动词 saw 带出宾语。句子的结构看似简单,却使译文整个句子的表达流畅起来,凸显了译文的"达"。

   "山路转折处"译为 round the bend in a mountain path。Bend 一词除用作动词外,也可用作名词,表"弯,拐角(尤指道路、赛场跑道、河流等)",相应的搭配有 a gentle/sharp bend(一个平缓的/急转弯)。

5. 愈指愈多。松林中射来零乱的风灯,都成了满天星宿。More and more lights came into sight as we kept pointing here and there. Lights from hurricane lamps flickering about in the pine forest created the scene of a star-studded sky.

   【注释】"愈指愈多"英译时增译了时间状语 as we kept pointing here and there,译文的用词明显比原文多了很多。这一译法看似不够"信",却把原文的隐含之意展现在读者面前。从上下文衔接的角度,我们也可以考虑将译文的语序加以调整,译成"As we kept pointing here and there, more and more lights came into sight.",这样与下一句的句首 lights from hurricane lamps 衔接得可能会更好一些。

6. ……将繁灯当作繁星,简直是抵得过。…the numerous lamplights now easily passed for as many stars.

   【注释】 短语 pass for 有"被看作、被当作"的意思。

翻译语篇 2

二　　马（节选）[8]

老舍

马威低着头儿往玉石牌楼走。走几步儿，不知不觉的就愣磕磕地站住一会儿。抬起头来，有时候向左，有时候向右，看一眼。他看什么呢？他不想看什么，也真的没看见什么。他想着的那点事，像块化透了的鳔胶，把他的心整个儿糊满了；不但没有给外面的东西留个钻得进去的小缝儿，连他身上筋肉的一切动作也满没受他的心的指挥。他的眼光只是直着出去，又直着回来了，并没有带回什么东西来。他早把世界忘了，他恨不得世界和他自己一齐消灭了，立刻消灭了，何苦再看呢！

猛孤丁的他站定不走啦。站了总有两三分钟，才慢慢地把面前的东西看清楚了。

"啊，今天是礼拜。"他自己低声儿说。

译前提示

本段材料节选自小说《二马》第一章的开篇。该小说是老舍客居伦敦时创作的最后一部长篇小说。通过《二马》，老舍批判了中国人自身的一些不足，如懒惰和不思进取等，也谴责了英国文化中的民族偏见。

1. 小说名《二马》指的是马则仁和马威父子，可译为 Mr. Ma & Son，将小说的主人公显性化。所选部分写的是马威知道自己心仪的女孩并不爱自己时的失魂落魄。
2. "愣磕磕地"可译为 mechanically，即"机械地"的意思。
3. "鳔胶" 可笼统地译为 glue。

本语篇的句子有长有短，有虚有实，翻译的难度较大。翻译时须灵活处理，不能逐字死译，否则很可能会造成理解障碍。

---

[8] 老舍. 2001. 二马. Julie Jimmerson, 译. 北京：外文出版社, 2.

参考译文

Mr. Ma & Son (Excerpt)[9]

Ma Wei walked toward Marble Arch with a bowed head and halted mechanically after a few steps to stare off in a daze. He raised his head and glanced about. It wasn't that he was looking for anything in particular, nor did he really focus on anything before him. His mind was preoccupied—absorbed by that something which seemed to permeate his heart like glue, impeding any penetration from outside. Even the movements of his muscles seemed directed by something other than his heart. His gaze drifted about, finding nothing to fix on. He had long since given up on everything, and wished that both he and the world could just vanish away, be extinguished in an instant—then he wouldn't have to endure the anguish of looking any longer.

He remained planted there in utter solitude for several minutes before slowly beginning to discern what was going on around him.

"Mmm, today's Sunday," he murmured to himself.

译文注释

本译文选自外文出版社出版的 *Mr. Ma & Son—A Sojourn in London*，由美国翻译家 Julie Jimmerson 翻译。原文内容有实有虚，如果按照字面意思一一翻译，英文读者恐怕无法理解。Jimmerson 的译文没有与原文一一对应，而是将一些信息进行了灵活处理，使得整个语篇的语言表达流畅，可读性强，较好地体现了朱生豪提倡的"神韵"，也较好地实现了钱锺书所追求的化境。

1. 马威低着头儿往玉石牌楼走。Ma Wei walked toward Marble Arch...

   【注释】Julie Jimmerson 将"玉石牌楼"译为 Marble Arch。"牌楼"作为普通名词，可译为 arch 或 archway。按照现在国内通行的英译方法，地名可以按照普通话的发音直接音译，如将"青岛市"译成 Qingdao City，而不是 Green Island City。

---

9 老舍. 2001. 二马. Julie Jimmerson, 译. 北京：外文出版社, 3.

在翻译人名和地名时，可参考中国对外翻译出版公司出版的《世界人名翻译大辞典》和《世界地名翻译大辞典》，这是国内进行人名翻译和地名翻译的重要依据。

2. 马威低着头儿往玉石牌楼走。走几步儿，不知不觉的就愣磕磕地站住一会儿。Ma Wei walked toward Marble Arch with a bowed head and halted mechanically after a few steps to stare off in a daze.

【注释】原文的两句话都不是很长，因此译文采用了合译的翻译技巧，将两句话合译在一起，并把"低着头儿"作为伴随状语处理，译为 with a bowed head，从而与译文第二句的 raise his head 相互呼应，衔接顺畅。

当然，也可以考虑按照原文内容译成两句话，但与参考译文第二句 He raised his head and glanced about. 的衔接性就减弱了。因此，学生在进行语篇翻译时，应有语篇意识和全局意识，即翻译时不能只考虑某个句子本身，还需要考虑该句子与上下文及整个段落，甚至整个语篇的呼应性和衔接性。只有这样，整个译文表达才能流畅连贯，否则很容易让人产生突兀感。

3. 他想着的那点事，像块化透了的鳔胶，把他的心整个儿糊满了；不但没有给外面的东西留个钻得进去的小缝儿，连他身上筋肉的一切动作也满没受他的心的指挥。His mind was preoccupied—absorbed by that something which seemed to permeate his heart like glue, impeding any penetration from outside. Even the movements of his muscles seemed directed by something other than his heart.

【注释】原句很长，翻译的难度较大。参考译文采用了断句的翻译技巧，将原文分成两句话来翻译。遇到长句翻译时，断句法是常用的翻译技巧。关于长句的翻译方法，请参见第十一章中翻译加油站的具体内容，本章节不加赘述。

Preoccupy 有"占据（某人）思想"之意，如"Health worries preoccupied him for the whole holiday."（整个假期他一直为健康状况担忧。）

另外，permeate 表"充满"和"遍布"之意，如"The smell of cooking permeates (through) the flat."（整个公寓都弥漫着做菜的气味。）

译文第一句将主语进行了变换，将原文中的主语"他"改成 his mind 作主语，与下一句的译文主语 the movements of his muscles 构成了并列关系，使译文读者更容易了解作者的意图。因此，这一调整使译文的逻辑性比原文更清晰。

4. 他的眼光只是直着出去，又直着回来了，并没有带回什么东西来。His gaze drifted about, finding nothing to fix on.

> 【注释】 这句话不宜逐字死译，特别是"他的眼光只是直着出去，又直着回来了"不能按照原文逐字翻译，否则读者会不知所云，产生很大的理解障碍。就这一类虚实结合的句子而言，翻译时将大意传达出来即可，一一对应反而是大忌。
>
> 本译文将这句话笼统地翻译成 His gaze drifted about, finding nothing to fix on. 虽然与原句的结构和措辞不同，但把原文的大意传达出来了，做到了"得意而忘形"。

翻译加油站

语篇与翻译

黄国文（1988）在《语篇分析概要》中指出："语篇通常指一系列连续的话段或句子构成的语言整体。它可以是独白、对话（dialogue），也可以是众人交谈（multiperson interchanges）；可以是文字标志（如交通标志），也可以是诗歌、小说。它可以是讲话，也可以是文章；短者一、二句可成篇，长者可洋洋万言以上。"[10] 在实际的翻译活动中，我们面对的往往不是孤立的词句，而是一些互相关联和制约的词句。这些词句为了达到一定的交际目的，按照一定的格式有机地组合在一起，就构成了语篇。

在进行翻译前，要认真分析将翻译的语篇，深度理解原文的内容。张美芳（1999）曾指出，"译者既是原文的接受者，又是译文的生产者。他在接受原文的过程要进行语篇分析，在生产译文时同样要进行语篇分析，而且要将两次分析的结果进行比较，才能较好地完成翻译任务"[11]。因此，树立明确的语篇意识，不论在翻译实践还是翻译研究中都十分重要。

Beaugrande 和 Dressler[12]（1981）认为，语篇具有以下七个特征：衔接性、连贯性、意向性、可接受性、语境性、信息性和互文性。其中，"衔接"和"连贯"是最为重要的特征，它们是语篇特征的重要内容，也是实现其他特征的基本手段。"衔接体现

---

10 黄国文 . 1988. 语篇分析概要 . 长沙：湖南教育出版社，7.

11 张美芳 . 1999. 从语境分析看动态对等论的局限性 . 上海科技翻译，（4）：11.

12 Beaugrande, R. & Dressler, W. (1981). *Introduction to Text Linguistics*. London: Routledge.

在语篇的表层结构上,是语篇的有形网络;连贯存在于语篇的底层,是语篇的无形网络"[13](方梦之,2002)。

一、语篇的衔接(Cohesion)

衔接,或称词语连接,是指一段话中各部分在语法或词汇方面有联系或两方面都有联系。这种联系可能存在于句子之间,也可能存在于一个句子的不同成分之间。英国语言学家韩礼德和哈桑(Halliday & Hasan,2001)把英语句子的衔接手段分成四种:指代(reference)、替代(substitution)和省略(ellipsis)、连接(conjunction)、词汇衔接(lexical cohesion)[14]。其中,指代、替代、连接及词汇衔接与词的使用有关,而省略则是语法手段。

(一)指代

指代关系表达的是一种语义关系,指词与所代表的事物、行为、事件及特性之间的关系。

例1 *Mrs. Thatcher has resigned.* She announced *her decision* this morning.
    撒切尔夫人已经辞职了。她是今天早上宣布这一决定的。

例1由两句话组成。第一句中提到 Mrs. Thatcher has resigned(撒切尔夫人已经辞职了),这一信息与第二句有什么关联?第二句 She announced her decision this morning(她是今天早上宣布这一决定的),两个句子通过 her decision 建立了联系。Her decision 的内容是什么?就是第一句话:Mrs. Thatcher has resigned.

(二)替代和省略

替代表达的是一种语法关系,指用一个语言项替换另一个语言项。省略则是指相关的词或短语因为前文已经提过,没有必要再出现了。

例2   A: I'll have *a glass of milk.*
        B: I'll have *the same.*

---

13 方梦之. 2002. 翻译新论与实践. 青岛:青岛出版社,326.
14 Halliday, M. A. K. & Hasan, R. (2001). *Cohesion in English.* Beijing: Foreign Language Teaching and Research Press.

A：我要一杯牛奶。

B：我也一样。

例 2 中，A 说想要一杯牛奶（I'll have a glass of milk.），B 也想要一杯牛奶，但英文的表达是 I'll have the same，没有直接说 a glass of milk，而是用 the same 替代了 a glass of milk。

例 3　Tom is a teacher and his wife an engineer.

汤姆是老师，他的妻子是工程师。

例 3 中省略了 be 动词，完整的表达应是 "Tom is a teacher and his wife is an engineer."。这里的 is 因为前面出现过，所以被省略了。

（三）连接

英文句子内及句子间大多用连词表示相互的逻辑关系，如递进、条件、原因等。汉语的句子关系往往是平行的，句子的各个成分之间不是用连词，而是通过其内在的逻辑、意义关系结合在一起的。

例 4　If you confer a benefit, never remember it; if you receive one, remember it always.

施恩勿记，受恩勿忘。

原文中用 if 一词表示条件关系，而中文没有将 if 一词译出，简练地译为"施恩勿记，受恩勿忘"，比较符合中文的表达习惯。

（四）词汇衔接

词汇衔接指语篇中出现的部分词汇相互之间存在语义上的联系，或重复，或由其他词语替代，或共同出现。

例 5　Studies serve for delight, for ornament, and for ability. Their chief use for delight, is in privateness and retiring; for ornament, is in discourse; and for ability, is in the judgment and disposition of business.

读书足以怡情，足以博采，足以长才。其怡情也，最见于独处幽居之时；其博采也，最见于高谈阔论之中；其才干也，最见于处世判事之际。

"Studies serve for delight, for ornament, and for ability" 中，for 出现了三次，阐释了读书的三大功用。另外，第二句 "Their chief use for delight, is in privateness and retiring;

for ornament, is in discourse; and for ability, is in the judgment and disposition of business." 解释了这三种作用分别适用的情况,句式一致,采用了 "(Their chief use) for sth., is in sth." 的结构,将意义传达出来。

汉语和英语都会使用一些衔接手段将语篇连接在一起,但衔接手段有所不同。比如,汉语较少使用代词,而采用省略和重复的情况较多。在进行汉英翻译时,就涉及调整衔接手段的问题。汉语原文省略较多,翻译成英语时就需要用代词等手段来补全信息。所谓"翻译腔",也许就是因为不进行调整,将原文的衔接手段照搬到译文中的缘故。

二、语篇的连贯(Coherence)

"连贯指的是语篇中语义的关联,它存在于语篇的底层,通过逻辑推理来达到语义连接;它是语篇的无形网络"[15](黄国文,1988)。衔接可以通过词汇或语法手段,使语篇获得形式上的联系;而连贯则是指信息接受者根据语境信息和背景知识,通过逻辑推理来掌握信息发出者的交际意图。二者的区别在于:前者指语言的表层形式和陈述之间的关系,而后者指语篇中的逻辑关系。译者必须透彻理解看似相互独立,实为相互照应的句内、句间或段间关系,并在此基础上加以充分表达才能传达原作的内容和信息。因此,为了使语篇连贯,语言层面的调整是必需的。

连贯的语篇一般都衔接良好,而表面衔接良好的语篇却未必是连贯的。比如:"I bought a *Ford*. *The car* in which Mary rode down the Champs Elysees was *black*. *Black English* has been widely *discussed*. *The discussions* between the presidents ended *last week*. *A week* has seven days." 这一语篇的衔接看似很好,却让人不知所云。

在翻译实践中,译文的构建应遵照目的语的衔接标准,不能简单采用一一对应的方法进行处理,而应该加以变通,使译文既准确地传达原文的意思,又符合目的语的语言规范,从而翻译出既衔接又连贯的语篇。

---

[15] 黄国文.1988.语篇分析概要.长沙:湖南教育出版社,11.

课后练习

∞ 试将下列语篇译成英文。

1. 一年年过去，我也不再是一个小女孩，母亲也有70多岁了。那双我认为很粗糙的手依然为我和我的家庭操劳着。她是我家的医生，去药橱给我胃疼的女儿找胃药或为我儿子擦伤的膝盖敷药。她能做出世界上最美味的炸鸡……能洗掉牛仔裤上那些我永远都弄不干净的污点……

2. 但是我是向来不爱放风筝的，不但不爱，并且嫌恶它，因为我以为这是没有出息孩子所做的玩意儿。和我相反的是我的小兄弟，他那时大概十岁内外吧，瘦得不堪，然而最喜欢风筝，自己买不起，我又不许放，他只得张着小嘴，呆看着空中出神，有时至于小半日。

第二章
翻译的过程

苏联翻译理论家巴尔胡达罗夫在《语言与翻译》一书中曾指出,"翻译"一词有两层含义,一是指"一定过程的结果",即译文本身;二是指"翻译过程本身",即翻译行为本身。在进行翻译研究时,研究重点应该是作为翻译行为结果的译文还是包含翻译行为的过程?这一问题也是翻译界关注的内容之一。

从近代翻译理论的研究成果来看,大部分研究集中于译文本身,而对翻译过程的研究却相对较少。有关翻译过程的讨论,较为知名的来自尤金·奈达、詹姆斯·霍姆斯(James Holmes)和罗杰·贝尔(Roger Bell)等人。

名家名说

❧ 尤金·奈达

尤金·奈达(1969)将翻译过程模式分为三个环节——分析(analysis)、转移(transfer)和重构(restructuring),其中转移阶段包含了语义调整和结构调整[1]。奈达认为首先需要分析原作的语言信息(包括各成分之间的语法关系、语义单位的外延意义、语法结构和语义单位的内涵值),将其剖析成结构上最简单明了的形式,并在这一基础上进行转移,最后再重新组织成正常的目的语。

❧ 詹姆斯·霍姆斯

詹姆斯·霍姆斯(1988)将翻译过程分为两个层面:序列层面和结构层面[2]。前者是译者逐句翻译层面;后者是译者抽象出原文的"心理构想",然后运用这种心理构想作为产生新的译文过程中检测每个句子的一般标准。

---

1 Nida, Eugene A. & Taber, Charles R. (1969). *The Theory and Practice of Translation*. Leiden: E. J. Brill, p.484.
2 Holmes, James S. (1988). *Translated!: Papers on Literary Translation and Translation Studies*. Amsterdam: Rodopi, p.84.

∞ 罗杰·贝尔

罗杰·贝尔从语义学、心理学、信息加工理论等角度,将翻译过程分为分析和综合两大阶段。分析阶段依次包括句法分析、语义分析和语用分析三个子过程;综合阶段与分析阶段的做法刚好相反,依次进行语用综合、语义综合和句法综合三大过程。贝尔的翻译过程模式(1991)较为复杂,涵盖了六大方面的内容,其中两种语言间的转换就包含了视觉词汇识别系统和写作系统、句法处理器、常用的词汇结构存储及语法分析机制、语义处理器、语用处理器和概念组织器[3]。该模式试图从认知的角度描述翻译的思维过程,但对大部分学生来说恐怕过于复杂,很难在实践中加以操作。

除上述抽象表述外,也有人将翻译过程分解为理解(understanding)、表达(expressing)、检查(checking)和修改(revising)四大步骤,相信这样的表述可能更易为大家理解和接受。当然,也有人将翻译过程表述为准备、理解、表达和校核四个步骤,或者分为理解、准备和校译三个步骤。表述虽有所不同,核心内容其实差不多。

所谓准备过程就是在开始翻译前要了解作品的相关背景,如时代背景;了解作者的生平简历、政治观点、创作意图和写作风格等;研读该作者其他作品的译本或其他相关的平行文本等。同时,准备相关的翻译软件和工具书,如各类词典等。

理解过程的关键就是在认真研读原文的基础上,理解和透彻把握原文所要表达的内容,为表达阶段打下坚实的基础。一般而言,正确的理解是好的译文的前提,但正确的理解却不一定能生成好的译文。能否将原文的信息准确地道地翻译出来,还取决于译者的个人素质,包括译者的语言水平、对翻译方法和翻译技巧的熟练掌握和运用程度、对所译作品的掌握程度以及与所译作品的契合度等。没有正确的理解,就不可能有译文的"信达雅",也不可能达到"传神"或"化境"。

表达是整个翻译过程中的关键一步,是实现原文信息到译文信息转化的关键。好的译文不仅要注重遣词造句,还应如实再现原作的风格。这也涉及译者的语言功底及与所译作品的契合度等诸多因素。

---

3 Bell, Roger T. (1991). *Translation and Translating: Theory and Practice*. Longman: London and New York, p.59.

校核过程也是产生高质量译文不可或缺的一步。译文完成后，一定要养成检查和修改的习惯，也就是要校核自己的译文，包括有无拼写错误、标点符号错误、语法错误（包括词性错误、时态错误、语态错误和名词的单复数等）、表达错误（如选词错误和搭配错误等）。

汉译英是对译者英语表达能力的检验，从词语到句子结构的选择，再到各层意思的组织，都直接考验译者的英语表达能力；另外，汉译英也是对译者汉语理解能力的检验，如对行文的逻辑分析能力、对词语含义的准确体会及对文体风格差异的敏锐辨识等。

就在校的学生而言，汉译英练习可以分三步走：

首先，通读并吃透原文，充分理解原文所要表达的意思。

在通读过程中，要特别关注语篇的大意、基本思路，段落安排的用意以及一些细节的描写意图。一般而言，原文的段落安排都有一定的意图，在英译过程中应尽量保持原状。但如果在译文中不进行调整意思就说不清楚或表达不准确，可以考虑在译文中进行相应的调整。

其次，以句子为单位，逐段翻译。

通读全文的过程中，可以结合上下文将句子大致划分一下。着手翻译每个句子时，首先要考虑的是句子的主体，即基本句型和主要信息点的安排，其依据是上下文的思路、逻辑关系等；其次才是适用的词和短语。在这一过程中一定不要遗漏重要信息的翻译。

需要注意的是，汉译英过程中判断句子的主要依据是意思，即语义，而不是标点。也就是说，汉译英中对汉语句子的判断不能全看标点。有些标点比较重要，如句号，它表示的是一个比较长的停顿，一般也是一个比较完整意思的结束。而逗号基本可以不考虑，该拆成几句话表述还是合译成一句话主要由内容决定。分号介于句号和逗号之间，主要看分号前后两句的关系是否紧密来决定该拆该合。汉英实践不多的学生往往不敢越雷池半步，原文有四句话就一定要译成相应的四句话，否则就觉得译文不忠实于原文。事实上，根据语义的需要进行相应的调整完全是可以的。

最后，检查和修改译文。

全文译完后，不要看原文，单纯从译文的角度看叙事说理是否清楚合理，行文是否流畅，用词是否妥当。译者必须认真检查句子连接能否使上下文连贯、通顺，译文中有什么词会给人重复、累赘或古怪的感觉。这一阶段，译者应把译文从头到尾多读几遍，如有可能，最好读给别人听或请他们通读一遍，看有无生硬、拗口或难懂的地方。修改时须确认译文在内容和文体上都忠实于原文，重要信息没有遗漏，且无技术性错误。

总之，汉译英过程中，一定要从语篇的整体出发处理局部问题，同时要把重点放在意义的传达上，而不是形式上。修改译文时，一定要从译文的角度看译文是否合适，是否地道。只有英文表达自然流畅，译文才算完成了。例如：

月光如流水一般，静静地泻在这一片叶子和花上。薄薄的青雾浮起在荷塘里。叶子和花仿佛在牛乳中洗过一样；又像笼着轻纱的梦。

译文一：Moonlight was flowing quietly like a stream down to the leaves and flowers. A light mist over-spread the lotus pond. Leaf and flower seemed washed in milk.

译文二：The moon sheds her liquid light silently over the leaves and flowers, which, in the floating transparency of a bluish haze from the pond, looks as if they had just been bathed in milk, or like a dream wrapped in a gauzy hood.

原文选自朱自清的散文《荷塘月色》。译文一来自《英语世界》1985 年第 5 期，译文二来自《中国翻译》1992 年第 2 期。就语言表达而言，两个译文都是正确的，或者说都是不错的，但这两种译文在用词和句法结构上差别较大，仔细比较起来，译文二似乎技高一筹。

在用词上，译文一似乎更接近原文，如"在牛乳中洗过"的"洗"直译为 washed，但这样的表达可能不太生动；译文二用词灵活生动，如 bathed in milk，sheds her liquid light，将荷塘月色的美成功地传递给了译文读者。

在句法上，译文一与原文一句对一句，而译文二将原文的三句话译成一个英语长句，在这个复合句中因果层次分明，逻辑关系紧密。另外，译文二的语言富于诗意，而译文一尚有一些需改进之处，如将 over-spread 改为 spread over 可能更好，seemed washed 之间加上 to be 可能会更为自然。

英文重形合，汉语重意合。相对而言，译文二的译者熟谙这一差异并恰当地运用于实践中，加上丰富的词汇表达，使得译文连贯、优美。

翻译语篇 1

我们的女子教育（节选）[4]

林语堂

古代中国闺女实际上比之欧美女子缺少接触社会的机会，不过受了较好家庭教育则她可以增厚一些培养为良母贤妻的基础。而她的一生也没有旁的事业，只有做做贤妻良母而已。中国男人们现在临到了一个难关，便是他的选择妻子，摩登女子与旧式女子二者之间孰优。最好的标准妻子有人说过：要有新知识而具旧德性的女子。摩登女子与旧式女子的思想上的冲突，需要常识的无情判断（新女子以妻为一独立的不依赖的人格而轻视良母贤妻的说法）。当作者将知识与教育之增进认为一种进步并尤接近女性典型之理想时，敢深信决非谓吾人将求一闻名世界的女子钢琴名手或女大画家。我深信她的调治羹汤，应较其作诗会有益，而她的真正杰作，将为她的雪白肥胖的小宝宝。依著者的愚见一位典型的女性还该是一位智慧仁慈而坚定的母亲。

译前提示

此段材料出自林语堂《吾国与吾民》的第五章。在《吾国与吾民》一书中，林语堂以冷静犀利的视角剖析了中华民族的精神和特质，向西方展示了一个真实而丰富的中华民族形象。

1. 本文的语言表达基本接近现在的白话文，但个别措辞在翻译时还需要揣摩，如"旧德性""常识的无情批判""尤接近"等。
2. 中文写作中时常会出现一些谦辞，如"鄙人""愚见"等。最后一句话中的"愚见"译成 my humble opinion 合适吗？

---

[4] 林语堂.2002.吾国与吾民.黄嘉德，译.西安：陕西师范大学出版社，138.

整个语篇用词较为正式，翻译时应尽量用明白晓畅的正式英语来表达。另外，翻译这一语篇时可多用长句，这样语言风格跟原文可能更加相似。

参考译文

Education of Our Daughters (Excerpt)[5]

The Chinese girl in ancient times was actually less socially accomplished than the Western girl, but under a good family breeding she had a better chance of succeeding as wife and mother and she had no career except the career of wife and mother. The Chinese men are now faced with the dilemma of choosing between the modern girl and the conservative girl for a wife. The ideal wife has been described as one "with new knowledge but old character." The conflict of ideals (the new one being the wife who is an independent being and who looks down upon the expression "helpful wife and wise mother") calls for a ruthless application of common sense. While I regard the increased knowledge and education as an improvement and approaching the ideal of womanhood, I wager that we are not going to find, as we have not yet found, a world-renowned lady pianist or lady painter. I feel confident that her soup will still be better than her poetry and that her real masterpiece will be her chubby-faced boy. The ideal woman remains for me the wise, gentle and firm mother.

译文注释

参考译文选自林语堂的 *My Country and My People*。这是林语堂在美国引起巨大反响的第一部英文著作。林语堂在书中用坦率幽默的笔调、睿智通达的语言娓娓道出了中国人的道德、精神状态与向往，以及中国的社会、文艺与生活情趣。

5　林语堂. 2000. *My Country and My People*. 北京：外语教学与研究出版社，152.

值得一提的是，My Country and My People 比《吾国与吾民》早出版。My Country and My People 的中文译本不止一个，如郝志东、沈益洪的全译本表达流畅，在国内出版时中译本名为《中国人》。本教材节选的中文由黄嘉德翻译，其语言风格更接近民国时期的语言，但有些表达可能存在翻译腔的问题。

1. 古代中国闺女实际上比之欧美女子缺少接触社会的机会……The Chinese girl in ancient times was actually less socially accomplished than the Western girl...

   【注释】"缺少接触社会的机会"转译为 less socially accomplished，与后半句的 succeed as wife and mother and she had no career except the career of wife and mother 相对应，逻辑上更加紧密和清晰。

   有学生可能会把这一部分直译成 have less chances of contacting with the society 或译成 have less social contact。就语法而言，这样的译文没有大问题，但与后文 succeed 一词的联系就不太紧密了。

2. 中国男人们现在临到了一个难关，便是他的选择妻子，摩登女子与旧式女子二者之间孰优。The Chinese men are now faced with the dilemma of choosing between the modern girl and the conservative girl for a wife.

   【注释】"旧式女子"译成了 conservative girl，与 modern girl 相对照。

   原文有三个小句，而译文仅用了一个复杂句，主谓宾结构是 sb. be faced with the dilemma，后用 of 引导的同位语解释这个难关是什么。中文表述相对比较松散，带有中文句式的典型特征；而英文表达则更符合英文读者的审美心理和英文句式的紧凑特点。因此，在汉译英过程中，一定要注意英文句子结构和句式的特点，不要拘泥于汉语的表述方式，否则很容易出现硬译和死译的问题。从这个意义上说，校译过程中应脱离中文，仅从英语的角度考虑译文的适切性。

3. 我深信她的调治羹汤，应较其作诗会有益……I feel confident that her soup will still be better than her poetry...

   【注释】"调制羹汤"在翻译时省略了动词，译成 her soup；"作诗"也省略了动词，直接译为 her poetry，因为英语的名词使用频率高于汉语。用 her soup will still be better than her poetry 来翻译"她的调治羹汤，应较其作诗会有益"，行文更加地道和自然。

汉译英时经常采用词性转换的方法，如将汉语的动词翻译成英语的名词；而在英译汉时，则将英语的名词翻译成汉语的动词，如"He is a good swimmer."，译成汉语时，一般是"他很会游泳"或"他游泳游得很好"，而不是"他是一个好的游泳者"。

4. 依著者的愚见一位典型的女性还该是一位智慧仁慈而坚定的母亲。The ideal woman remains for me the wise, gentle and firm mother.

   【注释】"依著者的愚见"并没有按照字面的意思翻译成 according to my humble opinion，而是用了符合英文读者习惯的表述 for me。

   汉语中有大量谦词，如"敝人""犬子""贱内""老朽""拙作""愚见"等；对他人也有诸多敬称，如"您""令尊""令堂""贵校""高见""大作""鸿论"等。然而英美文化中"自贬"成分较少。在汉译英过程中，一定要考虑到英语的行文习惯和文化习惯。

翻译语篇 2

儒林外史（节选）[6]

吴敬梓

这人姓王名冕，在诸暨县乡村里住。七岁上死了父亲，他母亲做些针指，供给他到村学堂里去读书。看看三个年头，王冕已是十岁了。母亲唤他到面前来说道："儿阿，不是我有心要耽误你，只因你父亲亡后，我一个寡妇人家，只有出去的，没有进来的；年岁不好，柴米又贵；这几件旧衣服和些旧家伙，当的当了，卖的卖了；只靠着我替人家做些针指生活寻来的钱，如何供得你读书？如今没奈何，把你雇在间壁人家放牛，每月可以得他几钱银子，你又有现成饭吃，只在明日就要去了。"王冕道："娘说的是。我在学堂里坐着，心里也闷，不如往他家放牛倒快活些。假如我要读书，依旧可以带几本去读。"当夜商议定了。

第二日，母亲同他到间壁秦老家。秦老留着他母子两个吃了早饭，牵出一条水牛来交与王冕，指着门外道："就在我这大门过去两箭之地便是七泖湖。湖边一带绿草，各家的牛都在那里打睡。又有几十棵合抱的垂杨树，十分阴凉。牛要渴了，就在湖边上饮水。小哥，你只在这一带玩耍，不必远去。我老汉每日两餐小菜饭是不少的，

6　吴敬梓．1996．儒林外史（上册）．杨宪益，戴乃迭，译．长沙：湖南出版社，4.

每日早上，还折两个钱与你买点心吃。只是百事勤谨些，休嫌怠慢。"他母亲谢了扰要回家去，王冕送出门来。母亲替他理理衣服，口里说道："你在此须要小心，休惹人说不是。早出晚归，免我悬望。"王冕应诺，母亲含着两眼眼泪去了。

译前提示

本段材料节选自清代吴敬梓的《儒林外史》，该书被认为是中国传统小说最优秀的代表之一。虽然书中个别语言表达与现代白话文有差异，但理解本文没有太大问题。因此，翻译本篇材料的难点在于如何用地道的英语进行翻译。

1. "针指"即"针线"，可译为 sewing。
2. "如今没奈何"可理解为"如今没有办法"。
3. "间壁"即"隔壁"的意思，但是"秦老"应该如何翻译？汉语中类似的称呼较多，如"王老""老王""小王"。这些称呼如何翻译才能符合英美读者的习惯？

本段材料篇幅较长。翻译这一语篇前，应对《儒林外史》有所了解，掌握王冕这一人物的设定背景，然后通读全文，将王冕的故事了然于心。翻译过程中，也应厘清整个语篇的逻辑线索，考虑如何用词汇、语法等手段来实现译文的连贯和衔接。

参考译文

The Scholars (Excerpt)[7]

His name was Wang Mian, and he lived in a village in Chuchi County in Chekiang. When he was seven his father died, but his mother took in sewing so that he could study at the village school. Soon three years had passed and Wang Mian was ten. His mother called him to her and said, "Son, it's not that I want to stand in your way. But since your father died and left me a widow, I have had nothing coming in. Times are hard, and fuel and rice are

---

7　吴敬梓. 1996. 儒林外史（上册）. 杨宪益，戴乃迭，译. 长沙：湖南出版社, 5-6.

expensive. Our old clothes and our few sticks of furniture have been pawned or sold. We have nothing to live on but what I make by my sewing. How can I pay for your schooling? There's nothing for it but to set you to work looking after our neighbor's buffalo. You'll be making a little money every month, and you'll get your meals there too. You start tomorrow."

"Yes, mother," said Wang Mian. "I find sitting in school boring anyway. I'd rather look after buffaloes. If I want to study, I can take a few books along to read." So that very night the matter was decided.

The next morning his mother took him to the Qin family next door. Old Qin gave them some breakfast, and when they had finished he led out a water buffalo and made it over to Wang Mian.

"Two bow shots from my gate is the lake," he said, pointing outside. "And by the lake is a belt of green where all the buffaloes of the village browse. There are a few dozen big willows there too, so that it is quiet, shady and cool, and if the buffalo is thirsty it can drink at the water's edge. You can play there, son; but don't wander off. I shall see that you get rice and vegetables twice a day, and each morning I shall give you a few coppers to buy a snack to eat while you're out. Only you must work well. I hope you'll find this satisfactory."

Wang Mian's mother thanked Old Qin and turned to go home. Her son saw her to the gate, and there she straightened his clothes for him.

"Mind now, don't give them any reason to find fault with you," she charged him. "Go out early and come back at dusk. I don't want to have to worry about you."

Wang Mian nodded assent. Then, with tears in her eyes, she left him.

译文注释

《儒林外史》已被译成英、法、德、俄、日、西班牙等多种文字，在世界上广泛传播，成为一部世界性的文学名著。参考译文选自杨宪益和戴乃迭所译的 The Scholars，该译本在英语国家流传甚广。

1. 年岁不好，柴米又贵……Times are hard, and fuel and rice are expensive.

   【注释】"柴米又贵"译为 fuel and rice are expensive，将"柴"转译成 fuel 而不是 firewood，主要是考虑到译文读者的接受性，让现代的英美人士更容易理解这一内容。

   类似的例子其实有很多，如将"二锅头"简单翻译成 spirits，将"粽子"简译为 dumpling 等。这样的译文不够精确，但可以减少英文读者的理解障碍。

2. 如今没奈何，把你雇在间壁人家放牛……There's nothing for it but to set you to work looking after our neighbor's buffalo.

   【注释】汉语中，"牛"的所指范围比英文更广，译法也较多，如 cattle（牛的总称）、cow（母牛）、buffalo（水牛）、ox（大公牛）、calf（小牛）等，此处译为 buffalo 较为合理。前文提到，王冕是诸暨县人。浙江诸暨属江南水乡，那里饲养的一般都是水牛。原文第二段中也提到，秦老"牵出一条水牛来交与王冕"，所以译者的理解没有出现偏差。

   翻译时，如遇到不确定之处，可以先从上下文甚至整个语篇寻找线索。如果上下文或整个语篇无法提供线索，再查找其他文献或网络资源。好的翻译一定是在正确理解原文的基础上才能达到的。

3. 小哥，你只在这一带玩耍，不必远去。You can play there, son; but don't wander off.

   【注释】"小哥"是对年轻男子的称呼，被翻译成了 son，因为说话人比王冕年长。Son 除了"儿子"之外，还有"孩子"的意思，表示 a friendly form of address that is used by an older man to a young man or boy。

4. ……还折两个钱与你买点心吃。I shall give you a few coppers to buy a snack to eat while you're out.

   【注释】对中文读者而言，理解该句并不难，但要准确翻译"两个钱"和"点心"可能并非易事。杨宪益和戴乃迭的译文中，用 copper 表示"钱"，用 snack 表示"点心"。的确，copper 有"铜币"之意，snack 是"点心"，但这些词的意象在中外读者的心里应该有一定的差异。比如，原文中的"点心"指的是中式的点心，而 snack 一词给英文读者的第一反应恐怕是饼干、蛋糕等西点。注释 1 中提到的"柴"其实也是类似的例子。中西方文化本身有很大差异，这给我们的汉译英造成了很大的困难。翻译时，从读者接受度来说，用他们熟悉的事物来翻译一些具有中国特色的事物，也不失为一种好的选择。

5. 母亲替他理理衣服……she straightened his clothes for him...

   【注释】"理了理衣服"译为 straighten one's clothes；straighten sth. out 有"（使）变直，变正""理顺"的意思。

翻译加油站

翻译策略：归化与异化

在《译者的隐身：一部翻译史》[8]（*The Translator's Invisibility: A History of Translation*）中，美国翻译理论家劳伦斯·韦努蒂（Lawrence Venuti）使用了一对关键术语"domesticating translation"和"foreignizing translation"（2004），中文译作"归化"和"异化"。该术语是基于德国哲学家及神学家施莱尔马赫（Friedrich Schleiermacher）1813 年 6 月 24 日在柏林皇家科学院所作的演讲，其题目为《论翻译的方法》（On the Different Methods of Translating）。

施莱尔马赫认为，要帮助译作的读者在不脱离目的语的情况下正确而完整地看懂原作，可以采取两种方法：一种是"尽可能地不打扰原作者的安宁，让读者去接近作者"，即韦努蒂所指的"异化"（foreignizing strategies）；另一种是"尽可能不打扰读者的安宁，让作者去靠近读者"，即"归化"（domesticating strategies）。

一、归化

归化（domestication）是指译者在翻译中采用透明、流畅的风格，最大限度地减弱译文读者对外语语篇的生疏感的翻译策略。它尽可能地使源语文本所反映的世界接近译文读者的世界，从而达到源语文化与目的语文化之间的"文化对等"。所以，又被后来的研究者称为"译者的隐身"（the translator's invisibility）。

归化法的译文地道流畅，易被译文读者接受，但往往会失去原有的意象和文化色彩。

例1　大禹陵是我国古代治水英雄、开国圣君大禹的葬地。

8　Venuti, Lawrence. (1995). *The Translator's Invisibility: A History of Translation*. London and New York: Routledge.

The Yu's Mausoleum is believed to contain the grave of King Yu, the legendary head of ancient Chinese chieftains and tamer of floods.

译者依据典籍记载对原文进行了改写，并用《亚瑟王传奇》中的相关表达 the legendary head of ancient Chinese chieftains 来解释大禹的身份，更易被译文读者理解和接受，但原有的意象和文化元素恐怕无法传递给译文读者。前面翻译语篇 2 中，杨宪益和戴乃迭将"柴"译成 fuel，将"点心"译为 snack，都是归化法的具体体现。

二、异化

异化（foreignization）是指刻意打破目的语的行文规范而保留原文的异域特色的翻译策略。它主张在译文中保留源语文化，丰富目的语文化和目的语的语言表达方式。所以，又被称为"译者的彰显/显身"（the translator's visibility）。

异化法可以丰富译入语的语言表达，保留原有的意象，有利于文化之间的交流。但对译文读者来说，译文恐怕比较生硬，容易受到译文读者的抵制。以电影《功夫》中的一段对话为例：

例 2　阿鬼："十二路谭腿，攻守并重，名不虚传！"
　　　　苦力强："铁线拳刚中有柔，可谓拳中之尊！"
　　　　裁缝："五郎八卦棍，千变万化，高深莫测！"
　　　　Doughnut: Twelve Kicks of the Tam School! Superb attack and defense!
　　　　Coolie: Iron Fist: Powerful yet delicate. Topnotch!
　　　　Tailor: Hexagon Staff, with its thousand moves. Mystical!

裁缝、苦力强和阿鬼平日里只是猪笼寨里做衣裳、扛大包和炸油条的，与敌方一交手才显出庐山真面目，原来三位分别是洪家铁线拳、十二路谭腿和五郎八卦棍的传人。所选部分是他们离开猪笼寨之前的对话。这里的"铁线拳"和"十二路谭腿"采用了异化策略，分别译为 Iron Fist 和 Twelve Kicks of the Tam School，英文读者恐怕一时无法理解。

总之，归化法要求译者向译语读者靠拢，采取译文读者习惯的译语表达方式来传达原文的内容；异化法则要求译者向作者靠拢，采取源语作者使用的表达方式来传达原文的内容。在归化或异化的翻译策略指导下，译者会通过采用直译或意译等翻译方法，借助一系列的翻译技巧完成自己的翻译任务。

课后练习

∽ **试将下列语篇译成英文：**

1. 手种牵牛花，接连有三四年了。水门汀地没法下种，种在十来个瓦盆里。泥是今年又明年反复用着的，无法取得新的泥来加入。

2. 说起清华人，我怀念我的老师们。大学一年级，俞平伯、余冠英两先生教我国文，一位教读本，一位教作文，都亲切而严格。有一次余先生指出我把爬山虎写成紫荆的错误，但又要我多写几篇给他。二年级，贺麟老师教我西洋哲学史，见了我长达百页的英文报告书不仅不皱眉，反而在班上表扬我；正是在他的指导下，我读了不少古希腊哲学家著作的英译，真有发现新星球的喜悦。

第三章
汉英语言差异

语言是人类沟通交流的重要工具，是一个民族的重要特征。据统计，汉语是世界上使用人口最多的语言，而英语是世界上使用最广泛的语言。这两种语言属于不同的语系：汉语属于汉藏语系（Sino-Tibetan family），而英语属于印欧语系（Indo-European family）。因此，汉英两种语言势必存在着一定的差异，如：英语表达的重心一般在前（如英语中很多主题句位于段首），而汉语表达的重心一般在后；英语的被动语态多于汉语的被动用法；英语重形合，而汉语重意合；英语多用名词，而汉语多用动词。

名家名说

∞ 潘文国

潘文国在《汉英语言对比概论》一书中，对中英文的语音、文字、词汇、语法、篇章、语用、修辞和文化进行了较为全面的对比。他（2010）提到，"在进行汉英双语对比时，最引人注意的差异是意合（parataxis）和形合（hypotaxis）。人们通常说，汉语重意合，英语重形合。但是，在讨论这个问题的时候，我们决不能以为，汉语只有意合而没有形合，英语只有形合而没有意合。比如，汉字的字形就起着形合的作用。另外，各种语篇衔接手段也是各小句和句子之间'形合'的手段"[1]。

此外，其他文献对汉英语言也进行了较为详细的对比。如王治奎主编的《大学汉英翻译教程》[2]（2005）指出，汉英词汇的语义有差别，如"鸡"对应的英语有 hen，chick，cock 和 rooster；而中文的"叔""伯"对应的都是 uncle。就词汇的语法而言，汉语大致有十类词，实词有名词、动词、形容词、代词、副词、数词和量词；虚词有连词、介词、助词、叹词。英语也有十大词类，其中实词有名词、动词、形容词、副词、数词、代词；虚词有介词、连词、冠词和感叹词。汉语的量词和英语

---

[1] 潘文国.2010.汉英语言对比概论.北京：商务印书馆，312.
[2] 王治奎.2005.大学汉英翻译教程.4版.济南：山东大学出版社.

的冠词是各自所特有的。从词类的使用频率来分析，汉语多用动词，英语多用名词。汉语的动词在使用频率上远远高于英语，因为英语动词的使用要受限制，一句话只有一个动词谓语，而汉语的动词不受此限制。英语中代词、介词、连词的使用频率比汉语高。英语数词的使用不如汉语多，因为汉语的成语及缩略语依靠数词（词素）构成。汉语的量词同英语的冠词一样，附属于各自的名词，使用频率也同名词。

✿ 连淑能

连淑能（1993）在《英汉对比研究》中提到：

"翻译教学和研究的经验表明：翻译理论和技巧必须建立在不同语言和文化的对比分析基础上。英汉互译的几项基本原则和技巧，如选词（diction）、转换（conversion）、增补（amplification）、省略（omission）、重复（repetition）、替代（substitution）、变换（variation）、倒置（inversion）、拆离（division）、缀合（combination）、阐释（annotation）、浓缩（condensation）、重组（reconstruction），以及时态、语态、语气、习语、术语等的译法，都集中体现了英汉语的不同特点。机器翻译是让计算机按照人们所制定的程序和指令进行不同语言的对比转换，也离不开对比分析。翻译之所以困难，归根结底是因为语言差异和文化差异。因此，对比、分析和归纳这些差异，便是翻译学的重要任务。

"不同语言的对比分析不仅有利于教学和翻译，也有助于语言交际。通过对比分析，人们可以进一步认识外语和母语的特性，在进行交际时，能够有意识地注意不同语言各自的表现方法，以顺应这些差异，防止表达错误，避免运用失当，从而达到交际的目的"[3]。

✿ 赵世开

赵世开（1990）在《英汉对比研究论文集》的序中也提到："通过对两种语言的对比，人们会发现它们结构上的差异，这些往往是外语教学中的难点和翻译中值得注意的地方；同时，通过对比也能进一步加深人们对语言的本质和共性的认识，有助于人们借助言语行为相互沟通思想和感情"[4]。

3　连淑能.1993.英汉对比研究.北京：高等教育出版社，4.
4　杨自俭，李瑞华.1990.英汉对比研究论文集.上海：上海外语教育出版社，3.

综上所述，了解汉英语言之间的差异在翻译过程中起着至关重要的作用。翻译实践证明，凡是汉英两种语言相同之处翻译的难度就低，而汉英两种语言不同之处翻译的难度就高。因此，了解汉英两种语言的差异对翻译质量的提高有极大的促进作用。

汉英两种语言存在着较多的差异，范畴词就是典型的例子之一。"方面""方式""问题""情况"之类的范畴词，在汉语中虽没有多少实际意义，但可以使句子表达更为流畅，因此使用频率很高。汉译英时，范畴词可以不译；英译汉时，可以酌情使用。例如：

中国有13亿多人口，陆地自然资源人均占有量低于世界平均水平。

China has a population of more than 1.3 billion, and its land natural resources per capita are lower than the world's average.

此处"水平"未译，如把"世界平均水平"译成 the world's average level 就犯了 Chinglish 的错误了。

翻译语篇 1

竹　马（节选）

绿杨

现在中年以上的人差不多都有过儿时骑"竹马"的历史，所谓"竹马"其实就是骑在胯下的一根竹竿，儿童的想象力在这根竹竿上得到了充分的张扬。两腿夹着竹竿便有了骑在马背上的感觉，左右顾盼，就能生出几分大将军的豪迈，拖着竹竿呼啸而奔，就好像骑士纵马驰骋，再挥舞着刀、枪、剑、棒之类，那就是一场高潮迭起的"战争"。若是控着竹马轻歌曼舞，那简直就是马术表演中的"盛装舞步"了。

唐代大诗人李白（701—762）在著名的诗篇《长干行》中，用女孩的口吻描述了儿童在一起骑竹马、弄青梅的游戏，从此"青梅竹马"这句成语流行开来，成为男女之间儿时友谊的代名词。一根竹竿被赋予了情感象征意义，从而在中国文化中永存。

译前提示

原文节选自2000年第4期《中国文学》上的《中国传统游戏趣谈（之一）》，后被收进教材[5]，作者绿杨对骑"竹马"的场面进行了生动描述，让人不禁回想起儿时的场景。同时，作者对"竹马"所引发的"青梅竹马"一词的文化含义进行了一定的解释。

1. "竹马"应该如何翻译？是不是可以直接翻译成 bamboo horse？
2. 李白的《长干行》描绘了一位商妇各个生活阶段的生活侧面，塑造出一个对理想生活执着追求和热切向往的商贾思妇的艺术形象。"长干"是地名，属现在的江苏南京，这一带商业比较繁华。许渊冲将《长干行》译为 Ballad of a Trader's Wife，而美国著名翻译家庞德（Ezra Pound）则将它译为 The River Merchant's Wife: A Letter。

参考译文

Bamboo Horses (Excerpt)[6]

Almost all middle-aged people have the experience of riding bamboo horses. The toy was actually a bamboo stick, which fed the children's imagination. Putting the stick between their legs and looking around them, they felt as though they were generals riding on horses. They would rush about with the stick, wielding toy knives, guns, swords and sticks, like cavalrymen darting around on the battle field. They would also dance to the music on the bamboo horses, just like the costumed dancing in a riding performance.

The great Tang-dynasty poet Li Bai (701–762 AD), in his famous poem "The Trader's Wife", described the game of riding bamboo horses and playing with green plums in the tone of a girl. Later, "bamboo horse and green plum" became a popular phrase to describe the friendship between a man and a woman that had begun in their childhood. Thus, the bamboo stick takes on romantic significance and lives forever in Chinese culture.

5　陈宏薇. 2009. 高级汉英翻译. 北京：外语教学与研究出版社，135-136.
6　同上。

第三章 汉英语言差异

译文注释

总体而言，译笔简洁明快，行文流畅。由于汉英语言的差异，译者主要采用了断句的翻译技巧，对语言内容适当进行了一些调整，传达了原文作者对"竹马"游戏的怀念和喜爱。

1. 现在中年以上的人差不多都有过儿时骑"竹马"的历史，所谓"竹马"其实就是骑在胯下的一根竹竿，儿童的想象力在这根竹竿上得到了充分的张扬。Almost all middle-aged people have the experience of riding bamboo horses. The toy was actually a bamboo stick, which fed the children's imagination.

   【注释】原文第一句话是一个长句，由三个分句组成。第一个分句的主语是"中年以上的人"，第二个分句的主语是"竹马"，第三个分句的主语是"儿童的想象力"。

   在翻译这一长句时，译者做了比较大的调整。他将第一个分句译成第一句话，保留了原来的主语"中年以上的人"；第二和第三个分句合译成一句，将第二分句的主语"竹马"译为 the toy，并把第三个分句处理成了定语从句，实现了句式的紧凑和行文的流畅。

2. 两腿夹着竹竿便有了骑在马背上的感觉，左右顾盼，就能生出几分大将军的豪迈，拖着竹竿呼啸而奔，就好像骑士纵马驰骋，再挥舞着刀、枪、剑、棒之类，那就是一场高潮迭起的"战争"。Putting the stick between their legs and looking around them, they felt as though they were generals riding on horses. They would rush about with the stick, wielding toy knives, guns, swords and sticks, like cavalrymen darting around on the battle field.

   【注释】原文的第二句话按照骑竹马的顺序，连用几个主谓短语和动宾短语作主语，将儿童骑竹马的乐趣逐步推向了高潮。译者将该句分译成两句，并前后三次用 they 指代"儿童"作主语，突出了 children's imagination（and pleasure），行文简洁明快。

   另外，长句的翻译过程中经常会使用断句法，这一点在前文中已提及过。如对长句的使用不够有把握，可以考虑将一个中文长句翻译成两三个英文短句。当然，这可能会导致译文的整个气势逊于原文。

   原文中四字格使用较多，如"左右顾盼""呼啸而奔""纵马驰骋""高潮迭起"和"轻歌曼舞"等，符合中文写作的习惯。翻译成英文时，因为两种语言的差异，可能很难在译文中保留下来。这也体现了中英两种语言差异对翻译造成的困难。

4. 唐代大诗人李白（701—762）在著名的诗篇《长干行》中……The great Tang-dynasty poet Li Bai (701–762 AD), in his famous poem "The Trader's Wife"...

【注释】译者在翻译《长干行》时，没有采用许渊冲或庞德的译文，而是译成 The Trader's Wife。

在翻译较有知名度的作品或内容时，一般可以照搬最广为人知的英文对应表达，而不需要自己翻译，以免引起英文读者的误解，以为是另一部作品或新的内容。

另外，"唐代大诗人李白"的表达不太好，可改成 Li Bai (701–762 AD), the great poet of Tang Dynasty, in his famous poem... 的形式。

翻译语篇 2

母亲的微笑（节选）[7]

小时候，母亲给过我一件礼物，那是用手摸不到的，却深深烙在我的记忆中。

那时是 1946 年，我才 6 岁。一个闷热的星期六上午，母亲对我和哥哥比利说要一起去科尼岛玩一天。我家住纽约，公寓四壁像窑壁一般把热气罩住，叫人难受，因而我对此行颇感雀跃。

坐地下火车一个小时便到达这丝绒般的白色沙滩。海滩上人头攒动，海滨散步道与大西洋之间那一片起伏的沙滩至少有 110 万人。

我们尽量朝海边靠近，铺上一条满是蛀洞的军用毯子，母亲说："虽然不怎么好看，但还能用。"生活本来就是凑合着过日子嘛。

大家脱去外衣，里面早就穿好了泳装。哥哥朝着海水跑去，这时候正好有个卖冰淇淋的小贩从身边走过，肩上挎着一只大箱子，喊道："卖冰淇淋啰！"

我心里暗想：冰淇淋？在海滩上就能买到！但他卖什么价钱呢？跟母亲在一起，

---

7 丹尼斯·史密斯. 2001. 母亲的微笑//《读者文摘》亚洲有限公司.《读者文摘》读本丛书（一）（中英对照）. 广州：广东世界图书出版公司，106-109.

第三章 汉英语言差异

不论买什么东西,最好还是先问清楚价钱,再求她买。

小贩已经到了沙滩中间,朝着散步道走去。我跟在他后面,在一张张毯子间绕来绕去,躲闪其他游人。终于追上他了,我用手拉他的衣袖,问道:"卖多少钱,先生?"

"小朋友,算你便宜些,今天卖一毛钱。"

"一毛钱!街上只卖五分钱。"

"小朋友,这里不是街上嘛。这里是海滩,你可以去别处看看。"

译前提示

本段材料节选自《母亲的微笑》的开篇,作者是美国人 Dennis Smith。所以,本语篇是从英文翻译而来,要求大家回译成英文。

1. 回译(back translation)指把译文译回原文的过程,即把一种语言翻译成第二种语言,然后根据第二种语言的译文再译回第一种语言。这是学习翻译时常用的好方法:在不知道原文的情况下,译者会努力去想原文可能是怎么说的,尽量把译文译回原来的模样,这样可以较好地提高译文的语言质量。

   第二章中翻译语篇1《我们的女子教育》,其实也是回译的练习,但因为英文作者也是中国人,因此没有专门提及这一信息。

2. 就回译而言,下列建议还是比较可行的:译者翻译时最好先不查词典,把原文通读几遍,在理解的基础上一口气译出来,当然翻译时应做到心中有数,不能乱译;然后再一句一句地仔细推敲,努力想象英文是如何表达的,尽力将译文修改到最好的状态。翻译过程中不查词典,一是可以提高速度;二是不会让查词典打断思路,有利于把注意力放在表达意思上而不是放在找对应词上,从而减少死译和硬译,行文也可能更流畅。译完后再仔细推敲其中的字词,尽最大的努力去提高译文的质量,这是翻译学习中非常可取的一种方法。

3. 第三段中的"地下火车"可理解为"地铁"。

参考译文

Smile of a Lifetime (Excerpt)

My mother gave me a gift when I was young. It wasn't something to touch, but I kept it seared in my memory.

I was only six at the time. It was a stifling hot Saturday morning in 1946, when my mother announced to my older brother, Billy, and me that we were going to Coney Island for the day. The walls of our New York City tenement embraced the heat like the walls of a kiln, and I cheered at the announcement.

It was an hour-long subway trip to the velvety white sand. The beach was mobbed—over a hundred thousand people packed together on the rolling sand between the boardwalk and the Atlantic Ocean.

We advanced as close to the water as we could, and spread out our moth-worn Army blanket. "This is not great," my mother said, "but it's okay." All life was making do.

We slipped out of our clothes to our bathing suits beneath. My brother ran toward the water, and just then an ice-cream man passed, a large box hanging from his shoulder. "Getcha ice cream!" he yelled.

Ice cream, I thought, right here on the beach! But what was the price? With my mother it was always better to know the price of something before you asked her for it.

The ice-cream man was halfway up the beach and heading toward the boardwalk. I ran after him, crisscrossing around the blankets, dodging people, kicking sand. Finally I reached him and tugged at his sleeve. "How much, mister?" I asked.

"Special for you, kiddo," he said. "Ten cents today."

"Ten cents! It's only a nickel on the block."

"Well there ain't no blocks here, kiddo. This is the beach, and why doncha just look around."

译文注释

1. 《母亲的微笑》Smile of a Lifetime

    【注释】想必很多学生会将标题直译成 Mother's Smile，但英文用的是 Smile of a Lifetime。为什么会用 lifetime 一词？

    在这一故事中，作者提到父亲因为患有精神分裂症，被送进了精神病院；一家的重担就落在了母亲的肩上，她靠给邻居打零工养活"我"和哥哥，生活的艰辛使她很少微笑，能够让她微笑的事情也很少。母亲的微笑"我小时候见过一次，后来又见到了第二次"。第一次微笑：六岁时，母亲带我们去科尼岛度假，"我"跟着卖冰淇淋的小贩一路走，询问冰淇淋的价格。但问完后，发现自己迷路了，找不到回去的路。"我"一边跑一边哭，突然看到母亲牵着哥哥在找"我"。"母亲看到我时，我看见她脸上掠过令我终生不忘的一丝微笑：这微笑，洋溢在她的全身，纯真、舒展而又欣喜，仿佛在说：'总算找到你了！'"之后，在"我"的成长过程中，母亲为"我"操碎了心。"我"逃学到街上鬼混，学别人吸毒。有一次还因为群体斗殴而被捕，律师告诉法官"我"打算去服兵役，这样才没有被起诉。服完兵役后，"我"深知母亲的不易，决心不再走老路，打算考消防员。母亲的第二次微笑就是在"我"成为消防员的时候，因为当时成为一名消防员是一个了不起的成就。

    因此，英文标题中使用 a lifetime 突出了母亲微笑之少、之可贵，以及她的微笑对"我"的终生影响。

2. 那时是1946年，我才6岁。一个闷热的星期六上午，母亲对我和哥哥比利说要一起去科尼岛玩一天。I was only six at the time. It was a stifling hot Saturday morning in 1946, when my mother announced to my older brother, Billy, and me that we were going to Coney Island for the day.

    【注释】从一句话中我们就可以发现中英文表达的不同。中文表述中习惯先说哪一年，"我"多大了，发生了什么事情。而英文的表达却未必如此。

    因此，看似非常简单的句子在翻译时却会成为一个陷阱。在英语学习过程中，学生应当有意识地关注英文的表达习惯，这样在用英语表达时才不会出现表达生硬或不够地道的问题。

3. 大家脱去外衣，里面早就穿好了泳装。We slipped out of our clothes to our bathing suits beneath.

【注释】 回译这一句话时，可能有学生会译成 We took off our clothes since we had been dressed in the swimsuit. 对照英文的表达，是不是觉得英文的表述更为简洁呢？这就体现了英语翻译成中文，再从中文回译成英语时会遇到的一些典型问题，也体现了汉英语言的差异。

在进行回译练习时，千万不要被中文的字词和结构束缚，而应该努力设想英文的表达是怎样的，英语母语者会用何种句式表达同一信息。只有这样，翻译出来的译文才可能是地道自然的。

4. 我和冰淇淋小贩之间的对话翻译可能也不简单。尽管我们对故事中讨价还价的场景很熟悉，但未必清楚地道的英文口语如何表述。Kiddo=kid, doncha=don't you，这些都是英语口语中很地道的表达。

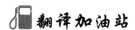翻译加油站

翻译方法：直译和意译

直译（literal translation）和意译（free translation）是英汉翻译中两种不同的方法。赞成用直译法的人认为，译文应尽力复制原文的语言形式，因为表达形式也反映了表达内容，形式的改变意味着意义的改变。只有保留原文的表达形式，才能忠实地传达原文的思想内容。普遍认为，在翻译中并非所有的句子都可以直译，如果直译行不通，可以尝试意译法。意译是指在忠实于原文内容的前提下，摆脱原文结构的束缚，使译文符合目的语的规范，将一种语言所表达的意义用另一种语言做释义性的解释，在转换过程中不必过分拘泥于原文的形式。

相对而言，直译更注重准确，而意译更注重通顺。但是，好的翻译应该既准确又通顺，达到两者的统一。一般而言，任何一个语篇的翻译都是由一定比例的直译和意译组合而成的。翻译过程中应采用哪一种方法，视具体情况而定。

第一，当汉语的句子结构和表达方式与英语相似时，应采用直译法。

汉语和英语在句子结构方面有一定的相似性。在英汉句子结构基本对应的情况下，应以直译为主。

例1　浑水摸鱼

to fish in troubled waters

例 2　不久，一九二四大革命爆发。

　　　Soon, the revolution of 1924 broke out.

例 3　我教他们英语。

　　　I teach them English.

例 4　失败是成功之母。

　　　Failure is the mother of success.

例 5　我已收到您的来信。

　　　I have received your letter.

　　上述例子中，中英文的句子结构基本对应，因此可以按照原文的形式直接译出。

　　第二，当汉语的句子结构和表达方式与英语差异较大时，可采用意译法。

　　汉语重意合，动词使用较多，没有词形变化、定语从句和独立主格结构，连接词和分词的使用也比英语少，逻辑关系不明显，且流水句较多；而英语句子重形合，经常使用词形变化、连接词、分词、定语从句和独立主格结构等手段表示成分之间的语法关系。当汉语的句子结构和表达方式与英语差异较大时，可以采用意译法。试看下面的例子：

例 6　望子成龙

　　　to expect one's child to be an outstanding personage

　　中国人认为龙能够喷云吐雾，行云布雨，神通广大，因而受人膜拜。在中国，龙还是皇权的象征，皇帝的身体叫"龙体"，穿的衣服叫"龙袍"，坐的椅子叫"龙椅"，睡的床叫"龙床"，就连皇帝的子孙也叫"龙子龙孙"。而英文读者眼中的 dragon 却是凶恶的象征。"亚洲四小龙"一般被译成 four tigers in Asia，而不是 four dragons in Asia。因此，"望子成龙"不宜直译成 to expect one's child to be a dragon，而是意译为 to expect one's child to be an outstanding personage。

例 7　那件令人不快的事件，已经搞得满城风雨、人人皆知了。

　　　There has been much publicity about the unpleasant case.

　　"满城风雨"如果直译为 wind and rain in the whole city，可能会让英文读者误以为是描述糟糕的天气，又是刮风又是下雨。这与原文想要表达的意思相差甚远，英文读者恐怕无法产生与原文读者相同的反应。因此，本句采用了意译的方法。另外，这句话如果意译为 This unpleasant case has been known to everyone，也是可以接受的。

例 8　一朝被蛇咬，十年怕井绳。
　　　　Once bitten, twice shy.

原文中的"蛇"与"井绳"在外形上有其相似之处，字面意思是"一旦被蛇咬过，看到井绳都可能感到非常恐惧"，比喻受过一次伤害后就害怕遇到同样或类似的事物或事件。如按照字面意义将该句译成英文，很可能表达不出其喻义，文字的美感也可能会消失殆尽。因此，译文采用的是意译法，文字表达非常精练。

上述三个句子的翻译均采用了意译的手法。如果直译这些句子的结构和表达方式，译文读者很可能会产生误解或者无法理解其内容，而用意译法翻译上述句子可以使译文更加地道，更符合译语的行文习惯。

课后练习

试将下列语篇回译成英文：

伦敦有许多美丽的公园和花园，但基尤植物园（Kew Gardens）景色最美。基尤植物园每天开放，乘公交车从伦敦市中心出发只需20分钟即可达到。这里一年四季都可以看到各种各样的花，基尤植物园里有10万种不同的植物是从其他国家采集而来的。喜爱炎热气候的植物生长在玻璃房中，我们把这些玻璃房称为温室，最大的是棕榈温室，它有近150年的历史。棕榈温室的构思很巧妙，大量的阳光能够射进来照在植物上。在温室内，你可以通过攀爬20米高的楼梯到达顶端，从上往下眺望棕榈树、橘子和香蕉，其景色令人心旷神怡。

第四章

中西文化差异

　　翻译不仅是语言的转换，也是文化的交流。每个民族都有各自的文化背景和价值取向。一个事物在一种文化中可能非常有美感，到了另一种文化中却可能因为价值取向和审美差异而失去原有的美感，甚至还会被曲解。

　　文化是什么？"文化"一词最早源于拉丁文 cultura，在拉丁文中的原义是"耕作、种植、作物"。现在所说的"文化"一词是19世纪末从日语中转译过来的。据《大英百科全书》统计，在世界各国的正式出版物中，关于"文化"一词的定义大约有160种。

　　目前对"文化"一词最权威的解释还是19世纪英国人类学家泰勒（Edward Tyler）在1871年出版的《原始文化》（*Primitive Culture*）一书中所给出的定义："从广义的人种论的意义上说，文化或文明是一个复杂的整体，它包括知识、信仰、艺术、道德、法律、风俗以及作为社会成员的人所具有的其他一切能力和习惯"[1]。

　　后来有学者认为这一定义强调了精神文化，却忽略了物质文化，因而对泰勒的定义进行了修订，补充了"实物"的文化现象。就这样，文化的定义被修正为："文化是一种复杂体，包括实物、知识、信仰、艺术、道德、法律、风俗以及其余社会上习得的能力与习惯"[2]。但这一新定义也存在一定的问题，如精神文化被细分为知识、信仰、艺术、道德、法律、风俗等诸多内容，而物质文化仅以"实物"一词加以替代，是否有失偏颇？

　　既然文化的内涵如此丰富，中国文化和西方文化各有什么特点？在翻译过程中，如果涉及文化因素，我们可以通过什么方式来处理？语言和文化之间又存在何种关系？

1　（英）泰勒.1988.原始文化.2版.蔡江浓，译.杭州：浙江人民出版社，1.
2　包惠南.2001.文化语境与语言翻译.北京：中国对外翻译出版公司，2.

名家名说

∞ 杨自俭

中华文化博大精深，就其特点而言，"张岱年先生在多篇文章中讲到了刚健有为、中庸、崇德利用、天人合一、有机整体观、知行合一、重义轻利、重德教轻宗教、爱国观念、人格意识、因循守旧、自由超脱、虚静思想、等级观念、男尊女卑、命运观念、鬼神迷信等。这些思想观念既包含高层次的学术思想，也包含低层次的社会心理"[3]（杨自俭，2000）。杨自俭（2000）认为，西方文化"在人与社会的关系上，西方一直是 individualism 占主导地位，主张人构成了社会，人是根本；不能牺牲个人利益成全社会利益；个人行为只要不损害他人与社会，任何人不能干涉；个人财产神圣不可侵犯。关于人与人的关系，西方讲人道主义的天赋人权，人生来自由平等，但不讲超出社会的人无所谓权利，全人类的人权现实是不存在的。后现代主义的全球化思潮推行人权高于主权，把人的生存权与发展权置于自由权之下"[4]。

∞ 邓炎昌、刘润清

在《语言与文化：英汉语言文化对比》一书中，邓炎昌和刘润清（1989）提到："现在人们认识到，语言至少有两套规则：一是结构规则，即语音、词汇、语法等；二是使用规则，即决定使用语言是否得体的诸因素。一句完全合乎语法的话，用于不恰当的场合，说得不合说话人的身份，或者违反当地的社会风俗习惯，就达不到交际的目的，有时甚至造成意想不到的后果。语言的使用规则实际上就是这种语言所属文化的各种因素。因此，学习和运用外语必须了解与这种外语有密切关系的文化。如果掌握语法知识有助于保证所造的外语句子结构正确，那么熟悉有关文化知识则有助于保证使用外语得当"[5]。

---

3 杨自俭. 2000. 关于中西文化对比研究的几点认识（代序）——英汉文化对比与跨文化交际学术研讨会开幕词 // 罗选民. 英汉文化对比与跨文化交际. 沈阳：辽宁人民出版社, 2.
4 同上，第4页.
5 邓炎昌，刘润清. 1989. 语言与文化：英汉语言文化对比. 北京：外语教学与研究出版社.

李运兴

就文化翻译模式而言，李运兴（2000）认为译者在处理文化成分时会采用如下模式[6]：

模式1. 文化直入（the Go-ahead Model），原语文化表达形式直接进入译文。

模式2. 文化阻断（the Block Model），原语文化表达形式消失，文化意义未进入译语语篇。

模式3. 文化诠释（the Annotation Model），为原语文化表达形式提供文化语境信息。

模式4. 文化融合（the Integration Model），原语文化表达形式与译语表达形式融合，以一种新的语言形式进入译语。

模式5. 文化归化（the Adaptation Model），原语表达形式略去，代之以译语表达形式，原语文化意义丧失。

李运兴从文化交流的角度将这五个模式分为两类：模式1、3、4促成不同文化的交流和沟通，而模式2和5则使原语文化成分被阻隔在目的语文化之外。这样的分类具有一定的意义。当然，就翻译实践而言，重点是如何在实践中行之有效地翻译与文化有关的词汇或篇章。

另外，就语言和文化而言，语言记录了一个民族和社会的历史发展进程，是一个民族历代智慧的结晶，但语言不能超越文化而独立存在，任何语言的生存发展都离不开其赖以生长的社会文化环境，社会文化又在一定程度上制约着语言使用者的思维方式和表达方式。因此，语言与生存环境、生活习惯、社会风俗、宗教修养、历史背景等文化因素有着千丝万缕的联系。

例如，英国是一个岛国，渔业和航海业在历史上和经济生活中占有很大的比重，因此，英语中有很多有关航海和海产的习语。如果将这些习语翻译成汉语，中国人恐怕很难找到完全对应的表达。例如：

rest on one's oars. 暂时歇一歇

---

6 李运兴. 2000. 翻译中的文化成分 // 罗选民. 英汉文化对比与跨文化交际. 沈阳：辽宁人民出版社，50-51.

keep one's head above water 奋力图存

as close/dumb as an oyster 守口如瓶

cast/lay/have an anchor to windward 未雨绸缪

all at sea 不知所措

a fish out of water 在陌生环境中不得其所的人

an odd/a queer fish 奇怪的人

neither fish nor fowl 不伦不类

have other fish to fry 有其他要事要办

drink like a fish 狂喝，牛饮

All is fish that comes to one's net. 捕到网里的都是鱼。/ 来者不拒。

Never offer to teach fish to swim. 千万不要班门弄斧。

There are plenty more fish in the sea. 还有很多一样好的人或事物。/ 天涯何处无芳草。

与英国不同的是，中国是一个农业大国，在农业生产中占据了重要地位的是牛，因此汉语中有很多表达与牛有关，如"力大如牛""汗牛充栋""九牛一毛""多如牛毛""老黄牛"，等等。

同时，汉语具有悠久的历史，不少地名在漫长的使用过程中逐渐被赋予了独特的历史文化内涵。例如，外国人可能知道泰山（Mount Tai）是中国的名山，但对泰山在汉语中的深刻喻义恐怕了解不多。泰山作为五岳之尊、群山之长，古人常以它为高山的代表，并把它比喻为令人敬仰的人物和极为重要的事物。正因为有了这样的历史渊源，汉语中才会有诸如"重如泰山""泰山压顶""有眼不识泰山"这样的习语。

另外，英语和汉语中都有部分成语源于各自的寓言或历史典故，包含特定的人名或地名。这类成语如果按照字面意思直译，译文读者通常无法理解。如果加上许多解释，又失去了成语的精练特色，成了翻译中的难题。例如：

毛遂自荐 to volunteer one's service

初出茅庐 at the beginning of one's career

东施效颦 crude imitation with ludicrous effect

南柯一梦 a fond dream or illusory joy

四面楚歌 to be besieged on all sides

这些译文仅仅译出了成语的喻义，其文化含义已经消失殆尽。因此，如何处理好翻译中的文化因素是提高译文质量的重要一步。

翻译语篇 1

祝　　福（节选）

鲁迅

有一年的冬初，四叔家里要换女工，做中人的卫老婆子带她进来了，头上扎着白头绳，乌裙，蓝夹袄，月白背心，年纪大约二十六七，脸色青黄，但两颊却还是红的。卫老婆子叫她祥林嫂，说是自己母家的邻舍，死了当家人，所以出来做工了。四叔皱了皱眉，四婶已经知道了他的意思，是在讨厌她是一个寡妇。但看她模样还周正，手脚都壮大，又只是顺着眼，不开一句口，很像一个安分耐劳的人，便不管四叔的皱眉，将她留下了。

译前提示

本段材料节选自鲁迅的短篇小说《祝福》。《祝福》写于1924年，鲁迅通过对祥林嫂一生悲惨遭遇的描写，刻画了一个被践踏、被愚弄、被鄙视的旧中国劳动妇女的典型形象。节选部分描绘了祥林嫂初到鲁镇的情景。

1. 本段中有很多称呼语，如"卫老婆子""祥林嫂""四叔"和"四婶"等，这些生活中常见的称呼应当如何翻译？
2. "白头绳"在中国文化中有着特殊的含义，这一细节描写与后面提及的"死了当家人"相互呼应，翻译时需要把暗含之意翻译出来吗？应如何翻译？
3. "蓝夹袄"和"月白背心"都是民国时期女性的典型衣饰，"袄"是否就是 jacket？

参考译文 1

The New-Year Sacrifice (Excerpt)[7]

Early one winter, when my uncle's family wanted a new maid, old Mrs. Wei the go-between brought her along. She had a white mourning band around her hair and was wearing a black skirt, blue jacket, and pale green bodice. Her age was about twenty-six, and though her face was sallow her cheeks were red. Old Mrs. Wei introduced her as Xianglin's Wife, a neighbor of her mother's family, who wanted to go out to work now that her husband had died. My uncle frowned at this, and my aunt knew that he disapproved of taking on a widow. She looked just the person for them, though, with her big strong hands and feet; and, judging by her downcast eyes and silence, she was a good worker who would know her place. So my aunt ignored my uncle's frown and kept her.

参考译文 2

New Year's Sacrifice (Excerpt)[8]

Early one winter, when my uncle was looking for a new maidservant, old Mrs. Wei—a middle woman in these sorts of transactions—brought her along to the house. Around twenty-five or twenty-six at the time, she wore a black skirt, a blue jacket and a lighter blue waistcoat, her hair tied up into a bun with a white cord. Though her face had a sallow, greenish tinge to it, her cheeks were pink. Mrs. Wei introduced her as Xianglin's wife, the neighbor of one of her mother's relatives. Her husband had died, so she'd left home to look for work. Uncle frowned; my aunt knew what was worrying him—the fact she was a widow. But seeing as she had a good sturdy look, with big, strong hands and feet, and kept her eyes docilely on the ground and let others do the talking for her, she seemed the kind of person who would know her place and do what she was told. And so, my uncle's scowl not withstanding, she was kept on.

---

7 鲁迅.2000.彷徨.杨宪益,戴乃迭,译.北京:外文出版社,20-21.

8 Lovell, Julia. (2009). *The Real Story of Ah-Q and Other Tales of China: The Complete Fiction of Lu Xun*. London: Penguin.

> 📖 **译文注释**

参考译文1是由杨宪益和戴乃迭翻译的,参考译文2是由研究中国历史和中国现代文学的英国学者Julia Lovell(蓝诗玲)翻译的。

1. 两个参考译文都将"卫老婆子"译成old Mrs. Wei,"祥林嫂"译成Xianglin's wife;当然,杨宪益的译本中wife的首字母用了大写。

    "卫老婆子"如译成old Mrs. Wei,是指她的丈夫姓卫。而《祝福》中提到,"大家都叫她祥林嫂;没问她姓什么,但中人是卫家山人,既说是邻居,那大概也就姓卫了"。这里的"中人"就是卫老婆子,由此可推断,卫老婆子自己姓卫,而不是她的丈夫姓卫。因此,将"卫老婆子"译成old Mrs. Wei是不妥的。

    那么,是否应该翻译成Lady Wei或者Ms. Wei呢?民国时期,称呼卫老婆子这种身份地位不高的中人为Lady或Ms.恐怕不合适。所以,"卫老婆子"可以考虑翻译成an old woman surnamed Wei。与old Mrs. Wei相比,an old woman surnamed Wei尽管有些拖沓,但至少与原文提供的信息相符。

2. 两个译本都将"四叔"和"四婶"译成了my uncle和my aunt,而没有把"第四"这一排行在英文中表达出来。这恐怕与文化差异有关系:中国人注重辈分大小和长幼有序,很多称呼,如"二爷""五婶""三弟""大舅""大伯""二叔"等,都体现了这一特点。当然,中国人也习惯按辈分和长幼关系将没有血缘关系的熟人称为"叔""伯""婶""姐""弟"等。此外,中国文化中严格区分父亲的亲戚和母亲的亲戚,父亲的兄弟叫叔叔和伯伯,而母亲的兄弟则叫舅舅;父亲的姐妹叫姑妈,而母亲的姐妹叫阿姨。英美文化中,称呼别人一般用某某先生(如Mr. Smith)、某某太太(如Mrs. Smith)和某某小姐(如Miss Smith)等;另外,在英美国家,父母的兄弟都叫uncle(如Uncle Tom),父母的姐妹都叫aunt(如Aunt Annie)。因此,这两个译本的作者都是按照西方人的称呼习惯来翻译的,没有在译文中把"第四"体现出来。

3. ……头上扎着白头绳……译文1:She had a white mourning band around her hair. 译文2:her hair tied up into a bun with a white cord.

    【注释】杨宪益和戴乃迭将"白头绳"译为a white mourning band,用mourning一词将白头绳在中国的文化含义翻译出来了;Julia Lovell仅将它译为a white cord,没有译出白头绳的文化内涵,这可能与译者没有意识到白头绳在中国文化中的含义有关系。

4. 两个译文都将"蓝夹袄"译成了 blue jacket。jacket 的英文释义是 a piece of clothing worn on the top half of the body over a shirt, etc. that has sleeves and fastens down the front；又或者是 a short, light coat，这与民国时期女性所穿的"夹袄"有一定的差异。

5. "月白背心"的译文 1 是 pale green bodice，译文 2 则是 a lighter blue waistcoat。Bodice 尤指 the top part of a woman's dress, above the waist，即"连衣裙的上身"。而 waistcoat 指 a short piece of clothing with buttons down the front but no sleeves, usually worn over a shirt and under a jacket, often forming part of a man's suit，即（西服）背心，特别是男士的西服背心，与祥林嫂穿在夹袄外的背心很不相同。

在翻译中国传统服饰时，我们会发现在英语中很难找到完全对等或者相对比较对等的词语，如"旗袍""长袍马褂"等都是典型的例子。在翻译时遇到涉及文化的词汇一般都比较棘手。如果条件允许，可以在正文之外加尾注或脚注，对该词进行进一步解释，以帮助译文读者了解该词的文化内涵。

翻译语篇 2

我不愿做女孩儿（节选）

王扶

如果你生就了是个女孩儿，如长得很不像个女孩儿的样，比如个子太高，脚太大，皮肤太黑，等等；

如果你是一个女孩儿，却生在一个全体都盼望生男孩儿的家庭里，你的命运恐怕就应该用另外两个字来代替——倒霉！

我，就是这么个倒尽了霉的女孩儿。

公平地说，妈妈算对我最好的，尽管因为生了我这个女孩儿，她遭尽了全家人的白眼。首先是父亲的。爸爸对妈妈从来就谈不上爱，只不过凑合生活罢了。用大人的话说，就是"过日子"。妈妈也盼生个儿子，来缓和一下这个"维持会"的紧张局面。没想到，儿子没生出却偏偏生了个不像女儿的女儿。这下儿，连爷爷奶奶也和爸爸构成了统一战线，极力主张爸爸和妈妈离婚。

妈妈姓马，她要我姓了她的姓，给我取名一个"力"字。妈说她盼我永远有力量，去争一口气。

> **译前提示**
>
> 本段材料节选自当代女作家王扶的小说《我不愿做女孩儿》的开篇，该小说通过一系列发生在"我"身上的不公正待遇，说明了"我"不愿做女孩儿的原因。这些不公正待遇无非是由于中国男尊女卑、重男轻女的思想在中国社会和某些家庭成员的头脑中作祟所引起的。
>
> 1. 原文第一段中有三个"太"，全部用 too 来表达吗？
> 2. "白眼"不能直译为 white eye，"翻白眼"可译为 roll one's eye 或者 look at sb. out the corner of one's eyes，"遭白眼"可译为 be given a disdainful look 或者 be treated with contempt。
> 3. "维持会"是带有抗日战争意味的讽刺性说法，翻译时不宜沿用这一说法。

参考译文

I Hate Being a Girl (Excerpt)[9]

If you're born a girl, but don't look like a girl—you're too large, your feet are oversized, and your skin is too dark.

If you're a girl like that, and born to a family desperate for a boy—well, I'm afraid your destiny can even be designated with two words—bad luck.

I am such a girl with the worst of all possible luck. To be fair, Mother has been very good to me, though she had been treated with the utmost contempt because of giving birth to me. The contempt came first from Father. He had never shown anything resembling love—they had made do with each other. In grown-ups' terms "they had passed their time from one day to the next". Mother had hoped to have a boy, too, thinking it might ease the tension in her precarious

---

9 刘士聪, 柯力诗. 2002. 汉英·英汉美文翻译与鉴赏（中英对照）. 上海：译林出版社, 349.

marriage. Instead, she had a girl, and one who wasn't even much of a girl. As a result, even my grandparents formed a united front with my father, urging him to get a divorce.

Mother's family name was Ma—Horse. She decided that I should take her family name and called me Li—Power, as my given name. She said she expected me to be a forceful woman, and make a good showing in the world.

译文注释

参考译文选自刘士聪和柯力诗合译的"I Hate Being a Girl",译文较好地把握了原文中那种夸张讽刺的口吻,达到了一定的翻译效果。

1. 如果你生就了是个女孩儿,如长得很不像个女孩儿的样,比如个子太高,脚太大,皮肤太黑,等等;If you're born a girl, but don't look like a girl—you're too large, your feet are oversized, and your skin is too dark.

   【注释】第一段中的"个子太高,脚太大,皮肤太黑"译成了 you're too large, your feet are oversized, and your skin is too dark,原文的三个"太"用两个 too 和 oversize 加以转换,避免语言表达过于单一。

   中文表达中习惯用一系列的排比来增加气势,但英文中应尽量避免用词的单调和重复。因此,汉译英过程中,千万不能忽视英文读者的审美习惯和表达习惯。

2. 爸爸对妈妈从来就谈不上爱,只不过凑合生活罢了。He had never shown anything resembling love—they had made do with each other.

   【注释】译文用 make do with each other 把父母亲之间缺乏爱意,只是搭伙过日子的感觉翻译出来了。

3. 用大人的话说,就是"过日子"。In grown-ups' terms "they had passed their time from one day to the next".

   【注释】"过日子"译成了 they had passed their time from one day to the next,把原文的意思进行了传达。不过,可以考虑在 had 和 passed 之间加上 merely 一词,这样效果可能会更好。

4. 妈妈也盼生个儿子,来缓和一下这个"维持会"的紧张局面。Mother had hoped to have a boy, too, thinking it might ease the tension in her precarious marriage.

【注释】"维持会"在此处属于讽刺性的说法,不宜直译出来。译文中将它转译成 her precarious marriage,表"岌岌可危的婚姻"之意。从整个语篇可以知道,"我"的爸爸妈妈感情不好,他们的婚姻随时可能破裂,因此这样的改译是有道理的。

在翻译过程中一定要熟悉原文的内容,透彻理解原文所要传达的意思,不能望文生义,以免让读者产生误解。

5. 妈妈姓马,她要我姓了她的姓,给我取名一个"力"字。Mother's family name was Ma—Horse. She decided that I should take her family name and called me Li—Power, as my given name.

【注释】在介绍"我"的名字时,译文采用汉字拆字加释义的译法,对全文主题的传达起到了较好的烘托作用。

当然,整个译文中,破折号的使用频率远远高于一般的英文写作,这一点应尽量避免。

翻译加油站

翻译技巧(一):选词

在汉译英过程中,基本句型确定后的重要一步就是要选择合适的英语单词、词组和句型来表达汉语的内容。因此,正确的选词是保证译文质量的重要一步。

一、根据上下文选词

一个词在新的语境中意义可能会发生改变。因此,在汉译英过程中,应根据上下文选择合适的单词或词组。

例1 她**追求**的是真理,而他**追求**的是荣华富贵。
What she *seeks* is truth, and what he *hankers after* is nothing but high position and great wealth.

原文有两个"追求",但感情色彩不同。第一个"追求"是褒义词,而第二个则是贬义词。译文中,第一个"追求"翻译成 seek,第二个则使用了 hanker after。Seek 属中性词,如 seek a more brilliant future(寻求更美好的未来);seek medical treatment(寻求医治);而 hanker after 则有"贪图"之意,如 hanker after power(贪图权力）。所以，在汉译英过程中切忌抱着一本词典，不顾上下文直接照搬照抄；一定要从上下文出发，考虑所选词语的褒贬色彩、词语表达的强烈程度、语体特征等内容，这样我们的译文才可能做到既忠实又准确。

例 2　A：这点小**意思**，请务必收下。

B：你这个人真有**意思**，怎么也来这套？

A：哎，只是**意思意思**。

B：啊，真是不好**意思**！

A: This is (a little gift as) *a token of my appreciation*. Please do take it.

B: Oh, aren't you a bit too *polite*? You should not do that.

A: Well, it just *conveys my gratitude*.

B: Ah, thank you (though I really do *not deserve* it).

这一对话中，"意思"的出现频率很高，表达的意思也各不相同，从英文斜体部分可以看出每一个"意思"所要表达的侧重点。另外，在翻译时不能仅着眼于某些词语的具体含义，还需要注意整个句子的社会功能和交际功能，如最后一句的"啊，真是不好意思！"。中国文化中，"啊，真是不好意思！"往往是说话人接受了礼物时的客套之词，翻译时就不需要把"意思"翻译出来，直接按照英美交际文化的习惯把将整个句子译成 thank you 即可。

例 3　这娃娃**头**真大。（就是指头，可选 head）

This baby has a big *head*.

例 4　她在梳**头**。（"梳头"指梳头发，应选 hair）

She is combing her *hair*.

例 5　她女儿在山**头**玩。（"山头"指山尖、山的顶端，可选 top 或 peak。当然，top 比 peak 更合适，因为 peak 给人的感觉是山很高，不太符合"她女儿"的人物设定。）

Her daughter is playing on the *top* of the hill.

例 6　一辆小车停在桥西**头**。（"桥西头"说明该桥东西向，"西头"指西边的桥头。但要注意，英语中用 end 表达桥的两头。）

A car was parked at the west *end* of the bridge.

例 7　让我再从**头**讲起。（"从头讲起"比较好理解，即"从一开始说起"，可译成 beginning。）

Let me tell the story from the very *beginning*.

例8　他把铅笔**头**扔了。（"铅笔头"的惯用法是 pencil stub。）

He has thrown away the pencil *stub*.

例9　他是我们组的**头**儿。（"头儿"即"领导"之意，可选的词较多，如 head、chief 和 leader 等。）

He is the *head/chief* of our group.

例10　事情不能只顾一**头**。（此处的"一头"应该是"一方面"的意思，可译成 aspect。）

We must not pay attention to only one *aspect* of the matter.

例11　这还是我**头**一次来杭州呢。（"头一次"即"第一次"，the first time。）

This is the *first* time that I have been in Hangzhou.

例12　我们有 30 **头**牛。（此处的"头"是量词。要注意，head 作量词时，单复数同形。）

We have thirty *head* of cattle.

"头"在汉语中属于高频单词，在不同语境中表达的意思也各有不同。这些译文主要根据上下文进行选词，以准确传达原文所要表达的意思。下面有关"运动"的例子也是如此。

例13　**运动**有益身心。（此处"运动"侧重表达"锻炼"之意，可选用 exercise。）

Exercise is good for health.

例14　足球是我喜欢的**运动**。（足球是运动项目中的一类，"某项运动"通常选用的是 sport。）

Football is my favorite *sport*.

例15　我国每年纪念"五四**运动**"。（"五四运动"并不陌生，国内翻译该词时多选用 May Fourth Movement 的表达。笔译过程中，碰到这一类专有名词时，可以上网查找以帮助确定译文。）

The May Fourth *Movement* is commemorated in our country every year.

例16　他们发动了一场戒烟**运动**。（为了一定的社会目的或政治目的而进行的运动，往往会首选 campaign 一词。）

They started a *campaign* against smoking.

例17 技术革新**运动**是成功的关键。（此处的"运动"是范畴词，没有实际含义，可不译。）

Technological *renovation* is a key to success.

例18 人们热烈响应筹款**运动**。（Drive 一般指团体为了特定目的而进行的有组织的活动。筹款运动一般都是有组织的，可以选用 drive。）

There was great enthusiasm for the donation *drive*.

二、根据词的搭配习惯选词

汉英两种语言各有自己的搭配习惯，汉译英时，应根据英语的搭配习惯进行翻译。例如：

送某人一本书 *Give* sb. a book

送礼 *present* a gift to sb.

送信 *deliver* a letter

送客 *see* a visitor out

送行 *see* sb. off

送命 *lose* one's life

送孩子上学 *take* a child to school

送某人回家 *escort* sb. home

送卫星上天 *launch* a satellite

汉语中，"送"属于常用动词，能搭配使用的词特别多。在翻译成英语时，一定要注意英语的搭配习惯，不能千篇一律地选用 give 进行翻译。

取消一次会议 to *cancel/call off* a meeting

取消决定 to *rescind* a decision

取消禁令 to *lift* a ban

取消诺言 to *kill* the promise

取消会员资格 to *deprive* sb. of his membership

与"送"一样，"取消"一词在汉语中使用频率也很高，英译时也应注意英语的搭配习惯，不能都译成 cancel。

汉英两种语言存在较多差异，汉译英时应按照英文的搭配习惯来处理汉语，因为英文中有些是固定的表达，有些则是可以逐字翻译的。翻译时应根据具体情况确定选词。

课后练习

> **试将下列语篇译成英文：**

1. 酷抠族，是悄然崛起于当今"族"语境下的一群时尚达人。人如其名，他们身上既有"酷"（cool）的超逸，也有"凡人"（carl）的简约。是当下一种时尚的抠门，这是一种褒义下的"抠"，因为酷抠族崇尚的是"节约光荣，浪费可耻"。酷抠族未必贫穷，也不是守财奴，他们具有较高的学历，不菲的收入。酷抠族精打细算不是吝啬，而是一种节约的方式。

2. 但到了第二天的早晨，肥皂就被录用了。这日他比平日起得迟，看见她已经伏在洗脸台上擦脖子，肥皂的泡沫就如大螃蟹嘴上的水泡一般，高高的堆在两个耳朵后，比起先前用皂荚时候的只有一层极薄的白沫来，那高低真有霄壤之别了。

中篇

实用翻译

第五章
商务广告的翻译

广告，就是广而告之，即广泛地告知公众某种事物的宣传活动。我国 1980 年出版的《辞海》给它下的定义是："向公众介绍商品、报道服务内容或文娱节目等的一种宣传方式，一般通过报刊、电台、电视台、招贴、电影、幻灯、橱窗布置、商品陈列的形式来进行"[1]。《中华人民共和国广告法》（1994 年版）"总则"中将广告解释为"商品经营者或者服务提供者承担费用，通过一定媒介和形式直接或者间接地介绍自己所推销的商品或者所提供的服务"的行为。著名的美国市场营销协会（American Marketing Association，即 AMA）给广告下的定义是："广告是由特定的广告主通常以付费的方式通过各种媒体对产品、劳务或观念等信息的介绍及推广。"因此，广告的主要功能就在于介绍和推销某一种商品或服务。

就广告的目的而言，美国广告协会（Association of National Advertising）将之归纳为 Awareness，Comprehension，Conviction 和 Action。Awareness 是指广告的作用在于引起公众对广告产品的注意力；Comprehension 是指广告必须使公众理解广告所要传达的信息；Conviction 是指广告应说服公众接受广告产品；Action 是指公众最终采取行动，购买广告产品。因此，广告必须在选词、措辞、句法上富有特色，才能实现其特定目标。

在如今的信息社会，各种各样的商务广告铺天盖地般地进入我们的视野。作为一种具有商业价值的应用文体，商务广告的最大特点就在于其推销性，即让消费者认识、理解某种商品或服务。因此，商务广告旨在满足消费者真实或潜在的需要，激发消费者的购买欲望，从而使消费行为成为现实。

一个完整的广告理论上包括标题、商标、口号、正文和插图五部分。本章主要探讨的是广告的正文部分。

---

[1] 《辞海》编辑委员会.1980.辞海·经济分册.2 版.上海：上海辞书出版社，401.

商务广告的语言特点

商务广告语言风格独特，富有感召力，不同的商务广告虽有其独特之处，但通常都有其共同点：极具吸引力、创造力、说服力和影响力。

在词汇上，商务广告有如下特点：

首先，中英文广告均喜欢创造新词、怪词，以吸引消费者的眼球。如一家旅行社推出的广告"TWOGETHER[2]"；又如山西汾酒的广告"汾酒必喝，喝酒必汾"[3]，也是典型的例子。

其次，频繁使用形容词，增加鼓动性和感染力，如北京烤鸭的广告"烤鸭色枣红、鲜艳、油亮、皮脆、肉嫩、味美适口；别有奇香，久吃不腻，营养丰富"。英文广告中还喜欢使用形容词的比较级和最高级，如一种洗发水的广告：There is a remarkable gel that can give your hair any look you want—sleeker, fuller, straighter, curlier, more natural...。

另外，英语广告中还经常灵活组词构成一些复合词，如 thrill-of-a-lifetime, environmental-friendly 等。

在语法上，商务广告有如下特点：

首先，多用简单句和祈使句，可口可乐的广告"Coca-Cola is it"和飞利浦的广告"Let's make things better"都是典型的例子。中文广告也多使用简单句和祈使句，如大宝的广告"要想皮肤好，早晚用大宝"。

其次，多用省略句，如佳洁士（Crest）的"Behind that healthy smile"和欧米茄（Omega）的广告"It is a moment you planned for. Reached for. Struggled for. A Long-awaited moment of success."。

另外，在广告中还经常使用各种修辞手法，如双关和文字游戏等，如摩尔（More）香烟的广告"I am More satisfied"，可奈牌冰箱的广告"可奈，可奈，人见人爱！"[4]

---

2 这是一则为夫妻提供休闲旅游的广告，该广告故意将"Together"错拼为"TWOGETHER"，强调了夫妇二人共享假期的快乐，以吸引消费者的注意力。

3 "汾酒"必"喝"的发音与"逢酒必喝"很相似。

4 该广告利用了"可奈"与"可爱"的谐音。

商务广告翻译的要点

广告作为一种信息载体，本身充满丰富的想象力、极大的创造性和很强的煽动性，译文也应当凸显这些特点，做到简洁、生动、形象，富于感情色彩和感染力。由于社会文化和语言等方面的原因，翻译广告时并非只是一一对应的语码转换，而是在保持深层结构的语义基本对等以及功能相似的前提下，重组原语信息的表达形式，尽可能运用多种翻译技巧从不同的角度进行多层次的处理，从而达到形、神、意兼顾的翻译效果。

商务广告翻译大致有如下翻译方法：

第一，直译，就是从形式、内容到文化色彩等都保留其原文特征，如"The taste is good"译为"味道好极了"；"Drive carefully—the life you save may be your own"译为"安全驾驶——救人一命即救己"。中文广告"高科技的产品，时代的精华"译为"A product of high technology, the quintessence of a new age"；北京烤鸭是一种风味独特的中国传统名菜，距今已有300多年的历史，最早是由金陵（南京）王府膳房流传出来的。译为"Beijing Roast Duck is a special traditional Chinese recipe which has a history of more than 300 years, originating from the imperial kitchen in Nanjing."

第二，意译，即保留内容而舍弃形式，如麦斯威尔（Maxwell）咖啡的广告"Good to the last drop"译为"滴滴香浓，意犹未尽"；诺基亚（Nokia）的"Connecting people!"译为"诺基亚，科技以人为本！"。中文广告中也不乏这样的例子，《环球》杂志的广告"一册在手，纵览全球"译为"*The Globe* brings you the world in a single copy"。

第三，套译，即直接采用形义都与原文对应的现成的广告套语，如将南方科技咨询服务公司的广告"有了南方，就有了方法"译为"Where there is South, there is a way."[5]

第四，转译，即依照目的语的习惯，对原文从视角、虚实和形象等方面进行转换的翻译，如将青岛牌电视的广告"不求今日拥有，但求天长地久"译为"Choose once and choose for good."

---

5 该译文套用了英语谚语"Where there is a will, there is a way."，这一译法恰到好处，令客户觉得该公司有无数的妙计。

第五章 商务广告的翻译

翻译语篇 1

您的肌肤有变黑、雀斑和色斑问题吗？您还在为此而烦恼吗？现在让欧莱雅帮助您。

经过多年专业研究以及同全球皮肤专家的合作，欧莱雅在护肤方面拥有了强大的专业优势。欧莱雅位于巴黎和东京的研发中心，特别针对亚洲女性肌肤进行研究，致力于开发革命性配方，以满足亚洲女性的需求。

皮肤专家高桥庆子博士建议您：不仅要在白天针对皮肤变黑的每一步进行保养，夜间的保养也同样重要；在夜间，黑色素仍然持续产生，而肌肤吸收有效成分的速度也会更快。因此，夜间是进一步美白的理想时间。

欧莱雅雪颜三重美白系列能够提供完善的全天候滋润，针对肌肤变黑过程的每一步，提供有效保护，全面抵御 UVA 和 UVB 紫外线。此外，它还包含多种皮肤修复成分，于夜间强化护理肌肤，增强肌肤对紫外线的抵抗力。每晚持续使用，令您的肌肤恢复自然光彩。

译前提示

本段材料是著名化妆品牌欧莱雅（L'Oréal）雪颜三重美白系列（White Perfect-Triple Whitening）的广告，属于典型的广告文体。

很多公司在广告中会强调公司的实力强大，产品效果好，而且物美价廉。在平时的学习中可以多积累相关的词汇，这样可以达到事半功倍的效果。

1. "雀斑"可译成 freckle，"色斑"是 color spot。
2. "高桥庆子博士"是 Dr. Keiko Takahashi。
3. "UVA 和 UVB 紫外线"可译成 UVA/UVB rays。

整段材料逻辑清晰，表达连贯，富有感染力。在进行翻译时，应尽可能选择富有感召力的英语表达，引起读者，特别是女性读者的注意，以达到推销这一化妆品的目的。

参考译文

Do you have the problem of skin darkening, freckles or color spots? Are you still worried about that? Now L'Oréal can help you to solve it.

For many years, L'Oréal has been developing a strong expertise on skincare through advanced research and partnerships with dermatologists worldwide. L'Oréal research centers in Paris and Tokyo are dedicated to perfecting the knowledge of Asian skin and issuing innovative formulas to meet the specific needs of Asian women.

Dr. Keiko Takahashi, a specialist in dermatology, gives you this piece of advice: an action at each step of the skin darkening process is essential in the morning but also in the evening; at night, the production of melanin goes on, and skin is more receptive to active ingredients. Hence, night is the ideal time to complete the day whitening action. In addition to a perfect all-day moisturizing action, which acts at each step of skin darkening process, providing an optimal protection against UVA/UVB rays, White Perfect-Triple Whitening contains Repair Complex, a powerful cell-repairing complex to strengthen skin during the night. It enhances skin resistance against UV rays and night after night, skin recovers its natural qualities.

译文注释

参考译文语言表达流畅，能够将原文广告中的信息较好地传递给译文读者，从而吸引读者购买欧莱雅的产品。

1. 您的肌肤有变黑、雀斑和色斑问题吗？ Do you have the problem of skin darkening, freckles or color spots?

   【注释】为了吸引消费者的注意力，广告中经常会在一开始时就使用一些疑问句。本广告用词比较正式，用了"您"，翻译成英语时用 you 即可，以拉近与消费者之间的距离，使消费者在看到广告后心生亲近之意。

2. 欧莱雅位于巴黎和东京的研发中心，特别针对亚洲女性肌肤进行研究，致力于开发革命性配方，以满足亚洲女性的需求。L'Oréal research centers in Paris and Tokyo are dedicated to perfecting the knowledge of Asian skin and issuing innovative formulas to meet the specific needs of Asian women.

【注释】"欧莱雅位于巴黎和东京的研发中心"在原文中是一个分句，译文翻译为 L'Oréal research centers in Paris and Tokyo，成了整个句子的主语。"位于……" 在商务广告中经常被翻译成 in 引导的地点状语或者是定语从句。

例如，"饭店位于城区较好的地段，是个舒适、宁静的庭院"，可翻译成：With a fine location in the city, this hotel is a homelike and tranquil courtyard. 在阅读英文材料时，可以关注一些英文的表达习惯；在日常生活中，对看到的中文标识、听到的新闻、读到的中文材料，试着思考一下其英文表达，让自己时时做翻译的有心人。

3. 欧莱雅雪颜三重美白系列能够提供完善的全天候滋润，针对肌肤变黑过程的每一步，提供有效保护，全面抵御 UVA 和 UVB 紫外线。此外，它还包含多种皮肤修复成分，于夜间强化护理肌肤，增强肌肤对紫外线的抵抗力。In addition to a perfect all-day moisturizing action, which acts at each step of skin darkening process, providing an optimal protection against UVA/UVB rays, White Perfect-Triple Whitening contains Repair Complex, a powerful cell-repairing complex to strengthen skin during the night.

【注释】原文的两个句子长度不短，但译者将这两个句子合译在一起，通过短语和从句，在句法结构上层层修饰，句中套句，再加上插入语、补充成分、同位语或独立成分等，组成了一个非常复杂的长句，发挥了英语句式的优点。

译文中包含定语从句及较长的同位语，是典型的英语长句。翻译时，如果对英语长句的表达没有把握，也可以按照原文的形式用两个句子加以表达。

4. 每晚持续使用，令您的肌肤恢复自然光彩。...night after night, skin recovers its natural qualities.

【注释】化妆品广告中经常强调产品对肌肤的改善作用，如"令肌肤白皙""焕发肌肤自然光彩""保持肌肤的清新滋润"等。如果平时较熟悉这一类表达，翻译时可以省不少时间。

翻译语篇 2

外出旅行时，您最喜欢的音乐也带上了吗？具有 FullSound 技术的飞利浦 GoGear 专为提升 MP3 音乐的播放音质而打造。

想让 MP3 音乐给您带来最大享受吗？凭借飞利浦 FullSound 技术，一切皆有可能。FullSound 技术丰富了音乐信号，让您能够听到丰富饱满的声音；它将音乐天才的每一丝情感和每个声音细节都表达得恰如其分，让人如痴如醉。这种独特功能提升了常规 MP3 的音质，使其成为高品质的音乐体验。结合品质卓越的飞利浦耳机，您的 MP3 音乐堪比天籁之音！

GoGear 轻盈小巧，方便随身携带，更具有简单易用的菜单。凭借 FullSound 技术，您可以体验到更具动感的音乐；与此同时，您可以欣赏高质量的视频，存储和查看照片，还可以收听 FM 收音机。GoGear 还有内置麦克风，您可以用它录音。

另外，GoGear 提供了直观的用户界面，导航既快速又简单，您还可对其自定义。当您对原有的歌曲感到厌倦，想找新的歌曲时，您可以轻松浏览音乐资料库，同时还可轻松控制音乐播放。这样，每个聆听时刻都可以成为一种全新的体验。

当今音乐的文件格式多种多样。但您不用担心，飞利浦 GoGear 播放机支持多种文件格式。无论您想聆听 MP3、WMA 还是 AAC 歌曲，完全没有问题。尽情享受吧！

从现在开始，您可以随身体验完美的音乐了。

译前提示

本段材料是飞利浦 MP3 的广告。总体而言，本广告篇幅较长，翻译时有一定的难度。翻译前可以参阅其他品牌 MP3 的广告进行参考或者搜索飞利浦相关产品的广告或介绍，尽量掌握一些英语的平行文本，从而使译文更加自然和地道。

另外，因为本语篇宣传的产品是 MP3，选词时应尽量选择富有科技含量、与高音质有关的单词和词组。

1. 因为宣传的是高科技产品，材料中有很多与科技有关的词汇，应搜索网络或其他的 MP3 广告确定正确的译文。另外，原文中一些英文表达夹杂其中，如 FullSound、WMA 和 AAC，英译时直接保留即可。
2. "内置麦克风"可译成 built-in microphone。

参考译文

When you're on the go, does your favorite music travel with you? The Philips GoGear with FullSound was created to enhance the sound quality of your MP3 music while you play it.

Want to get out everything from your MP3 files? With Philips FullSound you can. This unique feature upgrades the regular MP3 performance to a high quality audio experience. It enriches the music signal, so what you hear is the full sound; with every nuance of emotion and every detail of musical genius it puts back where it belongs. Together with Philips superior quality headphones, your MP3 music really comes to life!

The GoGear is lightweight and compact so you can carry it easily, with a simple-to-use menu. As well as listening to more dynamic sounding music with FullSound you can watch high quality video, store and view photos, and listen to FM Radio. There is also a built-in microphone so you can record your own voice.

Moreover, GoGear offers an intuitive user interface for fast and easy navigation, which you can also customize it. As you get bored of old favorites and want to discover new ones, you can easily browse your music library and still control your music playback. So every listening moment can be a new experience.

We all know music comes in many different file formats these days. But don't worry, Philips GoGear players offer a wide file format support. It really doesn't matter whether you want to listen to your MP3, WMA or AAC songs. Enjoy it!

Now you can experience your music on the go as never before.

译文注释

参考译文来自飞利浦 GoGear 的英文广告，语言颇为地道，且富有感染力，能够给译文读者留下较深刻的印象，从而促使他们购买这一产品。

1. 具有 FullSound 技术的飞利浦 GoGear 专为提升 MP3 音乐的播放音质而打造。The Philips GoGear with FullSound was created to enhance the sound quality of your MP3 music while you play it.

    【注释】译文中增加了 while you play it，使表达更具逻辑性。

    在翻译过程中，出于逻辑的考虑译者有时会增加一些原文隐含或省略的内容。在进行翻译时，译者应当对所译文本进行逻辑梳理，表达过程中可以酌情增加或删减某些信息，以帮助译文读者更好地理解相关内容。

2. 它将音乐天才的每一丝情感和每个声音细节都表达得恰如其分，让人如痴如醉。...with every nuance of emotion and every detail of musical genius it puts back where it belongs.

   【注释】"nuance"表示"（意义、声音、颜色、感情等方面的）细微差别"，将MP3的高品质凸显出来。

   商务广告中往往会选用一些新词或富有感染力的词语，涉及高科技产品的广告更是如此。进行翻译时，应注重选词，尽量实现广告的潜在目的。

3. 结合品质卓越的飞利浦耳机，您的MP3音乐堪比天籁之音！Together with Philips superior quality headphones, your MP3 music really comes to life!

   【注释】原文中的"堪比天籁之音"转译成your MP3 music really comes to life，这一表达同样生动并极具感染力。

   对不熟悉的文本类型，可以在翻译前多阅读一些平行文本，这样有助于译者更好地把握该类型文本的措辞、常用句式和文体风格。商务广告的平行文本很容易就能找到，只要搜索同行业大公司的网站，一般都能找到相关的内容。

4. GoGear轻盈小巧，方便随身携带，更具有简单易用的菜单。The GoGear is lightweight and compact so you can carry it easily, with a simple-to-use menu.

   【注释】中文广告中经常会使用很多四字格，如"轻盈小巧""方便耐用""价格公道""货源充足""新颖时尚"等，翻译成英文时一般选用一个相关意义的形容词即可。因此，词汇的积累对翻译速度和翻译质量而言非常重要。

5. 当您对原有的歌曲感到厌倦，想找新的歌曲时，您可以轻松浏览音乐资料库，同时还可轻松控制音乐播放。As you get bored of old favorites and want to discover new ones, you can easily browse your music library and still control your music playback.

   【注释】"音乐资料库"可译成music library，"音乐播放"翻译成music playback，即"音乐回放"，在该句中是一个可行的译法。尽管原文是一个长句，但翻译的难度并不高。只要掌握了这两个词，正确翻译这一句话不是难事。

🛢 翻译加油站

翻译技巧（二）：增词法

汉英两种语言在词法和句法上存在很大的差异，如英语中有词形变化，汉语中没有；英语中有大量的连词、介词、关系代词等，汉语中的各个成分却通过内在联系组合在一起，不一定或很少使用连词和介词。因此，翻译过程中不能逐词、逐句地翻译。

汉译英过程中，在表达同一思想时常需要在译文中增补一些原文中没有的词语，主要包括出于语法需要而增词、出于语义需要而增词和出于文化传递而增词三种情况。

一、出于语法需要而增词

汉译英时，往往会因为语法需要而增补冠词、介词、代词、动词和连词等。

（一）增补冠词

例 1　耳朵是用来听声音的器官，鼻子是用来嗅气味的，舌头是用来尝滋味的。

The ear is the organ which is used for hearing. *The* nose is used for smelling. *The* tongue is used for tasting.

英语中，提到独一无二的事物，如日月星辰，要选用定冠词 the。同时，在表达人体部位时也是如此。因此，译文中增加了三个 the。

（二）增补介词

例 2　1976 年 7 月 28 日，唐山发生了大地震。

On July 28, 1976, a big earthquake took place in Tangshan.

与中文不同，英文中提到具体的日期时，介词 on 是不能省略的。

例 3　你经常想到帮助别人是很好的。

It is good *of* you to be always thinking of helping others.

大部分学生在看到原句时，都知道应采用句型 It is adj. for/of sb. to do sth.。在表达人物的性格、品德、主观感情或态度的形容词后，如 good, kind, nice, clever 和 foolish, 应选用 of, 而不是 for。

（三）增补代词

例 4　大作已收到，十分高兴。

　　　I was very glad to have received your writing.（增补作主语的代词）

例 5　贵公司 7 月 9 日的来函已收悉。

　　　We acknowledge the receipt of the letter of your company dated July 9.（增补作主语的代词）

汉语可以用无主句表达；但英语中除了祈使句，一般的句子都有主语。因此，这两句话在翻译时各自增补了人称代词 I 和 We 作主语。

例 6　你越讲大道理，大家就越感到讨厌。

　　　The more you elaborate on empty theories, the more people feel disgusted with *them*.（增补作宾语的代词）

例 7　他发现要及时完成这一任务很难。

　　　He found *it* difficult to finish the task on time.（增补作宾语的代词）

例 6 中，be disgusted with sb./sth. 表示"厌恶某人 / 物""讨厌某人 / 物"；因此，出于语法需要，译文中增补了 with 的宾语 them。例 7 中，"发现某物 / 人怎么样"的英文表达是 find sth./sb. + adj., 译文中增补了形式宾语 it, 替代后面的不定式短语 to finish the task on time。

例 8　凡是在科学技术上有建树者，都是工作最勤奋，并且勇于创新的人。

　　　Those *who* have made original contributions to science and technology are the ones who have worked the hardest and have not been afraid to break new ground.（增补关系代词）

汉语中没有关系代词，但英语的定语从句经常需要使用它。例 8 中，译者增补了 who 做定语从句的主语，否则该从句就没有主语，犯了语法错误。

（四）增补动词

例 9　他眼明手快。

　　　He *is* quick of eye and deft of hand.

例 10　他们喜形于色。

　　They *beamed* with joy.

例 11　我对他敬而远之。

　　I *stood* aloof from him.

　　与英语不同，汉语中很多句子没有谓语动词，如"明天晴天""花很美"等，译成英语时就需要增补谓语动词。四字格，如"眼明手快""喜形于色"和"敬而远之"，在翻译成英文时也是如此，否则句子就缺少谓语。

（五）增补连词

　　汉语中经常会省略表示逻辑关系的连词，比如，人们往往会说"天冷了，多穿点"，而不是"因为天冷了，所以多穿点"。但在译成英文时，应根据英文的表达习惯，增加表示相关逻辑关系的连词。

例 12　不努力不成功。

　　One will not succeed *unless* one works hard.

　　原文没有主语，翻译时首先应增补主语 one 或 we 等，用于泛指。有的学生可能会译成"If one does not work hard, he will not succeed."。但仔细分析原句后会发现，原句是励志型的话语，表达的深层含义应是"人不会成功，除非他努力"。因此，选用 unless 可以将原句的含义更加准确地表达出来。

例 13　虚心使人进步，骄傲使人落后。

　　Modesty helps one to go forward, *whereas* conceit makes one lag behind.

　　原文的两个分句属对比关系，如果译文仅用一句话译出，就需要增补连词将前后两部分内容连接起来，只有这样才能符合英语语法。

例 14　早知他有病，我就不叫他来了。

　　If I had known he was ill, I would not have asked him to come.

　　"早知他有病，我就不叫他来了"是典型的虚拟语气，翻译时应想到要用 if 引导。另外，如果记不清虚拟语气的具体用法，应当及时复习。

二、出于语义需要而增词

例15 谁都知道朝鲜战场是艰苦些。

Everyone knows that *the life* on the Korean battlefield was rather hard.

战场本无艰苦这一说法，这里指的应该是战场上的生活艰苦些，因此译文中增加了 the life 这一内容。

例16 公司里一半以上的雇员表示要在今年买车。

More than half of the employees in the company have expressed *their desire* to buy a car this year.

译文中增加了 their desire，将 to buy a car this year 变成了后置定语来修饰 desire。当然，也可以将这句话翻译成宾语从句，如 "More than half of the employees in the company have said that they want to buy a car this year."。

例17 窝藏不报者，须受相当的处分。

Persons who shelter *undesirable elements* and do not report them to the *authorities concerned* shall be duly punished.

原文省略的内容较多，如窝藏的是什么东西？要报告哪个组织或机构？原文中没有交代这些具体的信息，但是译者需要根据原文内容进行适当的增补，从而使译文读者了解原文所要传达的信息。

例18 我希望，在座各位以及一切爱好和平的人民携起手来，为共同促进世界的持久和平和各国各地区的普遍发展与繁荣而努力。

I hope that all of us here today will join hands with all *other* peace-loving people and work for lasting world peace and the common development and prosperity of all nations and regions.

原文的表述是"在座各位以及一切爱好和平的人民携起手来"，如果译成 all of us here today will join hands with all peace-loving people，那么言下之意就是"在座的各位不爱好和平"。因此，other 一词是必须增加的内容。

三、出于文化传递而增词

例19 班门弄斧

Try to show off your proficiency with the ax before Lu Ban *the master carpenter*.

例 20 "黑孩子"

Black children, *who are born in violation of China's one-child policy*

英文读者未必知道鲁班是谁，所以例 19 中的斜体字部分解释了他的身份：他不是普通人，而是木匠中的行家；例 20 中将"黑孩子"一词直译为 black children，同时用斜体字增补了"黑孩子"的内涵，即"当时违反了中国独生子女政策的孩子"，这样英文读者能够更好地了解原文想要表达的信息。

课后练习

试将下列语篇译成英文：

1. 如果信息是力量，灵感就是一股使我们从按部就班到挥洒自如的潜能。康柏相信科技不再只是简单的信息工具，而是启发灵感的魔力。按动按钮，我们启动的不再只是计算机，还有无穷的想象力。现在，我们终于超越了信息科技的限制，迈进全新的科技境界。激发灵感的科技——康柏 Inspiration Technology，欢迎进入新的 IT 世界。

2. 青岛啤酒投巨资引进世界上最新的啤酒生产设备和世界一流的质量管理技术，确定操作方法并严格执行，所生产的啤酒品位高、档次高，自投放市场以来，以其口感新鲜、酒香清醇、口味柔和、品质上乘而深受广大消费者的喜爱。

　　优良的原料、先进的设备、严密的质量管理、严格的员工教育是酿造纯生啤酒的基础，青岛啤酒股份有限公司能够充分满足此条件，生产出更出色的啤酒。

　　青岛啤酒，激情欢动，为您干杯！

第六章
企业介绍的翻译

随着全球化进程的不断加快,越来越多的中国企业开始走出国门,融入世界的经济大潮,成为享誉世界的知名企业。国际化意识的不断加强及实际的商务需求促使许多企业开始用英文进行自我宣传,甚至建立企业的英文网页介绍公司的产品或服务,以寻找潜在的消费者和合作伙伴。因此,企业介绍的英译已成为中国企业接轨世界经济必不可少的一部分。

企业介绍一般向潜在的消费者和合作伙伴介绍企业的经营性质、经营范围、从业人员、产品的质量和性能、获奖情况等。它是企业宣传公司本身及其产品或服务的前沿阵地,是一家企业树立良好的公司形象和产品形象的重要手段。企业介绍一般会包含以下信息:公司概况,如公司的成立时间、占地面积、员工人数、企业宗旨等;公司的发展状况,如公司已获得的奖项或机构的认证;公司的主要产品或服务;建立合作的意愿,等等。一般而言,中文的企业介绍往往面面俱到,从企业的经营性质到从业人员、产品的相关情况,甚至负责人的照片也会被附上,信息的涉及面较广。

⌘ 企业介绍的语言特点

"企业介绍作为一种对外宣传资料,属于实用性很强的经济应用文,注重信息的传递和促销的效果,因此具有信息性、表达性、交际性和诱导性等功能特点"[1](印晓红,杨瑛,2010)。在语言上,中文的企业介绍有如下特点:

首先,追求华丽的辞藻,文字工整对仗、整齐划一,喜用四字格增加音韵美。

企业为了树立形象或说服顾客,经常会夸大企业的信誉和产品质量,喜欢采用华丽的文辞对自己的企业及其产品和服务进行修饰和夸大。中文的企业介绍"表现为平铺直叙,长篇大论,喜欢重墨渲染一些枝节信息,大量使用概念式及空洞夸大的描述性套话,如'历史悠久''人杰地灵'等;习惯罗列权威机构的认证及大到全

---

1 印晓红,杨瑛.2010.商务口译入门.上海:上海交通大学出版社,1.

国、小到地县的各种奖项,并加以细节描述"[2](陈小慰,2006)。而英语的企业介绍则更注重事实,要求文字表达逻辑清晰,言简意赅。因此,英文的企业介绍语言一般简洁明了,朴实清晰;在介绍企业情况时,英文的企业介绍喜欢用数字说话,用数字来表述公司规模、员工数量和营业额等。另外,英文的企业介绍表达更为灵活,句型多变。

其次,喜欢使用一些套话和空洞的口号,以突出公司的社会形象,强调产品或服务的吸引力。

中文的企业介绍中经常会出现如下词语,如"名列前茅""全国领先""本公司产品质量可靠,价格公道""以顾客为中心""服务海内外客户""质量第一、信誉第一",等等。

企业介绍翻译的要点

企业介绍的英译属外宣类翻译,尤金·奈达的等效翻译理论(Principle of Equivalence)、德国功能派的目的论(Skopos Theory)等都可以指导这一翻译实践。

尤金·奈达在《翻译科学探索》(*Toward a Science of Translating*)一书中指出,"在动态对等翻译中,译者所关注的并不是源语信息和译语信息的一一对应关系,而是一种动态关系,即译语接受者和译语信息之间的关系应该与源语接受者和原文信息之间的关系基本相同"[3](马会娟,1999)。在与查尔斯·泰伯(Charles Taber)合著的《翻译理论与实践》(*The Theory and Practice of Translation*)一书中,奈达进一步将动态对等定义为"译语中的信息接受者对译文信息的反应,应该与源语接受者对原文的反应程度基本相同"[4]。因此,尤金·奈达提出的等效翻译强调以读者为中心,也强调了翻译的交际功能。他认为,翻译就是从语义到语体在译语中用最切近而又最自然的对等语言再现源语的信息;翻译时,最重要的是翻译信息的内容,兼顾信息的语体,功能对等优于形式对等。因此,在进行企业介绍的英译时,应主要考虑外国读者的反应,只有这样,才能达到企业介绍英译的目的。

---

[2] 陈小慰.2006.新编实用翻译教程.北京:经济科学出版社,98.
[3] 马会娟.1999.对奈达的等效翻译理论的再思考.外语学刊,3:74.
[4] Nida, Eugene A. & Taber, Charles T. (1969). *The Theory and Practice of Translation*. Leiden: E. J. Brill, p.25.

20世纪70年代兴起的德国功能派翻译理论认为，翻译是一项有目的的交际活动，代表人物有赖斯（Katharina Reiss）、弗米尔（Hans Vermeer）和诺德（Christiane Nord）。

赖斯主张将文本功能列为翻译批评的一个标准，即从原文、译文两者功能之间的关系评价原文。赖斯的学生弗米尔在行为理论的基础上发展并创立了功能目的论，她认为翻译是一种有目的的行为活动，翻译时译者应根据客户的要求，结合翻译的目的和译文读者的特殊情况，从原作所提供的多源信息中进行选择性的翻译。诺德则强调译文应贴近读者（receiver-oriented），翻译时译者应使用符合译语文化观念和习用语言结构模式的表达方式，对原文作必要的调整。因此，功能派强调把翻译看作一种需要考虑读者和客户要求的全新的目的性交际活动，译者在整个翻译过程中的参照系应是译文在译语文化环境中所要达到的一种或几种交际功能。

综上所述，企业介绍的英译应注意一些要素，如译文语体、读者反应和译入语文化。首先，英译时应考虑译文的语体，因为企业介绍的英文译本是该企业与外国读者进行交流的手段，译文是否符合他们的语体规范直接影响到它能否为读者理解和接受，也直接影响其沟通和宣传功能。其次，企业介绍的英译应以读者为中心，注重读者反应。企业介绍英译的成功与否往往可以通过读者的认可度以及由此而引发的商务沟通行为的广泛度来衡量。最后，企业介绍的英译还应尊重译语文化。各国的政治、经济、文化、风俗习惯、价值观及行为模式都存在着差异，都有各自独特的文化特性和语言表达方式，翻译过程中应该考虑到思维方式和文化习惯等各方面的差异，以确保跨文化交际的实现。

具体的翻译过程中，企业介绍的英译有如下几种方法：

一、直译，译文既保持原文的内容又保持原文的形式。

例1　目前，本公司经营各类中药三千余种，中药机械十余种。

Now our company handles over 3,000 traditional Chinese medicines and more than ten kinds of machinery for manufacturing Chinese medicines.

例2　中国煤炭进出口总公司于1982年7月成立，是中国煤炭行业唯一从事对外经济和贸易的全国性专业化公司，统一经营全国煤炭、煤炭技术和机电设备及矿产品的进出口业务。

China National Coal Import & Export Corporation, founded in July

1982, is the sole company specialized in foreign trade and international cooperation of coal industry in China. It is engaged in exclusive import and export of coal, coal technology, electrical & mechanical equipment and other minerals.

上述两个例子不仅保留了原文的内容，也保留了原文的形式，翻译时难度不大。

二、改译，原文中有一些内容直译后会令人费解或引起误解，这时译者可以不拘泥于原文的形式，对部分内容加以改变以达到语用等效。

例 3　公司拥有雄厚的技术力量，大、中专毕业以上的技术、管理人才占员工总人数的百分之三十以上……

Boasting tremendous technological strength, the company owns a well-qualified management and staff.

原文摘自福建某公司的企业介绍。"大、中专毕业以上的技术、管理人才占员工总人数的百分之三十以上"如果直译出来，恐怕无法给英文读者"拥有雄厚的技术力量"这一印象，因此改译成 the company owns a well-qualified management and staff。

三、减译，汉语强调声律对仗，行文工整；另外，中文习惯罗列大大小小的奖项，译文应考虑英文读者的文化和心理认知特点，除了一些国际认可、级别较高的获奖信息外，其他可以考虑删去不译。

例 4　自 2003 年以来，我公司已荣获广西玉林市"副会长单位"称号，并先后荣获技术进步等 2 项省级奖项。

Since 2003, our company has been awarded the local honorary title and many prizes, including 2 provincial prizes.

原文提到了荣获的称号——"副会长单位"，但译成英文恐怕外国读者根本无法理解。因此，译文没有将这一信息具体化，只翻译成"获得当地的荣誉称号"。另外，译文中也没有提到"技术进步"等具体信息，只翻译了"2 项省级奖项"的内容。

四、增译，汉语中有许多具有中国文化特色的浓缩词语，这些浓缩的语言形式后隐藏了大量被省略的信息，如果译者在翻译过程中不补足这些省略成分，英文读者可能很难理解这些信息。因此，翻译浓缩词语时需要增译，把省略的内容翻译出来。

例5　对不同的地区，伊利采取了不同的营销战略。在打入北京市场时，鉴于北京冷饮品牌众多的情况，采取"农村包围城市"的战略，逐步向内扩展。

Yili adopts different strategies for different regions. In Beijing, where there was fierce competition, it adopted an encirclement strategy (starting from the suburbs and gradually expanding into the downtown area).

该译文将"农村包围城市"进行了增译，解释其具体含义，帮助英文读者更好地了解伊利的营销模式。

翻译语篇 1

我们的企业精神很简单：顾客永远至上。正是这一精神推动我们去丰富日常生活。从石油化工制品到各种抗生素，从开创性研究到遗传工程，都有我们的产品，我们使生活变得更加健康和舒适。我们认为这才是"顾客至上"的真正含义。正是这种"顾客至上"的宗旨，才使得我们公司成为遍布世界120个国家，资产达320亿美元的大型公司，涉足化学、电子、贸易、金融、建筑以及公共服务诸多领域。未来总是带来变化，但是我们公司将永远恪守让顾客满足的宗旨。

译前提示

本段材料是某公司的企业介绍，看到这一语篇时会发现很多表达可以复制到其他企业的介绍中。因此，在平时的翻译练习中，可以有意识地积累一些相关的语言表达和常用的句子结构，以备不时之用。

1. "无懈可击"可译成 impeccable。
2. "抗生素"是 antibiotics。
3. "遗传工程"可译成 genetic engineering。

本语篇围绕"顾客至上"的企业精神，给中文读者塑造了一个正面的企业形象，同时还宣传了企业的强大实力。翻译时，应用简洁明了的语言将原文的内容传递给英文读者。

第六章 企业介绍的翻译

参考译文

Our corporate formula is simple: Customers always come first. It is this formula that drives us to enhance everyday living, making life healthier and more comfortable by creating everything from petrochemical products to antibiotics and pioneering research to genetic engineering. We believe this is what putting you first really means. Our customer-first philosophy is the reason why our company today is a corporation of 32 billion dollars working in over 120 countries and involved in every aspect of chemistry, electronics, trade, finance, construction and public service. The future always brings change, but our formula for customer satisfaction remains consistent.

译文注释

该译文语言表达紧凑，长短句结合，较为符合英文读者的阅读习惯和行文习惯，较好地传达了原文的内容。

1. 我们的企业精神很简单：顾客永远至上。

   【注释】很多企业都强调"顾客至上"的企业精神。"顾客至上"如译成短语，可以采用 customer first 的表达。"我们的企业精神很简单：顾客永远至上"的译文是 Our corporate formula is simple: Customers always come first，将这一成分译成一个句子，自然也是可以的。

2. 从石油化工制品到各种抗生素，从开创性研究到遗传工程，都有我们的产品，从而使生活变得更加健康和舒适。...making life healthier and more comfortable by creating everything from petrochemical products to antibiotics and pioneering research to genetic engineering.

   【注释】原文行文相对比较松散，在英译过程中，可以通过使用现在分词、过去分词、短语、从句等形式将译文组织得更为紧凑些。

   参考译文中，该句译为 making life healthier and more comfortable by creating everything from petrochemical products to antibiotics and pioneering research to genetic engineering，与前一句话合译在一起，使上下句的衔接更为连贯，逻辑也更为明晰。

3. 正是这种"顾客至上"的宗旨，才使得我们公司成为遍布世界 120 个国家，资产达320亿美元的大型公司，涉足化学、电子、贸易、金融、建筑以及公共服务诸多领域。Our customer-first philosophy is the reason why our company today is a corporation of 32 billion dollars working in over 120 countries and involved in every aspect of chemistry, electronics, trade, finance, construction and public service.

【注释】原文中罗列了一些并列名词，在翻译时要一一对应并不难。但需要注意的是，译文的语序有了调整：将"资产达320亿美元"放在了"遍布世界120个国家"之前。这一调整的主要目的在于给读者留下深刻的印象，突出公司的雄厚实力。

另外，译文是一个长句，突出了英文句子结构的长处，通过同位语、现在分词等手段，将众多信息放在同一个句子中，从而使译文表达比原文更为紧凑。

翻译语篇 2

中国北京同仁堂集团公司进出口公司

中国北京同仁堂集团公司进出口公司是中国北京同仁堂集团公司直属全民所有制企业，为自主经营、独立核算、自负盈亏的企业法人。

"同仁堂"是北京最古老、声誉最高的一家堂号。它创建于公元1669年，至今已有三百多年的历史。其制药宗旨为："炮炙虽繁必不敢省人工，品味虽贵必不敢减物力"，所制产品以"配方独特，选料上乘，工艺精湛，疗效显著"而驰名中外。

"同仁堂"商标为国家驰名商标，已在"马德里协定"国家及其他四十多个国家和地区注册，受到特别保护。

中国北京同仁堂集团公司进出口分公司主要经营中国北京同仁堂集团公司所属企业自产产品及相关技术的出口业务，经营生产所需原辅材料、机械设备及技术的进口业务；开展对外合资经营、合作生产、"三来一补"业务；经贸部批准的其他商品的进出口业务。

目前，经营各类药品三千余种，中药机械十余种。药品行销全国及四十多个国家和地区，出口额居全国同行之首。

本公司热诚欢迎各国朋友前来洽谈贸易，建立各种形式的经济合作关系。

地址：中国北京丰台区南三环中路 15 号

电话：67620827 传真：67635193

电挂：7654BMMC 邮编：100075

译前提示

本段材料是中国北京同仁堂集团公司进出口公司的相关介绍。相信大家都听说过同仁堂，但是如何翻译"同仁堂"？

1. 集团一般用 group 表达。
2. 全民所有制企业是指企业财产属于全民所有的，依法自主经营、自负盈亏、独立核算的商品生产和经营单位。全民所有制企业又称为国有企业，但广义的国有企业还包括国家控股的股份有限公司、有限责任公司和国有独资公司，全民所有制企业只是国有企业的一种。因此，全民所有制企业可以译成 state-owned enterprise。
3. "马德里协定"由阿尔巴尼亚、阿尔及利亚、亚美尼亚等 53 个成员国共同缔结而成，是《商标国际注册马德里协定》的简称，其内容是关于简化商标在其他国家注册手续的国际协定。"马德里协定"可译成 Madrid Agreement。

本语篇在介绍同仁堂的运作形式和相关业务时运用了很多四字格，如"自主经营、独立核算、自负盈亏"、"配方独特，选料上乘，工艺精湛，疗效显著"和"合资经营、合作生产、三来一补"等。英译时，可选用多变的句型和正式的英语文体来进行翻译，突出其高大上的感觉，顺利实现原文的交际目的。

参考译文

Beijing Tongrentang Group Co., Ltd., Import & Export Company

Beijing Tongrentang Group Co., Ltd., Import & Export Company is a state-owned enterprise directly under Beijing Tongrentang Group Co., Ltd. It operates independently and assumes independent accounting and sole responsibility for its profits and losses.

Established in 1669, Tongrentang is the most long-standing and prestigious pharmaceutical factory in Beijing, with a history of over 300 years. It follows the principle of "making the best medicines, irrespective of the cost of materials and time consumed". Tongrentang's medicines are famous for unique prescriptions, superior medicinal materials, excellent technology and successful curative effect in the world.

The trademark Tongrentang is well-known in the country. It is registered in the countries of Madrid Agreement and also in more than 40 other countries and regions. It is under strict protection.

The scope of business includes:

Export of products and technologies from the enterprises under Beijing Tongrentang Group Co., Ltd.

Import of raw and processed materials, machinery equipments and technologies which are needed in production.

Engaging in joint venture, cooperative production, compensation trade, processing with customer's materials, imported materials and assembling with customer's parts.

Import and export of other commodities approved by MOFTEC.

Now the company deals in over 3,000 kinds of Chinese medicines and 10 kinds of machinery for manufacturing Chinese medicines. The medicines sell well in China and in more than 40 countries and regions. The export value of traditional Chinese medicine is the largest in China.

We warmly welcome all friends from various countries to do business with us and establish relations in various forms of economic cooperation.

Add: No. 15, South Third Ring Road (Central), Fengtai District, Beijing 100075, China

Tel: 67620827   Fax: 67635193

Cable: 7654 BMMC

第六章 企业介绍的翻译

译文注释

参考译文较忠实地传达了原文的相关内容，语言表达流畅自然，是一篇值得学习的企业介绍英译材料。

1. ……为自主经营、独立核算、自负盈亏的企业法人。It operates independently and assumes independent accounting and sole responsibility for its profits and losses.

   【注释】原句是全文第一句话的后半句，译文采用了断句法，将第一句话断成了两句，后半句用一句话加以表达。

   "自主经营"翻译为 operate independently，"独立核算"是 assume independent accounting，"自负盈亏"译成 (assume) sole responsibility for its profits and losses。"企业法人"的翻译有 legal entity 或 business corporation，本句中该词可以不译，因为意思已内含于整句话中。

2. 其制药宗旨为："炮炙虽繁必不敢省人工，品味虽贵必不敢减物力"，所制产品以"配方独特，选料上乘，工艺精湛，疗效显著"而驰名中外。It follows the principle of "making the best medicines, irrespective of the cost of materials and time consumed". Tongrentang's medicines are famous for unique prescriptions, superior medicinal materials, excellent technology and successful curative effect in the world.

   【注释】因涉及专业知识，且行文紧凑，"炮炙虽繁必不敢省人工，品味虽贵必不敢减物力"的翻译很有难度。参考译文将这一内容进行了减译，翻译成 making the best medicines, irrespective of the cost of materials and time consumed，即"生产最好的药物，而不计原料的成本和所费的时间"。

   "配方独特，选料上乘，工艺精湛，疗效显著"采用四字格的形式，翻译时可以考虑用"形容词＋名词"的形式来表达。

   汉语中很多四字格都可以用"形容词＋名词"的形式进行英译，如"风景优美"（beautiful scenery）、"空气清新"（fresh air）、"质量上乘"（superior quality）等。

3. ……开展对外合资经营、合作生产、"三来一补"业务。Engaging in joint venture, cooperative production, compensation trade, processing with customer's materials, imported materials and assembling with customer's parts.

   【注释】"三来一补"最早出现于 1979 年，是中国大陆在改革开放初期尝试的一种企业贸易形式，指来料加工、来样加工、来件装配和补偿贸易。翻译时可以增译，加上具体的解释，让英文读者更好地了解这一信息。译文中先说了"一补"compensation trade，再解释了什么是"三来"。

在翻译过程中如遇到不熟悉的固定表达，建议通过搜索网络或相关文献，确定其意义，从而准确译出该词的意思。

4. ……经贸部批准的其他商品的进出口业务。Import and export of other commodities approved by MOFTEC.

【注释】 经贸部，即对外贸易经济合作部，英文的完整表达是 Ministry of Foreign Trade and Economic Cooperation。译文中用了缩写，日常的学习中可以适当关注著名机构和组织的缩写，如 IMF（世界货币基金组织）、WTO（世界贸易组织）和 WBG（世界银行）等。

5. 本公司热诚欢迎各国朋友前来洽谈贸易，建立各种形式的经济合作关系。We warmly welcome all friends from various countries to do business with us and establish relations in various forms of economic cooperation.

【注释】 类似的表达经常出现在企业介绍和广告的结尾，学生可以有意识地记忆和背诵相关的译文表达。

除参考译文这一表达，也可以对此稍加改动，变成 Friends all over the world are welcomed to do business with us and establish relations in various forms of economic cooperation.

翻译加油站

翻译技巧（三）：减词法

翻译中词的省略也是常见的翻译手段，我们称之为减词法。减词法的目的在于使译文通顺、意思清楚，避免重复和累赘，使译文更符合目的语的表达习惯。但要注意，词的省略不是原文思想和内容的任意删减。

词的省略适用于以下几种情况：第一，在译文中看来是可有可无的或是多余的词语；第二，其意思已经包含在上下文中的词语；第三，其含义在译文中是不言而明的词语。

常常省略的词有原文中表示范畴的词语、原文中重复出现的词语，以及原文中的一些近义词。

一、省略范畴词

汉语中常用范畴词表示行为、现象、属性等概念所属的范畴。这些范畴词一般放在动词或形容词之后，也可放在名词之后，有时前面加助词"的"，有时没有。常用的范畴词包括"问题""状态""情况""工作"等。范畴词本身没有实际意义，英译时可以省略不译。

例 1　中国足球的落后**状态**必须改变。
　　　The (state/condition of) backwardness of the Chinese football must be changed.

例 2　外国人申请各种签证，应当提供有效护照，必要时提供有关证明**材料**。
　　　When applying for various visas, foreigners shall present valid passports and, if necessary, provide pertinent evidence.

例 3　目前就经济和社会发展**领域**而言，中国面临三大挑战。
　　　At present, China faces three major challenges in its economic and social development.

例 4　各地领导部门要努力开拓就业**门路**。
　　　Local authorities should work hard to create jobs.

例 5　关于利益分配**问题**，我就说这些。
　　　On profit distribution, that is all I have got to say.

汉语中习惯用"状态""领域""问题"等范畴词，但这些词本身没有实际的意义，翻译时只需将范畴词前面的动词或形容词译成名词即可，范畴词则可以省略，如"落后状态"译成 backwardness，"利益分配问题"译成 profit distribution。如果范畴词前面是名词，直接将该名词翻译出来即可，如"证明材料"直接译成 evidence，这样可以避免译文的冗余和中式英语的出现。

二、省略重复出现的词

为了追求行文的气势或增强音韵效果，汉语中常常采用重复法。对汉语而言，重复手法的频繁使用并不会影响文字的简洁性，但译成英文时，可能会造成行文的累赘感。因此，在汉译英时会省去中文里重复出现的词语。

例6 这些**问题**就是他提出的关于美国政治制度的**问题**。

These are his questions on the American political system.

原句中有两个"问题"，译文出于简洁性的考虑，将主语"这些问题"译成代词 these，省略了"问题"一词，第二个"问题"直接译出。

例7 我们说，**长征**是历史记录上的第一次，**长征**是宣言书，**长征**是宣传队，**长征**是播种机。

We answer that the Long March is the first of its kind in the annals of history, that it is a manifesto, a publicity force, and a seeding machine.

原句中有四个"长征"，译文将第一个"长征"直译成 the Long March，后面的三个"长征"统一用代词 it 来指代。

例8 刚进大学时，**陌生**的环境，**陌生**的人群，甚至宿舍楼下的磁卡电话也是**陌生**的。

When I first entered the university, everything seemed new to me: the environment, the crowd of people, and even the magnetic card telephone booth below our dormitory building.

原句中有三个"陌生"，译文表达非常精练，用一句话 everything seemed new to me 加以概括，避免了该词的一再重复。

例9 发展新兴**产业**和高科技**产业**，把开发**新**技术、**新**产品、**新产业**与开拓市场结合起来，把发展技术密集型**产业**和劳动密集型**产业**集合起来。

We should develop rising and high-tech industries. We should combine the efforts to develop new technologies, products and industries with the efforts to open up markets and integrate the development of technology-intensive with labor-intensive industries.

原句包含的信息较多，且重复出现的词较多，有五个"产业"和三个"新"。译文将句首的前两个"产业"合在一起翻译，"新兴产业和高科技产业"译为 rising and high-tech industries；句尾的两个"产业"也是如此，将"技术密集型产业和劳动密集型产业"译成 technology-intensive with labor-intensive industries。三个"新"只用一个 new 衔接，译文中"新技术、新产品、新产业"的英文表达是 new technologies, products and industries，使译文显得精练。

例10　我们可利用的矛盾**存在着**，对我们有利的条件**存在着**，机遇**存在着**，问题是善于把握。

There are contradictions that we can use, (conditions) that are favorable to us, opportunities that we can take advantage of—the problem is to seize them at the right moment.

原句中有三个"存在着"，译文用 there be 结构翻译了第一个"存在着"，同时将后面的两个省略掉，使译文表达更为通顺和精练。

三、省略近义词

汉语喜欢用字对仗工整，常使用意义较为相近的对称结构，如四字词组，读起来朗朗上口。而英语则不同，如果把这些对称结构的四字词组照搬到英语中，反而显得多余。因此，在翻译意义相近的汉语四字词组时，只需要翻译其中一个同义或近义词组，或进行概括化翻译即可。

例11　孔子的家里很穷，但是他从小就**认真读书，刻苦学习**。

His family was very poor, but Confucius worked hard at his studies even in early childhood.

例12　若不然，叫她趁早**回心转意**，也对她多些好处。

Otherwise, the sooner she changes her mind the better for her.

例13　花园里面是人间的乐园，有的是吃不了的**大米白面**，穿不完的**绫罗绸缎**，花不完的**金银财宝**。

The garden was a paradise on earth, with more food and clothes than could be consumed and more money than could be spent.

例14　今年生产计划的顺利完成，是全体职工共同努力的结果，是加强本行业横向联系的**同心协力**的结果，也是市局机关大抓**宏观管理**和全局**安排、运筹**的结果。

The production plan was carried through due to the concerted effort of the staff, the coordinated cooperation between factories in partnership and the effective management of the government sectors concerned.

例 11 中，"认真读书"与"刻苦学习"属近义词，因此减译成 work hard at his studies，避免重复。例 12 中的"回心"与"转意"也是如此。例 13 中的"大米白面""绫罗绸缎"和"金银财宝"分别译为上义词 food, clothes 和 money 进行概括化翻译。

例 14 中的"同心协力"用了 coordinated 一词,"安排""运筹"没有翻译出来,而是包含在 management 一词中。

课后练习

∞ 试将下列语篇译成英文:

1. 本公司是一家中外合资的综合性经济实体,为国内首家专业生产各类礼物和纪念品的企业。本公司规模宏大,技术力量雄厚,机械设备、生产原料进口,产品自行设计生产。

2. 海尔集团是世界第四大白色家电制造商、中国最具价值品牌。海尔在全球建立了 29 个制造基地,8 个综合研发中心,19 个海外贸易公司,全球员工总数超过 5 万人,已发展成为大规模的跨国企业集团,2008 年海尔集团实现全球营业额 1190 亿元。

第七章
旅游文本的翻译

"旅游文本"原指旅游（接待）一线人员（尤其是导游翻译）在工作中经常碰到的、约定俗成的那些应用型文本[1]（陈刚，2004）。本章的"旅游文本"主要指旅行社或政府有关部门以正式或非正式形式出版（及网上发布）的旅游手册、旅游指南等语篇，主要是对旅游景点、旅游资源、服务设施等情况的介绍。

从广义上讲，旅游文本可分为专业文本和普通文本。旅游专业文本是针对旅游领域专业人士的文本，如旅游研究论文；旅游普通文本是针对普通大众（特别是潜在的旅游者）的文本，其中包括旅游标示语（告示标牌）、导游词、旅游广告、旅游宣传册、旅游宣传单、旅游指南、旅游景点介绍、旅游行程介绍、旅游合同、旅游地图、旅行见闻等[2]（丁大刚，2008）。本章主要探讨的是普通文本的翻译。

旅游文本的功能可归纳为指示功能、信息功能和描写功能。所谓指示功能，是指文本发出指令性或诱导性信息，并产生明显的"语后效果"，即直接刺激旅游者的旅游欲望。信息功能，即文本提供相关介绍和信息，包括对景区和景点的介绍，对旅行路线、设施和费用等的介绍，也包括对景点历史、文化和风土人情等的介绍。描写功能是指在传达上述信息时做到生动具体，富有美感，使读者能够感受到人文之美和自然之美。

旅游文本的三大功能中，指示功能是隐性的，但它却是整个文本最重要的功能。与指示功能不同，信息功能和描写功能是显性的，存在于整个语篇的词、句、段之中。简言之，旅游文本的功能虽然多样，但其最终目的就是通过对旅游景点和景区的细致描写，使文本内容生动形象，富有感染力，给读者（特别是潜在的旅游者）提供丰富信息的同时，使其得到美的享受，进而产生一睹为快的欲望。因此，就这一目的而言，旅游普通文本的目的与广告的目的非常相似。

---

1 陈刚．2004．旅游翻译与涉外导游．北京：中国对外翻译出版公司，309．
2 丁大刚．2008．旅游英语的语言特点与翻译．上海：上海交通大学出版社，14．

∞ 旅游文本的语言特点

旅游文本"短小精悍,生动活泼,通俗易懂,信息量大,又不失文学性、艺术性、宣传性和广告性"[3](伍锋,何庆机,2008)。中英文旅游文本的用词虽然与其他文本相比有相似之处,但也存在着一些特性:

首先,词汇涉及众多领域,如政治、历史、地理、文学、艺术,甚至天文和考古等。

伍峰等在《应用文体翻译:理论与实践》(2008)一书中指出,旅游文本最显著的特征就体现在词汇上,其词汇特点又体现在丰富性上。旅游词汇涉及文化、经济、政治、宗教、地理、历史、民俗、休闲与娱乐等,有时甚至会涉及某一领域的专业术语,如 pyramidal steep(锥形屋顶)、Karst topography(喀斯特地貌)等;另外,旅游文本还大量使用特定文化的专有名词,例如苏堤(Sudi Causeway)、西子(Xishi)、玉皇山(Yuhuang Mountain)等。

其次,使用大量的描述性词汇,如描述性的形容词(特别是比较级和最高级)和名词频繁出现。描述生动形象,引人入胜。语言活泼风趣,给人以美的享受,激发游客的旅游欲望。

《应用文体翻译:理论与实践》一书中也提到,中文旅游文本的文字比较文学化,常用夸张的手法;而英语旅游文本常用文化用语和大量描述性文字,力求体现艺术性和美感,常常使用优美和文学性较强的形容词,如 picturesque(风景如画的)、idyllic(田园诗般的)等。

"这些描述性的词汇在译成汉语时往往比较容易,因为汉语更注重文辞的华美,但中文的一些四字描述词汇在译成英文时往往要打一定的折扣,当然要尽量挑选一些描述类英文形容词或动词表述出来,不过要注意避免语义重复"[4](彭萍,2010)。

另外,介绍具体信息时,会使用相对简单的词汇来表达。

旅游文本属于宣传类文本,为达到最好的宣传目的,吸引更多的读者到宣传的景点、景区一游,购买或享受所宣传的旅游服务,旅游文本就必须使用一定的简单

3　伍锋,何庆机.2008.应用文体翻译:理论与实践.杭州:浙江大学出版社,319.
4　彭萍.2010.实用旅游英语翻译(英汉双向).北京:对外经济贸易大学出版社,30.

词汇，以满足不同教育程度的读者需求。因此，在介绍信息时，尤其是涉及具体信息时，旅游文本会使用一些简单的词汇。中英文都有这样的现象。

在句式上，中英文旅游文本各有自己的特点。英语多用短句，有时又夹杂几个长句，句型长短不一，灵活多变；而汉语则多用并列结构，读来朗朗上口，富有节奏感。中英文旅游文本有如下共同特点：

首先，中英文旅游文本均会使用祈使句。

旅游文本也属于号召类文本，即号召读者采取行动，享受某一旅游服务或游览某一旅游景点和景区，因此中英文旅游文本中都会使用一些祈使句来增强号召力，因此在汉译英时可以直译出来。如："齐来参与，一起爱护湿地，保护湿地"可直译为 Let's all cherish and protect the wetland.

其次，中英文旅游文本也经常使用疑问句。

旅游文本中经常会使用疑问句（包括一般疑问句和特殊疑问句），目的在于启发读者，引起读者的注意，从而发挥旅游文本的号召作用。同时，疑问句的使用能够让读者产生一种仿佛在与文本对话的感觉，使读者增加亲切感，从而使译文更好地贴近读者。汉语的这些疑问句可以直接翻译成英文，如"你是否想步行 20 分钟或者 2 个小时去欣赏美景呢？"可译成 Do you want to walk 20 minutes or 2 hours to enjoy the beautiful scenery?

∞ 旅游文本翻译的要点

旅游文本翻译属于实用翻译的一类，对促进中外旅游文化的交流和推动旅游经济的发展起着举足轻重的作用。因此，旅游文本的翻译是一种跨文化活动，英译旅游文本时，译者需要对原文信息进行完整传达，或对原文信息进行必要的增补，或对原文信息进行删减，或对原文信息的表达方式进行调整，以符合英文读者的文化背景、认知习惯和审美情趣。

第一，全译。如果汉语中的所有信息是全人类所共有的信息，完整翻译后能被英文读者所接受，不会引起歧义或误解时，全译不失为旅游文本翻译的首选。

例 1 拉萨是西藏自治区的首府，是西藏政治、经济、文化的中心和交通枢纽。

本句选自《拉萨旅游指南》。原文的信息完整翻译成英文不会造成歧义或误解，因此可以全译。译文如下：Lhasa is the capital city of Tibetan Autonomous Region. It is also the political, economic and cultural center of Tibet as well as its transport hub.

例2 卢沟桥也叫马可·波罗桥。它坐落在北京西南15公里处的地方。它原是北京八大景之一，于1189年开始修建，1192年完工。桥是用汉白玉建的，全长266.5米，宽7.5米，有十一个桥洞。

例2对卢沟桥进行了具体介绍，也没有引起理解障碍的内容，因此可以全译为：Lugouqiao, also known as Macro Polo Bridge, is located about 15 kilometers southwest of Beijing. It used to be one of the eight major scenes in Beijing. Construction of the bridge was begun in 1189 and completed in 1192. It is built of white marble, 266.5 meters long, 7.5 meters wide with 11 arches.

第二，增译。当旅游文本中某些信息带有较强的文化个性，如历史典故，或某些信息需要进一步解释时，英译时经常会增加一些原文隐含的信息，以激发英文读者的兴趣，引起他们的共鸣。例如，在介绍当地元宵节的习俗时，原句是"元宵节那天，人们都吃元宵"。译成英文时，可以增译"元宵节"和"元宵"的相关信息，以帮助英文读者更好地理解。译文如下：On *Yuanxiao Jie* or the Lantern Festival, which falls on the fifteenth day of the first lunar month, it is a common practice to eat *Yuanxiao*, a kind of glutinous rice-flour balls filled with bean paste, sugar or some other sweet things.

第三，减译。旅游文本英译过程中，减译的方法使用较多。汉语的旅游文本经常会堆砌很多华丽的辞藻，或对某一景观的描写显得过于累赘和拖沓，在英译过程中就需要对这部分信息进行一定的省略。这样做一方面是使英文表达自然流畅，另一方面还可以使英文读者直截了当地获取重点信息。大部分外国游客阅读英文版的旅游指南时是为了了解中国的一些风土人情，获取一些实用的具体信息，增加旅游的乐趣，而不是进行考古或民俗研究。当然，在翻译实践中，减译这一方法应慎用。

例3 从花溪城镇中心南行12公里，就是青岩了。青岩是中国历史文化名镇，汉、苗、布依等勤劳淳朴的人民在600多年的岁月里共同写就了小镇的历史。

她选址于九脉之隘，坐落于五峰之中。是我国冷热兵器过渡时期巧妙运用地形地貌、依山就势、合理布局、投入少而城市攻防能力强的营城杰作，攻防体系完善。几百年来经历无数战争，有"攻不破的青岩城"之誉。大旅行家徐霞客游历青岩留下了贵州"南鄙要害"的评说[5]。

本段内容选自中英对照的《花溪旅游指南》，是对花溪附近一个叫做"青岩"的古镇的介绍。《花溪旅游指南》提供的英译本如下：Located in the joint spot of nine mountains 12 km south of Huaxi Town, the important military fortress of Qingyan Ancient Town has suffered numerous military attacks in a history of more than 600 years and invited the title of Unbreakable Castle and the Key Military Spot in the South China.

本译文大刀阔斧，很多信息，如小镇的布局和徐霞客的评述等都没有翻译。就译本的文字而言，表达流畅，突出了青岩古镇在军事上的重要性。但在英译过程中，减译的方法还需慎重使用，能够翻译的内容和信息还是应当尽量翻译出来。

第四，改译。中华民族和英美人士的思维方式、文化传统及审美情趣上都存在着一定的差异，写作方法和描写手段也迥然不同。汉语旅游文本中"多以意象感人，追求客观景物与主观情感的和谐之美，在对景点描写时，常把景物的内在意蕴依附在外在的表象之上，努力做到情景交融，意境相谐。而英语中对于景物的描写重在形象可感，在很多情况下，不是对意境进行深化，只是简单地罗列具体形象，从而传达出景物的质朴之美"[6]（辛凌，王婷，2009）。在进行汉英翻译时，可在这类形象与意象之间进行适当的转换和调整。

例4 大理风光宏博壮丽，以大理市辖区内的苍洱旅游区为代表，自古以来有着"风花雪月地，山光水色城"的美称。

此例选自《大理旅游指南》。大理因下关的风、上关的花、苍山的雪、洱海的月被中国人称为"风花雪月地"，又因苍山和洱海被称为"山光水色城"。原文中的意境如果直译出来，未必能达到好的翻译效果。因此，翻译时可以将这些意境转换成英美人士易于接受或感兴趣的内容。这句话被译为：Dali is a beautiful city in Yunnan Province. Based on its Cangshan Mountain and Erhai Lake, the city has long enjoyed the reputation of "Land of Romance and Scenic Beauty".

---

5 金颖若，楚湘黔. 2006. 花溪旅游指南. 贵阳：贵州人民出版社，40.
6 辛凌，王婷. 2009. 大学英语实用翻译教程. 重庆：重庆大学出版社，224.

翻译语篇 1

乌镇——中国最后的枕水人家

乌镇，地处中国浙江桐乡市北部，位于上海、杭州、南京三大城市中间，位于东经 120°54′，北纬 30°64′。全镇总面积达 71.19 平方千米，总人口为 6 万人，常住居民 1.2 万人。

乌镇被纵横交错的河流分为四个区域，京杭大运河穿镇而过，是中国唯一与运河毗邻的水乡古镇。乌镇位于杭州—嘉兴—湖州淤积平原，无山丘，河流纵横交织，气候温和湿润，雨量充沛，光照充足，物产丰富，素有"鱼米之乡、丝绸之府"之称。

乌镇于公元 872 年建立，至今已有 1000 多年的历史。然而，对谭家湾遗址（国家重点文物保护遗址）出土的史料研究表明，乌镇的先民早在约 7000 年就在这块土地上繁衍生息了。古运河滋养了乌镇灿烂的文明，悠久的历史积累使得乌镇有着丰富的文化底蕴。

1000 多年来，乌镇从未改过名，迁过地址，改变过水乡生活方式。历经沧桑岁月，乌镇的传统建筑至今保存完好。镇内有着密集的水网和码头，民居邻河而建、傍桥而市；石栏拱桥、过街券门、深宅大院、河埠廊坊保存完好，一派原生态江南水乡的怡然风情。

镇内 19 世纪晚期的原建筑占到了 40 多亩，有 100 多座形状各异的古石桥。乌镇好比一座古建筑的自然博物馆，水道、石板街纵横交错。当地居民就像他们祖先一样，在古房子里过着安宁的生活。

乌镇由于其悠久的历史、深远的文化、优雅的水乡风景、独特风味的美食、多种多样的民俗和节日，已经成为东方古代文明的活化石。这是自然赋予的美。乌镇在向我们展示其中国古文化的独特魅力和东方生活的灵魂的同时，也是中国传统文化的传播者和沟通中国和外国的使者。

乌镇的历史、文化、自然风景、先进完备的服务设施、热情好客的人们和服务团队融为了一体，使乌镇成为中国最佳的旅游景点。无论是观光、休闲、度假和商业活动，乌镇都是您的首选。

第七章 旅游文本的翻译

📖 译前提示

本段材料是乌镇的宣传材料。乌镇是典型的江南水乡古镇，有"鱼米之乡、丝绸之府"之称，是全国二十个黄金周预报景点及江南六大古镇之一。1991年乌镇被评为浙江省历史文化名城。

本段材料中有一些词汇和表达是旅游文本的常用内容，翻译前可以先查找类似的旅游文本，如周庄和苏州的英文介绍进行参考。

1. "常住居民"是 permanent resident。
2. "鱼米之乡、丝绸之府"可译成 the town of fish, rice, and silk。
3. "券门"一般指圆拱形的小门。"过街券门"在本篇中可译成 arched gate across the street。

这一语篇信息含量大，把乌镇的相关信息和历史完整地呈现在读者面前。英译时如何将这些信息体现出来？如何措辞才能吸引英文读者来乌镇一游？在翻译时，应注意到英文的旅游文本在介绍基本信息时喜用简单词汇和句型，描述风景时会使用大量的描述性词汇。另外，翻译时也要注意传达原文的号召力和感染力，激发读者游览乌镇的欲望。

📖 参考译文

Wuzhen—The Last Resting-on-water Town in China

Wuzhen lies at the north of Tongxiang City of Zhejiang Province, China, and at the center of the triangle formed by Shanghai, Hangzhou and Nanjing, for its location of 120 degrees 54 minutes east longitude and 30 degrees 64 minutes north latitude. The town covers an area of 71.19 square kilometers, with a total population of 60,000 and permanent residents of 12,000.

The town is divided into four zones by a cross-shaped river, with the Beijing–Hangzhou Grand Canal running across the town, making it the only ancient water town adjacent to the canal. The town lies on the Hangzhou–Jiaxing–Huzhou Alluvial Plain, with no hills but interlaced rivers. Due to its warm and humid climate, and abundant rainfalls and sunshine, the products here are rich, making Wuzhen well-known as "the town of fish, rice, and silk".

Wuzhen enjoys a history of over 1,000 years since its establishment in 872 AD. However, according to the textual research of the Tanjiawan site, one of the important cultural relics under state protection, ancestors of Wuzhen had lived here at the New Stone Age 7,000 years ago. The ancient Grand Canal nurtured the splendid culture of Wuzhen, and the long historic accumulation endowed Wuzhen with sound cultural deposits.

For more than 1,000 years, Wuzhen has never changed its name, address, or lifestyle. The traditional buildings are still well preserved after so many rough years. Within the town, with a dense network of rivers and wharves, people build their houses along the river and establish markets close to bridges. Stone railings and arch bridges, arched gates across the street, imposing dwellings and spacious courtyards, river banks and verandas are well preserved, presenting an original ecological scene of a water town in Jiangnan, the south of the Yangtze River.

Within the town, there are now more than 40 acres of late 19th century original buildings, and more than 100 ancient stone bridges of different shapes. It is just like a natural museum of ancient architecture. In the town, watercourses and flagstone streets extend in all directions and intercross here and there. The native residents live peacefully in their old houses by water, just like their ancestors did before a long time.

Wuzhen has become a living fossil of ancient oriental civilization for its profound history and culture, graceful water town scenery, unique flavored delicious foods, various and colorful folk customs and festivals. It's a kind of beauty that naturally endowed. While displaying the extraordinary charming of Chinese ancient culture and the soul of the oriental life, Wuzhen has become a disseminator of traditional culture and an emissary of the communication between China and foreign countries.

With a good integration of history, culture, nature and surroundings, advanced and complete service facilities, warmhearted people and service team, Wuzhen deserves to be your best destination in China for your sightseeing, leisure or business activities.

第七章 旅游文本的翻译

> 📖 **译文注释**
>
> 本参考译文来自乌镇的英文宣传材料，个别字词稍有改动。总体而言，该译文可读性较强，语言表达流畅，能将乌镇的形象较好地传递给英文读者。

1. 乌镇位于杭州—嘉兴—湖州淤积平原，无山丘，河流纵横交织，气候温和湿润，雨量充沛，光照充足，物产丰富，素有"鱼米之乡、丝绸之府"之称。The town lies on the Hangzhou–Jiaxing–Huzhou Alluvial Plain, with no hills but interlaced rivers. Due to its warm and humid climate, and abundant rainfalls and sunshine, the products here are rich, making Wuzhen well-known as "the town of fish, rice, and silk".

   【注释】原句是典型的长句，表述的内容较多。译文将原句断成了两句话：第一句话侧重说明乌镇位于杭嘉湖平原，有河无山；第二句话的重点则是乌镇"物产丰富"，因此有"鱼米之乡、丝绸之府"之称。

   汉语中多流水句，一个小句接着一个小句，很多地方可断可连，与英文的句式结构形成很大差异，并对汉译英造成了很大的困难。翻译时，需要根据原句的语义联系进行切分或合并，分析原句的信息重点，将之处理成译文的主干结构，其他次要信息翻译成短语或从句。"区分主从"的具体技巧请见"散文翻译"一章的翻译加油站部分。

2. 镇内有着密集的水网和码头，民居邻河而建、傍桥而市；Within the town, with a dense network of rivers and wharves, people build their houses along the river and establish markets close to bridges.

   【注释】译文将"有着密集的水网和码头"译成了状语；同时，将"民居邻河而建、傍桥而市"的主语改成了"人"，"邻河而建、傍桥而市"的主语实现了一致化，从而使行文更为流畅。

3. 石栏拱桥、过街券门、深宅大院、河埠廊坊保存完好，一派原生态江南水乡的怡然风情。Stone railings and arch bridges, arched gates across the street, imposing dwellings and spacious courtyards, river banks and verandas are well preserved, presenting an original ecological scene of a water town in Jiangnan, the south of the Yangtze River.

   【注释】原句中有较多的并列名词，没有把握的话可以搜索相关的词典和网站，确保译文的准确性。

   "一派原生态江南水乡的怡然风情"在译文中被处理成了现在分词，与前面的"保存完好"构成了内含的因果关系;另外,"江南"一词有不同的译法,有些人直接翻译成 Jiangnan,不过英美读者可能理解不了,可以考虑译成 the south of the Yangtze River。

翻译语篇 2

杭州——人间天堂

意大利著名旅行家马可·波罗曾这样叙述他印象中的杭州:"这是世界上最美妙迷人的城市,它使人觉得自己是在天堂。"在中国,也流传着这样的话:"上有天堂,下有苏杭。"

杭州的名气主要在于风景如画的西湖。西湖一年四季都美不胜收,宋代著名诗人苏东坡用"淡妆浓抹总相宜"的诗句来赞誉西湖。在杭州,您可以饱览西湖的秀色,也不妨漫步街头闹市,品尝一下杭州的名菜名点,还可购上几样名特土产。

苏堤和白堤把西湖一分为二,仿佛两条绿色的缎带,飘逸于碧波之上。湖中心有三个小岛:阮公墩、湖心亭和小瀛洲。湖水泛着涟漪,四周山林茂密,点缀着楼台亭阁,是我国最有名的旅游景点之一。

杭州人观看西湖有个说法:"晴湖不如雨湖,雨湖不如夜湖。"您在杭州,一定要去领略一下西湖的风韵,看看此说是否有道理。

杭州是中国著名的六大古都之一,已有二千多年的历史。杭州不仅以自然美景闻名于世,而且有着传统文化的魅力。不仅有历代文人墨客的题咏,而且有美味佳肴和漂亮的工艺品。

杭州是中国的"丝绸之府",丝绸产品品种繁多,其中以织锦尤为引人注目。杭州还生产黑纸扇和檀香扇。其他特产有西湖绸伞和中国十大名茶之一的西湖龙井。

杭州有许多有名的餐馆,供应各帮菜点,还有一百多家旅馆酒店,为游客提供舒适的住宿。

一般来说,游览西湖及其周围景点花上两天时间较为合适。到杭州旅游,既令人愉快,又能得到文化享受。

译前提示

本语篇与语篇1颇为类似，翻译这一语篇时可以参考翻译语篇1的做法。本段材料是有关杭州的简介，涉及杭州的景色、特产、历史、美食、住宿及旅游日程等信息。随着G20在杭州的召开，相信会有更多的外国游客希望亲眼见到这一天堂之城，感受中国文化的底蕴和风情。

1. 原文使用了一些描述性词汇、短语、诗句及比喻等手段恰到好处地宣传杭州，从而唤起读者想去杭州旅游的欲望。在翻译较为知名的诗句或熟语时，可以上网查找相关的资料，找出对应的英文表达。
2. 原文中并列短句较多，读来朗朗上口，通俗易懂，翻译时要特别注意。
3. "丝绸之府"可以译成 the home of silk。
4. "黑纸扇和檀香扇"的英文是 black paper fans and sandalwood fans；"绸伞"是 silk parasol。

参考译文

Hangzhou—Paradise on Earth

The famous Italian traveler Marco Polo was so impressed by the beauty of Hangzhou that he described it as "the most fascinating city in the world where one feels that one is in paradise." In China, there has been a century-old popular saying praising the city: "There is paradise in heaven and there are Suzhou and Hangzhou on earth."

Hangzhou's fame mainly lies in its picturesque West Lake. As it is beautiful all the year round, the West Lake was compared by Su Dongpo, a celebrated poet of the Song Dynasty, to a beauty "who is always charming whether she is richly adorned or plainly dressed". In Hangzhou, you will find the lake not only a perfect delight to the eye but also a joy to stroll along the busy streets, taste famous Hangzhou dishes and buy some special local products.

The West Lake is bisected by the Su Causeway and the Bai Causeway which look like two green ribbons floating gracefully on the blue waters. In the center of the lake are three isles—Ruangongdun Isle, Huxinting Isle and Xiaoyingzhou Isle. With ripples on the water's surface and thickly wooded hills dotted by exquisite pavilions on its four sides, the West Lake is one of China's best known scenic spots.

Hangzhou residents have their way of enjoying the beauty of the West Lake. According to them, "the West Lake looks more delightful on rainy days than on clear days, but it is at its best after darkness has fallen". When you are in Hangzhou, you'd better go and take in the charm of the lake for yourself to see if the comment is true.

As one of China's six ancient capital cities, Hangzhou has a history of more than 2,000 years. It is famous not only for its natural beauty but also for its cultural traditions. Apart from a large number of poems and inscriptions in its praise left behind by scholars and men of letters throughout the centuries, it also boasts delicious food and pretty handicrafts.

Hangzhou is the home of silk in China. Its silk products come in a great variety, among which its brocade is especially attractive. Hangzhou also specializes in making black paper fans and sandalwood fans. Other specialties include silk parasols and West Lake Longjing Tea, which is among the top ten produced in China.

In Hangzhou, there are many fine restaurants, serving a wide range of cuisines. Meanwhile, there are more than a hundred hotels in the city, providing tourists with comfortable accommodation.

It is advisable for you to have a two-day tour of the West Lake and scenic spots around it. As a tourist, you will find the trip to Hangzhou both pleasant and culturally rewarding.

译文注释

参考译文选自彭萍编著的《实用旅游英语翻译（英汉双向）》[7]一书，个别表达稍有改动。

1. 意大利著名旅行家马可·波罗曾这样叙述他印象中的杭州："这是世界上最美妙迷人的城市，它使人觉得自己是在天堂。" The famous Italian traveler Marco Polo was so impressed by the beauty of Hangzhou that he

---

7　彭萍. 2010. 实用旅游英语翻译（英汉双向）. 北京：对外经济贸易大学出版社，6-7.

described it as "the most fascinating city in the world where one feels that one is in paradise."

【注释】翻译时，首先应确认马可·波罗的英文拼写。另外，可以上网搜索有无相关信息直接对应"这是世界上最美妙迷人的城市，它使人觉得自己是在天堂"的英文表达。如果网上找不到现成的英文，就需要自己翻译。

2. 上有天堂，下有苏杭。There is paradise in heaven and there are Suzhou and Hangzhou on earth.

【注释】"上有天堂，下有苏杭"的英文表达其实比较多，如 There is paradise in heaven and there are Suzhou and Hangzhou on earth； Above is the paradise, and below are Suzhou and Hangzhou； Paradise in heaven, Suzhou and Hangzhou on earth 等。选择一个合适的译文就行。

如果网上或文献中找不到完全对应的表达，可以试着套用某些名句的表达进行适当修改。

翻译时，要学会从网上搜索相关信息，并对收集到的信息加以甄别和判断，专有名词和俗语锦句应符合通行的说法，使译文尽量地道自然。

3. 西湖一年四季都美不胜收，宋代著名诗人苏东坡用"淡妆浓抹总相宜"的诗句来赞誉西湖。As it is beautiful all the year round, the West Lake was compared by Su Dongpo, a celebrated poet of the Song Dynasty, to a beauty "who is always charming whether she is richly adorned or plainly dressed".

【注释】翻译"宋代著名诗人苏东坡"时，按照一般的习惯，是将"宋代著名诗人"处理成同位语。

"欲把西湖比西子，淡妆浓抹总相宜"是非常有名的诗句，很多名家翻译过该句。如罗郁正将之译为 Compare West Lake to a beautiful girl, she will look just as becoming—lightly made up or richly adorned. T. K. Tsai 的译文是 For varied charms the West Lake well may I compare, to Xizi, who, adorned or not, alike was fair. 许渊冲将这句诗译为 West Lake may be compared to Lady of the West, whether she is richly adorned or plainly dressed. 本参考译文选用的是许渊冲的译法。

4. 湖中心有三个小岛：阮公墩、湖心亭和小瀛洲。In the center of the lake are three isles—Ruangongdun Isle, Huxinting Isle and Xiaoyingzhou Isle.

【注释】"阮公墩、湖心亭和小瀛洲"可以直接音译；如果篇幅允许，也可以添加脚注，介绍这三个岛的由来或相关信息。

翻译加油站

翻译技巧（四）：词类转换

词类转换是指在翻译过程中，按照目的语的规范，把原文中某些词类的词转换成另一种词类的词。

英语和汉语的词类大部分是重合的。但汉语中，一个词可充当的句子成分比英语多。例如，英语中充当主语的只有代词、名词或相当于名词的动名词或不定式，充当谓语的只有动词；而汉语中，名词、动词、形容词都可以做主语、谓语、宾语和表语[8]（司显柱，曾剑平等，2006）。

因此，翻译时要灵活处理，不一定要拘泥于原文中所用的词性，而是要根据目的语的特点进行调整。

一、动词的词类转换

汉语中动词的使用非常频繁，在一个句子中可以出现几个动词在一起连用的情况；在英语中，一般一个句子中只有一个动词可以作为谓语。因此，在翻译过程中，汉语动词经常转译成其他词性的词，如名词、形容词和介词等。

（一）转换成名词

例1　他总爱**喝**很多的酒。
　　　He is a great *drinker*.

例2　他妹妹老是**说谎**。
　　　His sister is a great *liar*.

例3　我们一贯**认为**他是一个很不错的学生。
　　　It has been our long-held *view* that he is a very good student.

前三个例子中，汉语动词译成了名词，如"喝"转换成名词 drinker，"说谎"转换成名词 liar，"认为"也译成了名词 view。汉语中喜用动词，所以动词的使用频率

8　司显柱，曾剑平，等.2006.汉译英教程.上海：东华大学出版社，96.

很高，译成英语时应该按照英语中喜用名词的习惯，将其转换成名词。

例 4　他们片面地**注重**重工业，**忽视**农业和轻工业，因而市场上货物不够，货币不稳定。

Their lopsided *stress* on heavy industry to the *neglect* of agriculture and light industry results in a shortage of goods in the market and an unstable currency.

与前几个例子一样，"注重"和"忽视"在原文中都是动词，翻译成英语时都转换成了名词，result in 是译文的谓语动词。

（二）转换成形容词

例 5　我们决不**满足**于现有的成就。

We are not *content* with our present achievement.

例 6　获悉贵国遭受地震，我们极为**关切**。

We are deeply *concerned* at the news that your country has been struck by an earthquake.

"满足"和"关切"在原句中都是动词，翻译成英语时经常译成形容词词组，分别是 be content with 和 be deeply concerned at/with。一般而言，状态动词在汉译英时会译成形容词。

例 7　他读书时**不加选择**。

He is *indiscriminate* in reading.

例 8　他们迫切地想**弄到消息**。

They are *news-hungry*.

例 9　那个家伙老是滔滔不绝**讲个不停**。

That fellow is very *talkative*.

"不加选择""弄到消息"和"讲个不停"分别用形容词 indiscriminate, news-hungry 和 talkative 来翻译，用词精练，也符合英语的用词习惯。

（三）转换成介词或介词词组

例 10　我们全体**赞成**他的建议。

We were all *in favor of* his suggestion.

"赞成"除译成 be in favor of 外，也可以用 be for 加以表达，与之对应的"反对"是 be against。

例 11　11 点时他已**睡在**被窝里。

He was *between* sheets by eleven.

"睡在被窝"用介词词组 between sheets 来表达，是不是很形象生动？

例 12　这种人**闹**什么？**闹**名誉、**闹**地位、**闹**出风头。

What are these people *after*? They are *after* fame and position and want to be in the limelight.

"闹"在汉语中可充当动词，使用的频率很高；另外，也可以和其他词组合构成新的词，如"吵闹""闹别扭""医闹"，等等。译成英文时，"闹"没有统一的译法，须根据上下文的实际含义来选词。就本句而言，"闹"做贬义词，表"追求"之意，译文用介词 after 来表达。

例 13　他们**吃着**粗茶淡饭，**住着**寒冷的窑洞，**点着**昏暗的油灯，长时间地工作。

They worked long hours *on* meager food, *in* cold caves, *by* dim lamps.

原句用"吃着粗茶淡饭，住着寒冷的窑洞，点着昏暗的油灯"描写了早期共产党领导人的艰苦生活。该句的信息重点是"长时间地工作"，所以译文中的谓语动词是 work，而"吃着""住着"和"点着"这些表示状态的词分别用介词 on，in 和 by 来表达。

二、名词的词类转换

在汉译英过程中，汉语的动词可以转换成英语的名词，而有时汉语的名词也可能会转换成英语的动词。

例 14　他的演讲给听众的**印象**很深。

His speech *impressed* the audience deeply.

"印象"可做名词和动词，译文将原文中的名词"印象"翻译成了动词，用词较为精练。当然，也可以保留名词形式，译成 His speech left a deep impression on the audience.

例15 该厂产品的主要**特点**是工艺精湛，经久耐用。

The products of this factory *are* chiefly *characterized by* their fine workmanship and durability.

例16 辛亥革命的**目的**在于推翻满清王朝。

The Revolution of 1911 *aimed at* overthrowing the Qing Dynasty.

"……的特点"译成英文时，一般用动词词组 be characterized by 来表达。对应的，"目的在于"也经常用动词词组 aim at 来表达。在翻译学习过程中，可以关注一些中英文对应的表达，这样既可以提高翻译速度，又可以使译文更地道。

课后练习

试将下列语篇译成英文：

1. 自由女神像是世界上最有名的纪念碑之一，它是19世纪时由法国人民赠送给美国人民的。这一伟大雕刻由雕刻家 August Bartholdy 设计而成，花了10年时间才完工。对那些经过纽约港在美国安家落户的数百万人来说，这一伟大纪念碑已成为了自由的象征。

2. 百年前，香港仅是一个小小的渔港，时至今日已发展成为世界上最繁荣的大都会之一。这城市汇聚了中西文化，华洋共处，是亚洲的金融中心及通往中国内地市场的入口，并享有"东方之珠""美食天堂"和"购物天堂"之美誉。香港地方虽小，却拥有不少世界之最，当中最有名的包括青马大桥和天坛大佛。购物玩乐之余，亦不乏传统文物与观光好去处。

第八章
科技文本的翻译

随着社会的不断发展和进步，科技文本几乎涵盖了政治、经济、军事、社会、文化等诸多领域，它是随着科学技术的发展而形成的一种独立的文体形式。

"在对科技文本的定义上，国内相关参考文献大多指：科技著作、科技论文和报告、实验报告和方案；各类科技情报和文字资料；科技实用手册和操作规程；有关科技问题的会谈、会议、交谈的文字资料；有关科技的影片、录像、光盘等有声资料的解说词以及描写和解释大自然现象的语篇等。科技文本的格式非常固定，大有国际化、标准化的趋势，如实验报告和科学论文的格式是世界通用的"[1]（韦琴红，2006）。科技文本可分为专门的科技文本和通俗的科技文本。专门的科技文本专业性较强，翻译时往往需要较为专业的词典，同时也需具备某学科的专业知识，对多数普通学生来说，恐怕难以胜任英译的任务。本章主要探讨的是如何翻译通俗的科技文本，如科普文本。

∽ 科技文本的语言特点

科技文本虽然形式多样，但在词汇和句法上却有着许多共同的特点，如表达准确、客观、简洁、规范；因此，科技文本的翻译也在一定程度上有别于其他类文本的翻译。

在词汇上，科技本文表现为词汇的专业性强，大量运用专业术语。

科技文本表述的是科技概念、科技理论和科学事实，所以专业性较强，专业术语的大量应用也成为其应有的特点。

"科学技术以揭示、开发和利用外在客观世界的事实及其规律为宗旨，纷繁复杂的客观世界需要一套系统规范的词汇供人们去交流认知世界的经验和实践"[2]（罗左毅，2012）。因此，科技文本会大量使用专业术语以简明扼要地阐述自然和社会现象的性质、特点及其发生和发展过程。另外，随着新技术、新发明、新设备、新工艺的不断涌现，科技文本也在不断地构建新的科技术语。英文科技文本中的很多

1　韦琴红.2006.英汉科技文本的语篇特征对比分析.杭州电子科技大学学报（社会科学版），2：30.
2　罗左毅.2012.英汉实用翻译教程.南京：南京大学出版社，120.

新术语是将普通词汇通过合成法构成的。通过这种方法构建的科技术语，其学科意义有些可以根据其构成成分的常见意义进行翻译；有些则不行，必须根据相关学科术语特定的表述形式进行翻译。在英译过程中，可以关注这一现象。

在句法上，科技文本，特别是英文的科技文本，表现为：

首先，频繁使用被动结构。

科技文本往往追求客观的阐述和准确清晰的表达，因此，英文的科技文本会频繁使用被动结构。因为英文的被动结构有叙述客观、行文紧凑严密的表达效果。虽然中文的科技文本没有像英文的科技文本那么明显，但英译时就需要将一些主动句译成被动句，少用人称代词及描述性形容词，以避免叙述的主观色彩，力求行文简洁、客观和严密。

其次，大量使用名词化表述。

名词化结构用词简洁、信息容量大，给人以静态的客观事实而非捉摸不定的动态感觉，在科技英语中使用较为普遍。"科技英语的名词化倾向是与科技文体的基本要求密切相关的。科技文章的任务是叙述事实和论证推断，因而要求言简意赅，这中间，基本问题之一就是语言结构的简化。"[3] 这就意味着，在英译科技文本时，可以适当采用名词化表述，如"照明强度测定"可以翻译成 illumination intensity determination，"乳腺癌普查计划实施总结"译成 breast cancer survey program evaluation。

另外，普遍使用一般现在时。

刘宓庆（1998）提到[4]，科技英语倾向于多用动词的现在时，尤其是多用一般现在时，来表述"无时间性"（timeless）的"一般叙述"（general statement），即通常发生或并无时限的自然现象、过程和常规等。一般现在时在科技英语中用于表述科学定义、定理、方程式、公式的解说以及图表的说明，给人以精确无误的"无时间性"，排除任何与时间牵连的误解。所以，英译科技文本时首选一般现在时。

∞ 科技文本翻译的要点

科技翻译属"信息型"文本翻译，就目的论而言，科技文本的翻译应有效突出

---

3 刘宓庆. 1998. 文体与翻译（增订版）. 北京：中国对外翻译出版公司，328.
4 同上，第 330-331 页。

文本的信息功能，保证信息传递的真实性和准确性。换句话说，"信息的有效传递、内容的精确和表达的规范是科技语篇翻译的核心，功能对等、信息准确是科技翻译的最高原则"[5]（辛凌、王婷，2009）。因此，译文的语言必须做到客观准确、明白易懂，使译文读者能有效获取相关的科技信息。

就翻译标准而言，科技文本的翻译要做到：

第一，内容忠实。

一般情况下，科技文本表达客观，用词精确，结构严谨，信息浓缩，逻辑性强，不允许有任何歧义。因此，"忠实"这一标准对科技文本的翻译来说尤为重要，否则会引起误解。翻译专业术语时，应采用相关学科通用的统一译名，或广为接受的译名，力求译名的规范化，避免因译名混乱而造成概念和信息错误。

同时，"忠实"还体现在原文风格的传达上。在科技文本的翻译过程中，传达原作风格也十分重要。翻译时应尽量避免主观渲染，避免表露个人感情，少用带感情色彩的词汇和修辞手段，做到说理叙事清晰明白，用词造句简洁准确，并尽量使用专业术语。

第二，语言通顺。

"通顺"主要指译文的语言必须通顺易懂，符合目的语的表达特点。"在汉译英过程中应按照英语的语法和表达习惯来选词、造句，避免条理不通、结构混乱、逻辑层次不明的现象。同时，要做到行文流畅，注意避免死译，生搬硬套汉语句式；应该在深刻领会中文意思的基础上，尽量摆脱中文形式的束缚，重新进行结构整合、理清逻辑层次，用符合英语习惯的表达方法把原文信息流畅地表达出来。"[6]（魏羽、高宝萍，2010）

第三，逻辑清晰。

科技文本往往信息量大，描述性和阐释性功能突出。汉语表达一般是按事情的因果逻辑顺序、事件发生的先后顺序等，将内容逐项交代出来。而英语表达则通常按所表达意义的主次关系依序排列，因此中心句领先、从句随后，或中心词在前、

5　辛凌，王婷. 2009. 大学英语实用翻译教程. 重庆：重庆大学出版社, 233.
6　魏羽，高宝萍. 2010. 汉英科技翻译教程. 西安：西北工业大学出版社, 8.

修饰语在后的句型结构非常普遍。在具体翻译过程中，必须仔细分析原文结构，理顺逻辑关系，有效发挥目的语的优势，做到逻辑层次清楚，语义连贯明确。

翻译语篇 1

磁悬浮列车：走什么样的道路（节选）

从远处迎面看，这种未来列车就像是一架在高架上滑行的超大雪橇。当它从距地面 23 英尺高的轨道上驶近时，几乎使所有的辨识试验都失灵：看不到火车头，听不到隆隆声，也听不到尖叫声。当列车疾驶而过时，只听到巨大的嘶嘶声，那是列车以近 300 英里的时速行驶时，排开空气所发出的声音。

这种新列车叫做"maglev"，是磁悬浮列车（magnetic levitation）的缩写。磁悬浮列车不像火车那样枯燥，它由巨大磁铁的磁力支持着浮在空中。它不是靠轮子在轨道上行使，而是利用磁铁推进，实际上它是在飞。除了风的阻力之外，它不受任何阻碍，所以能够达到普通陆上交通——最快的常规列车——所不能达到的速度。法国的高速列车 TGV 仅创造了每小时 186 英里的速度。有一列磁悬浮列车已经在运行。它是英国的一条短途慢速（每小时 25 英里）线路，穿梭行驶在伯明翰机场与火车站之间。但是，速度快得多的磁悬浮列车原型正在试验中，而且，雄心勃勃的工程明年即可开工，其中包括连接洛杉矶地区和赌城拉斯维加斯的 230 英里线路。

译前提示

本段材料的关键词是悬磁浮列车。磁悬浮技术研究源于德国：早在 1922 年，德国工程师赫尔曼·肯佩尔就提出了电磁悬浮原理，并于 1934 年申请了磁悬浮列车的专利。我国第一辆磁悬浮列车就是从德国购买的，2003 年 1 月开始在上海运行。

如今我们对悬磁浮列车已不陌生，但本段材料选自严俊仁 2004 年出版的《汉英科技翻译》，当时人们对悬磁浮列车的了解并不多。

1. 本文中的"雪橇"可以翻译成 bobsled, 即"双连大雪橇"，更符合语境。
2. "辨识试验"可以用 test of recognition。

这一语篇对磁悬浮列车的工作原理及实际运用进行了简单的介绍，英译时应注意英语科技文本的一些特点，如多用被动语态和一般现在时；同时，也须理顺原文的逻辑关系，使整个译文做到忠实通顺、逻辑清晰、富有科学性。

参考译文

Floating Trains: What a Way to Go (Excerpt)

Viewed head on and from a distance, the train of the future looks like an overgrown bobsled on stilts. As it approaches its track 23 feet above the ground, it fails almost all the tests of recognition: there are no engines, no rumble, and no screech. As the train hurtles by, there is only a vast whoosh, the sound of air being parted by a vehicle traveling at close to 300 miles per hour.

The new train is called a maglev, a contraction of magnetic levitation. The vehicle lacks that litany of trainlike properties because it floats in the air, supported by the force of immensely powerful magnets. Instead of rolling on rails, it actually flies, using magnets for propulsion. Unhindered by any friction except wind resistance, the maglev can attain speeds unheard of in ordinary land travel—the fastest conventional train. France's TGV hits only 186 miles per hour. One maglev is already running: a short, slow-moving (25 miles per hour) line in Britain that shuttles people from Birmingham's airport to the railway station. But much faster prototypes are being tested, and ambitious projects could get under way next year, including a 230-mile link between the Los Angeles area and the gambling mecca of Las Vegas.

译文注释

原文和译文均选自严俊仁编著的《汉英科技翻译》[7]，个别词汇有改动。相对其他类型的文本，大部分学生对科技文本的接触可能并不多，

---

7 严俊仁. 2004. 汉英科技翻译. 北京：国防工业出版社，284.

翻译的难度也就随之增加了。如果对科技本文感兴趣，可以在平时多阅读相关材料，这样，翻译类似的文本时就会变得简单多了。

1. 当列车疾驶而过时，只听到巨大的嘶嘶声，那是列车以近300英里的时速行驶时，排开空气所发出的声音。As the train hurtles by, there is only a vast whoosh, the sound of air being parted by a vehicle traveling at close to 300 miles per hour.

   【注释】"疾驶而过"可以用 hurtle by 这一表达，相关的例句有：The train often stopped to let really important trains bawl and hurtle by.（列车常常停下，让那些重要的列车呼啸疾驰而过。）

   原句和译文都是长句。科技文体频繁使用长句，其目的是使概念表达严密准确，叙述条理主次分明。一般说来，英文科技文本的长句多由复合句构成，复杂的复合句往往从句套从句、短语带从句，相互依附、环环相扣。翻译时，需要理清逻辑线索，用多样化的表达形式表述原文的复杂内容。

2. 磁悬浮列车不像火车那样枯燥，它由巨大磁铁的磁力支持着浮在空中。The vehicle lacks that litany of trainlike properties because it floats in the air, supported by the force of immensely powerful magnets.

   【注释】Litany 后面跟 of sth. 时，有"（对一系列事件、原因等）枯燥冗长的陈述"之意。如：He provided a long litany of development problems and challenges facing China.（他长篇累牍地陈述中国面临的发展问题和挑战。）

   原句中的"由巨大磁铁的磁力支持着"语序有调整，放在了句尾，用 supported 一词把前后部分有序地连接起来。另外，根据语篇的内容可以推断出这里的因果关系，所以译者增加了表示因果关系的连词 because。这样不仅语言表达更为流畅，逻辑关系也更加清晰。

3. 但是，速度快得多的磁悬浮列车原型正在试验中，而且，雄心勃勃的工程明年即可开工，其中包括连接洛杉矶地区和赌城拉斯维加斯的230英里线路。But much faster prototypes are being tested, and ambitious projects could get under way next year, including a 230-mile link between the Los Angeles area and the gambling mecca of Las Vegas.

   【注释】Prototype 有"原型"之意，后面可以跟 for sth. 或者 of sth.。如："一种文学体裁的原型"可以翻译成 the prototype of a literary genre。

   Mecca 本身是指位于沙特阿拉伯的城市麦加，它是先知穆罕默德的出生地，被世人视为伊斯兰的圣地，因此该词有"圣地""向往之地"的意思。与注释1一样，此话的原文和译文都是典型的长句。科技文本中频繁使用长句，在翻译时应重视这一现象。将汉语的长句翻译成英语的长句时，一定要认真检查有无语法错误，逻辑有无问题等。

翻译语篇2

宇宙中的生命

"宇宙中的其他地方有没有生命？"

要回答这个问题，我们首先必须考虑生物，无论是植物和动物，是由什么构成的。然后再考虑生命生存所需要的条件。生物体和其他物质一样，都是由原子构成的。原子结合形成分子。分子是一切物质可以被分割的最小单位。例如分解水分子后，水就不再存在，剩下的只是构成水的原子——一个氧原子和两个氢原子。生物的分子不是由两三个原子构成的，而是由成千上万个原子以多种复杂的形式组合而成的。

处于高温环境中时，构成生物的复杂分子就会分裂成各种原子而死亡。因此，太阳或其他任何恒星上面不可能有生命，因为那里太热了。

X射线会破坏活的分子，紫外线对多种分子也有杀伤力。由于接近太阳或其他恒星的行星没有抵挡这些射线的大气层，因此在这些行星上面不大可能会存在生命。

生物的呼吸、成长、移动，都需要能量。地球上的动植物都是直接或间接地从太阳那里获得能量。因此那些远离太阳、温度极低的行星上不可能有生物生存。

看起来要得到一个令人满意的答案，我们还有相当长的路要走。

译前提示

本段材料从"宇宙的其他地方有无其他生命"这一问题出发，探讨了生物的构成。文章没有涉及过于高深或专业的内容，相信大部分学生都能正确理解原文的内容。因此，翻译本段材料的最大难点就在于如何用通俗客观的英文将之传达给英文读者。

1. "原子"是atom，"分子"是molecule。
2. "氧原子"是atom of oxygen，"氢原子"是atom of hydrogen。

> 参考译文

Life in the Universe

"Are there living things anywhere else in the Universe?"

To answer this question, first we must consider what makes a living thing, whether plant or animal, and then what conditions living things need in order to go on living. Living things, like everything else, are made of atoms, which are grouped into molecules. A molecule is the very smallest possible bit you can have of any substance. When you break up a molecule of water, for example, you no longer have water at all, but only the atoms of which water is made—one atom of oxygen and two of hydrogen. The molecules of living things are made, not of two or three atoms, but of hundreds or thousands in different complicated patterns.

If they become too hot, these complicated molecules of living things break up into separate atoms and cease to be living. Therefore, there cannot be life on the Sun or any of the stars because they are far too hot.

Living molecules are also damaged by X-rays, and many of them by ultra-violet rays, so they are not likely to exist on a planet close to the Sun or any other star where there is no atmosphere to keep off these radiations.

Living things also need energy to make them breathe, grow and move. On Earth plants and animals get their energy, directly or indirectly, from the Sun. So planets, which are far from the Sun and extremely cold, are not places where living things could exist.

It seems that we still have a long way to go before we get a satisfactory answer.

> 译文注释

参考译文选自魏羽、高宝萍编著的《汉英科技翻译教程》[8]，整个语篇读来颇有科普文本的感觉。

---

[8] 魏羽，高宝萍. 2010. 汉英科技翻译教程. 西安：西北工业大学出版社，128.

1. 生物体和其他物质一样，都是由原子构成的。Living things, like everything else, are made of atoms, which are grouped into molecules.

    【注释】Like everything else 是插入语，起补充说明作用。插入语是英语句子中的一种独立成分，它与句子的其他部分没有任何语法关系，只是作为某种附加的说明，或起承上启下的作用，也常用来表示作者的态度和看法等。插入语的位置灵活，可位于句首、句中或句尾。

2. 例如分解水分子后，水就不再存在，剩下的只是构成水的原子——一个氧原子和两个氢原子。When you break up a molecule of water, for example, you no longer have water at all, but only the atoms of which water is made—one atom of oxygen and two of hydrogen.

    【注释】For example 也是插入语。of which water is made 是定语从句，修饰 the atoms，of 是 be made of 中的 of 提到 which 之前了。为了避免重复，two 的后面省略了 atoms。

3. 由于接近太阳或其他恒星的行星没有抵挡这些射线的大气层，因此在这些行星上面不大可能会存在生命。...so they are not likely to exist on a planet close to the Sun or any other star where there is no atmosphere to keep off these radiations.

    【注释】"没有抵挡这些射线的大气层"的译文是 where there is no atmosphere to keep off these radiations，变成了定语从句，修饰 star。

4. 因此那些远离太阳、温度极低的行星上不可能有生物生存。So planets, which are far from the Sun and extremely cold, are not places where living things could exist.

    【注释】本句包含了两个定语从句，第一个从句 which are far...cold 修饰主语，第二个从句由关系副词 where 引导，修饰 places。原文"因此那些远离太阳、温度极低的行星上不可能有生物生存"也可以译成存在句的否定句形式，即 there be 结构中用 cannot 表示否定的推断。多变的译文句型可避免译文显得呆板。

5. 看起来要得到一个令人满意的答案，我们还有相当长的路要走。It seems that we still have a long way to go before we get a satisfactory answer.

    【注释】中文中经常可以看到"还有相当长的路要走"类似的表达，一般可以翻译成 sb. still has a long way to go。

翻译加油站

翻译技巧（五）：语态转换

语态转换是指翻译中汉英两种语言之间主动语态与被动语态之间的互换。

英语的被动语态比汉语的被动语态使用频率高得多。英语中使用被动句的主要原因有：强调被动动作；强调动作的承受者；不知道或者无须说出动作的执行者；便于上下文连贯、衔接；为了突出客观性，避免使用人称主语（常见于科技学术论文中）；为了措辞得当，语气委婉；固定用法的被动句结构。

一、汉语的被动句译为英语的被动句

（一）汉语中典型的被动句（被、受、遭受、给、挨、叫、让、加以、予以、为……所、被……所，等等）译成被动句

例1　他被选为学生会主席。
　　　He *was elected* Chairman of the Student Union.

例2　这个问题必须在适当的时候以适当的方式予以处理。
　　　The problem must *be dealt with* by appropriate means at an appropriate time.

例3　一些古老的传统和价值观不再为年轻人所珍视。
　　　Some old traditions and values *are* no longer *cherished* by youth.

"被""予以"和"为……"都是汉语典型被动句的标识词，译成英语时一般还是采用被动句式。

（二）简化被动句

汉语中的简化被动语态是由主语和谓语配合起来，自然表示被动意义，句子中没有任何表示被动的词语。汉语的简化被动句也可译成被动句。

（4）有些问题还需要澄清。
　　　Some questions have yet to *be clarified*.

原句看似主动句，但主语"问题"与谓语"澄清"搭配在一起，内含的是一种

被动意义。因此，英译时使用了被动。

例5 狡兔死，走狗烹；飞鸟尽，良弓藏；敌国破，谋臣亡。

When the cunning hares *are killed*, the good hound *is thrown* into the cauldron（大锅炉）; when the soaring birds *have been caught*, the good bow *is put away*; when the enemy states *are overthrown*, the wise minister *is killed*.

没有古文功底或古文功底较弱的学生，在理解原文时可能有一定的困难。用白话文解释，其含义是：狡猾的兔子死了，用来抓兔子的狗就会被杀了吃掉；天上飞翔的鸟儿被打尽了，好的猎弓就会被藏起来；敌对的国家被攻破了，用来出谋划策的大臣就要被杀掉。从这一解释中，可以清楚地看出其被动意义，因此翻译时也采用了被动语态。

（三）"是"字句

例6 马路两旁是整齐的梧桐树。

The avenue *is lined* with neatly-spaced plane trees.

例7 世间万物都是由原子构成的。

Everything in the world *is built up* from atoms.

部分"是"字句也表被动概念，如马路两旁被梧桐树排列，世间万物被原子构成，在英译时都要采用被动语态。当然，在翻译"是"字句时应加以辨析，不是所有的"是"字句都用被动。

二、汉语的被动句译成英语的主动句

有些汉语句子，虽然形式上像被动结构，实际上是把主语省略了。这种句子译成英语时还是应当用主动形式来表达，如果译成被动结构就不太自然。另外，即使出现了"被"等被动标志词，有时也译成主动形式。

例8 这种竹席摸起来很光滑。

The bamboo mattress *feels* smooth.

在英语中，feel 表"摸"时很少用被动语态，而 be felt 往往表示"被感受"的意思，如：The best and most beautiful things cannot be seen or touched. They must be felt with the heart.（最美好的东西通常不是看到或触摸到的，必须要用心感受。）所以，尽管竹

席是被摸，但翻译时仍用主动语态，而不是 The bamboo mattress is felt smooth.

例9　台风"罗莎"过后，由于措施得力，损失已被减少到最低程度。

Effective measures *have reduced* the losses to the minimum after the typhoon Krosa.

译文将"措施得力"作为主语，整个句子自然而然就应该使用主动语态。当然，本句也可以考虑使用被动语态，如 After the typhoon Krosa, losses have been reduced to the minimum owing to the effective measures. 但与参考译文相比，用词较多。

三、汉语的主动句译成英语的被动句

（一）出于习惯或礼貌上的考虑

例10　广州的地铁三号线将在明年年底建成。

The construction of Metro Line 3 in Guangzhou *will be completed* by the end of next year.

例11　每年十月，杭州的西湖都要举行国际马拉松赛。

An International Marathon *is held* around the West Lake in Hangzhou in October every year.

上述两个例子中，汉语的主动句都译成了英语的被动句。需要注意的是，例10中增译了 the construction，例11则用 around the West Lake 来表达国际马拉松赛的举办地点，千万不要将这部分译成 in the West Lake。

（二）为了回避施事者

例12　据说今晚有一个重要会议。

It is said that there will be an important meeting this evening.

例13　据报道这起交通事故中大约有10人丧生。

It is reported that about 10 people have lost their lives in the accident.

例14　应当指出，这些指控是毫无根据的。

It should be pointed out that the accusations are groundless.

例15　众所周知，这些岛屿向来归中国管辖。

It is known to all that these islands have always been under Chinese jurisdiction.

"据说"和"据报道"在译成英语时，一般采用固定表达，分别是 be said 和 be reported。"应当指出"一般可以译成 should be pointed out；而"众所周知"则是 it is known to all 或 as is known to all 的句式。此类表达一般都采用被动语态，省略施事者。

（三）为了加强上下文的连贯和衔接

例16 人的思想形成了语言，而语言又影响了人的思想。

Language *is shaped by, and shapes,* human thought.

如果不使用被动语态，译文可能是 The human thought shapes the language. Meanwhile, the language shapes the human thought. 或者 The human thought shapes the language and the vice versa. 这样的译文与参考译文相比，连贯性和精练性都略逊一筹。

例17 他出现在台上，观众给予热烈鼓掌。

He appeared on the stage and *was warmly applauded by the audience.*

试将这一译文与如下译文作一比较：When he appeared on the stage, the audience applauded warmly. 哪个更好一些？当然是参考译文更胜一筹，因为它更连贯、更通顺。

课后练习

试将下列语篇译成英文：

1. 微波炉的维护

   一、清洗微波烘箱前，须关闭烘箱，并从插座上拔下插头。

   二、保持烘箱内部清洁。如溅出的食物或溢出的液体积在烘箱壁上，则请用湿布擦去。烘箱较脏时，可以使用软性洗剂。最好不要使用烈性清洁剂或研磨剂。

   三、请用微湿布来清洗微波烘箱表面部分，为防止损伤烘箱内的操作部分，不要让水分由通口渗入。

   四、要防止弄湿控制面板，如果潮湿，则请用柔软湿布抹擦，不能用洗涤剂、研磨剂或衣垢喷雾剂等擦洗控制面板。擦拭控制板时请将炉门打开，以防止不小心启动烘箱。

2. 在各门科学之中，生物学对于了解人类关系最大。1859 年，也就是稍多于一个世纪以前，达尔文提出了本书所涉及的革命思想——人类以及所有其他生命体，乃是进化发展过程的产物。但是，人类不仅已经进化，而且依然在不断进化。人类的进化不完全是过去的事情，它同时也是现实，而且关系着未来。人类由于处在辐射威胁之下，其中包括原子武器实验产生的放射性散落物所造成的辐射威胁之下，很可能遭到基因损伤。这一问题近年来已经理所当然地引起人们的广泛重视。

下篇

非实用翻译

第九章
小说翻译

"文学翻译与非文学翻译的区别,首先表现在对象的不同。文学翻译的对象是文学作品,具体地说,就是小说、散文、诗歌、纪实文学、戏剧和影视作品。而非文学翻译的对象是文学作品以外的各种文体,如各种理论著作、学术著作、教科书、报刊政论作品、公文合同,等等。其次表现在语言形式的不同。文学翻译采用的是文学语言,而非文学翻译采用的是非文学语言。第三是翻译手段不同。文学翻译采用的是文学艺术手段,带有主体性、创造性,而非文学翻译采用的是技术性手段,有较强的可操纵性。鉴于文学翻译与非文学翻译的区别,我们对二者的要求也大不相同。如果说,我们要求非文学翻译要以明白畅达、合乎该文体习惯的语言准确地传达原作的内容,那么对于文学翻译,这样的要求就远远不够了。文学作品是用特殊的语言创造的艺术品,具有形象性和艺术性,体现作家独特的艺术风格,并且具有能够引人入胜的艺术意境。所以,文学翻译要求译者具有作家的文学修养和表现力,以便在深刻理解原作,把握原作精神实质的基础上,把内容与形式浑然一体的原作的艺术意境传达出来"[1](黄忠廉,2000)。

小说翻译是文学翻译中的常见形式。在中国早期历史中,小说主要用于娱乐和消遣。到了清末民初,随着维新派提出"小说界革命"的口号,小说的作用被重新界定,被赋予了重塑民族精神的重任。当然,维新派对小说功能的重视也源于西方文化的影响,西方文化常将文学的欢愉功能和认知功能结合在一起。随着"小说界革命"的提出,西方文化对中国文学的影响初见端倪。与此同时,中国文学在外译的过程中,对西方文学也产生了一定的影响。

中国小说在英语世界的翻译由来已久。根据《高级文学翻译》[2](胡显耀,李力,2009),中国小说翻译不仅范围广,而且数量多,既有欧美译者也有中国译者,同一部小说会出现多种译本。早在1938年,伦敦阿瑟普洛斯坦因公司就出版了爱德华

---

1 黄忠廉.2000.翻译本质论.武汉:华中师范大学出版社,10.
2 胡显耀,李力.2009.高级文学翻译.北京:外语教学与研究出版社.

兹（Evangeline Dora Edwards）英译的 *Chinese Prose Literature of the Tang Period*（《中国唐代散文作品》），该书收有《搜神记》《李娃传》《太平广记》等小说。

四大名著的译介更是突出。欧美各国对《三国演义》的片断译介始于19世纪初，译者多为在华的外交官和传教士，如英国的汤姆斯（Peter P. Thoms）和汉学家翟理斯（Herbert A. Giles）及美国传教士卫三畏（Samuel W. Wells）等。1925年，上海别发洋行（Kelly & Walsh Ltd.）出版了英国汉学家邓罗（C.H.Brewitt-Taylor）翻译的 *San Guo, or Romance of the Three Kingdoms*，是《三国演义》的第一个英文全译本。1933年美国出版的 *All Men Are Brothers*（《四海之内皆兄弟》）可以说是《水浒传》在西方最好的全译本，译者是1938年诺贝尔文学奖得主、美国女作家赛珍珠。她的翻译准确生动、忠于原著，鲁迅也对其赞誉有加。后来加拿大学者张亦文所译的 *Romance of the Three Kingdoms*（中国友谊出版公司，1985）和美国翻译家罗慕士（Moss Roberts）的 *Three Kindoms*（外文出版社，1994）全译本也得以出版，在英文读者中颇受欢迎。目前，中外合作出版的第一部古典名著英译本《水浒传》(*Outlaws of the Marsh*）也已问世，译者为美国翻译家沙博理（Sidney Shapiro）。

此外，《西游记》在西方也得到了广泛译介，如英国浸礼会教士李提摩太（Timothy Richard）将其英译为 *Journey to the West*（《圣僧天国之行》），1913年由上海广学会出版；英国学者海斯（Helen M.Hayes）的译本名为 *A Buddhist Pilgrim's Progress*（《佛教徒的天路历程：西游记》），1930年分别在伦敦和纽约出版；亚瑟·韦理（Arthur Waley）的英译本名为 *Monkey*，1942年由纽约艾伦与昂温（Allen & Unwin）出版社出版，在学术界颇负盛名。

根据黄鸣奋（1997）的《英语世界中国古典文学之传播》[3]，《红楼梦》的英译始于1830年。当时英国人 J. E. Davis 译出了《红楼梦》第三回中的两首《西江月》词。之后陆续有片段译文见诸报刊。《红楼梦》的全译本有大卫·霍克思（David Hawkes）与其女婿约翰·闵福德（John Minford）的合译本 *The Story of the Stone*（1973），及杨宪益、戴乃迭的合译本 *A Dream of Red Mansions*（1978）。1991年，黄新渠的缩译本《<红楼梦>：一个中国贵族家庭的长篇故事》亦面世。相对而言，杨氏夫妇译本较尊重原作，一方面注意用词和特殊的语义搭配，另一方面喜用短语，

3　黄鸣奋. 1997. 英语世界中国古典文学之传播. 上海：学林出版社.

较贴近原作的形式风格，也符合英语的会话语体习惯；霍克思翁婿不太注重用词和语义的精简搭配，习惯于在长句中表达原作意境和传达自己的译者风格。

与四大名著的英译相比，中国现代文学在西方的译介较晚，始于20世纪上半叶。这一时期，鲁迅、茅盾、巴金、老舍等人的作品得到了译介，且大多被优先译成法文而后转译为英文。如英国人密尔斯（E. Mills）将《中国当代短篇小说家作品选》译成英文，1930年和1931年先后在英美两国出版，其中包括鲁迅的《阿Q正传》《孔乙己》和《故乡》。另外，茅盾的《子夜》《春蚕》，巴金的《家》《寒夜》，老舍的《骆驼祥子》《牛天赐传》亦先后被英译而广为传播。至于中国当代小说，由于文化环境日益宽松，大众传媒日新月异，在文化全球化潮流推动下，译介空前活跃，一些意识流作家如王蒙，寻根派作家如韩少功、王安忆，后现代派作家如余华等人的作品也被大量传译到西方[4]（胡显耀，李力，2009）。

✧ 小说翻译的要点

就文学翻译而言，很多人认为译诗最难，译小说比较容易，因为译小说的比译诗的多。文学翻译大师翁显良（1982）则认为，写是创作，译是再创作，说难都难，说易都易。难易不在于是诗歌还是小说，而在于作品艺术价值的高低。原作艺术价值越高就越难；以为容易，随便译出，恐怕难免在艺术上对原作不忠实[5]。

在该文中，翁显良提到小说翻译"最好坚持三个前提：一曰熟，二曰近，三曰得。所谓熟，指的是熟悉原作者，熟悉小说的背景，熟悉其中的人物。所谓近，指的是作为译者，应与原作者性情相近，阅历相近，从而风格相近。所谓得，指的是读了原作有所感受，产生共鸣，得之于心。凡是自己不熟不近而无所得者，则以不译为宜。未经研究而贸然动笔，固然容易出错。虽经研究而仍与作者心怀不相契，勉强翻译也难望成功"[6]。另外，翁显良也指出，从不熟到熟有一个过程。要熟悉某一作者，虽然未必通读其全部作品，但至少也要读过几部代表作，而不是仅读一篇。对其作品有比较全面的认识，才能知其人。知其人，才能减少自己与作者之间的隔阂。对所译的作品应多读几遍，才会有更深刻的感受。动笔翻译，处理各个特殊问题时

4　胡显耀，李力. 2009. 高级文学翻译. 北京：外语教学与研究出版社，231.
5　翁显良. 1982. 见全牛又不见全牛——谈文学翻译（上）. 翻译通讯，3：35-38.
6　同上，35。

才比较有把握。

翻译小说时应注意哪些内容？首先，小说往往注重人物形象的塑造，人物形象的塑造与其语言又紧密相连，因此在翻译人物语言时应与其身份和角色相对应。

小说中的人物语言是塑造人物个性化性格的主要手段，也是表现艺术主题的重要因素。作家笔下一个个栩栩如生、光彩照人的人物形象，他们的喜怒哀乐、悲欢离合，无不在读者心中产生强烈的共鸣。小说中人物的塑造除了直接或间接描写外，还通过人物对话来实现，即作家让笔下的人物通过本人之口来表现自己的个性，不同的人物以各自不同的方式说着各自的话。张保红（2010）认为，再现人物语言时需考虑以下因素："一是人物语言要切合人物自己的社会地位、职业、修养、性别、年龄等身份特征，符合其性格特点与思想观点。二是在特定环境下人物语言要表现人物特定的心理状态与个性特点。也就是说，既要关注人物语言个性的'常态'，也要注意到不同于'常态'的'变异'表现。三是人物对话要彰显人物各自独特的表达方式和语气、语调，避免'千人一腔'。"[7]

不同身份的人在不同场合使用的语言各有不同。有身份、有地位的人在公共场合往往言辞谨慎，唯恐"失言"而有损自己的形象；没有受过多少正规教育的普通老百姓说起话来就没有那么多讲究了。

《红楼梦》语言优美生动，塑造了一大批具有典型性格的艺术形象，其中有主子，也有奴才。身份不同，他们的语言也不一样。主子在奴才面前盛气凌人，但若对方地位比自己高，却又极尽卑躬屈膝之能事。黄粉保（2000）认为贾政就是这样一个人物，他对贾政与北静王的对话进行了评论[8]。原文如下：

> 北静王见他语言清朗，谈吐有致，一面又向贾政笑道："令郎真乃龙驹凤雏，非小王在世翁前唐突，将来'雏凤清于老凤声'，未可量也。"
> 贾政陪笑道："犬子岂敢谬承金奖，赖藩郡余恩，果如所言，亦萌生辈之幸矣。"

黄粉保认为，北静王尽管身为王爷，为了体现自己的教养，在贾政面前使用了"小王""唐突"等词以示自谦，并称贾宝玉为"令郎""龙驹凤雏"，称贾政为"世翁"。而贾政也没有了往日贾府里的那种威风，用了"犬子""萌生辈"等词来自

---

7 张保红. 2010. 文学翻译. 北京：外语教学与研究出版社，132.
8 黄粉保. 2000. 论小说人物语言个性的翻译. 中国翻译，2：44-46.

贬。在翻译上述谦辞及敬语时，译者应力求在译文中使用能同样反映人物身份地位以及为人处世态度的词语，让译文读者也能同原文读者一样，感受到当事人的微妙心态。

杨宪益和戴乃迭的译文如下：

The clarity and fluency of Pao-yu's answers made the Prince turn to observe to Chia Cheng, "Your son is truly a dragon's colt or young phoenix. May I venture to predict that in time to come this young phoenix may even surpass the old one?"

"My worthless son does not deserve such high praise," rejoined Chia Cheng hurriedly with a courteous smile. "If thanks to the grace of Your Highness such proves the case, that will be our good fortune."

黄粉保认为杨宪益夫妇的译文较好，译文中的 May I venture to，My worthless son，the grace of your Highness 以及译者所添加的 courteous 等词，能够恰如其分地体现讲话人的自谦和对对方的敬重。但美中不足的是，用 a dragon's colt or young phoenix 直译"龙驹凤雏"，且没有加注，恐怕难以被英美读者所接受，因为在西方文化中 dragon 是"凶恶"的象征。

其次，很多人阅读小说可能出于消遣和娱乐。除小说情节是否跌宕起伏、扣人心弦外，其语言是否流畅、是否吸引人，能否吸引读者读下去也成了小说吸引读者的重要因素之一。因此，译文的可读性是小说翻译过程中需要重视的一大问题。在小说翻译过程中，译者需要考虑到译本的可读性，也就是说译者承担着使作品靠近读者的任务，使译文通顺可读。

如何增强译文的可读性？译者可以在翻译过程中使用一切可行的方法使自己的译文做到流畅自然。众所周知，莫言在 2012 年获得了诺贝尔文学奖，成为获此殊荣的第一位中国籍作家。美国著名翻译家葛浩文（Howard Goldblatt）是莫言获奖作品的英文译者。他在翻译小说中的一些特殊表达时，主要采用以下三种方法提高译文的可读性[9]（张艳，2013）：

第一，如果原文中有一些词是碍于母语习惯，或出于反复或无特定目的的特殊

---

[9] 张艳. 2013. 陌生的葛浩文与熟悉的葛浩文——葛浩文小说翻译艺术究指. 广东外语外贸大学学报，4：79-82.

手法，予以删除不译，以消除文化陌生化和不必要的异国情调。如姜戎《狼图腾》中的一个例子：

  杨克反驳说："可中国人绝大多数是农民，或者是农民出身，汉人具有比不锈钢还顽固不化的小农意识，他们要是到了草原，不把狼皮扒光了才怪了呢。"

"不锈钢"是具有中国特色、强化语言效果的类比说法，译者删除的目的主要是减少英美读者的理解障碍，避免不必要的误导，既无伤大雅，也不悖原意。

葛浩文的译文是："But the vast majority of Chinese are peasants," Yang encountered, "or were born to peasants. The Han have a peasant mentality that's impossible to break down, and if they were transported out here, I'd be surprised if they didn't skin every last wolf on the grassland."

第二，对具有特定目的的作者自创的特殊手法，葛浩文并不拘泥于原文语言结构，而是梳理语境关系，大胆组合、变形与再创造，寻找最合适的表达方式。如王祯和《玫瑰玫瑰我爱你》中的一个句子：

  "对，还有那些台北破婊，他妈的，还讲什么，你知莫？我讲出来，你准气瘦。这些破婊居然说不来花莲主要是怕碰上地震！""什么？！"董老师倒没气瘦，只惊讶得大起声音来。

原文"气瘦"是典型的夸张手法，独创说法只可意会，英语并无对应搭配。葛浩文没有牵强照搬原文意象，而是通过灵活的换喻手法，使用 blow one's cool"（俚语，意为"失态，慌乱，激动或气愤"）和 blow one's stack（俚语，意为"发脾气，大发雷霆"）两个意思相近，但程度略有差别的同义短语，不仅描述生动，而且忠实表达了原意。

葛浩文的译文是："Oh, and that's not all. What do you think those skuzzy goddamned Taipei whores said? You'll blow your stack at this. They said their biggest worry about coming to Hualian was earthquakes!" "What did you say?" Dong Siwen blurted out, blowing his cool, not his stack.

第三，提取原文中特殊表达之神韵，寓其意义于上下文语境中，在其他相关语言符号中建构熟悉的意义，寓"神似"于"形"。如毕飞宇《青衣》中的一个例子：

酒席上笑了，同时响起了掌声。老板拍了几下巴掌。这掌声是愉快的，鼓舞人心的，还是继往开来的、相见恨晚和同喜同乐的。大伙儿一起干了杯。

原文运用了词语重复的修辞手法，把貌似不搭调的三个形容词与"掌声"搭配，构成反常的语言效果，包含了独特的审美考虑。针对这种变异，葛浩文一方面增添"an implication"一词解释掌声背后涵盖的意义，帮助读者理解；另一方面则在形式上补充"that...and that...but that"并列结构再现原文重复，力求类似的艺术效果。

葛浩文的译文是：Everyone laughed and clapped, including the factory manager himself. The applause was joyful and rallying, an implication that there was more to come, and that it was a pity they hadn't met earlier, but that it was wonderful they were sharing a good time now. They raised their glasses in a toast.

就当今中国文学外译现状而言，葛浩文的翻译理念具有重要意义。我们在外译过程中往往多偏重忠实，不敢也舍不得舍弃一些形式上的元素，唯恐丢掉了中国的民族特色。但事实上，我们是否更应保留精神和思想的元素，力求最佳的译文效果？

翻译语篇 1

三体·周文王·长夜（节选）

汪淼拨通了丁仪的电话，对方接听后，他才想起现在已是凌晨一点多了。

"我是汪淼，真对不起，这么晚打扰。"

"没关系，我正失眠。"

"我……遇到一些事，想请你帮个忙。你知道国内有观测宇宙背景辐射的机构吗？"汪淼产生了一种倾诉的欲望，但旋即觉得幽灵倒计时之事目前还是不要让更多的人知道为好。

"宇宙背景辐射，你怎么对这个有雅兴？看来你真的遇到一些事了……你去看过杨冬的母亲吗？"

"啊——真对不起，我忘了。"

"没关系。现在科学界，很多人都像你说的那样遇到了一些事，心不在焉的，不过你最好还是去看看她，她年纪大了，又不愿雇保姆，要是有什么费力气的事麻烦你帮着干干……哦，宇宙背景辐射的事，你正好可以去找杨冬的母亲问问，她退休前是搞天体物理专业的，与国内的这类研究机构很熟。"

"好好，我今天下班就去。"

"那先谢谢了，我是真的无法再面对与杨冬有关的一切了。"

打完电话后，汪淼坐到电脑前，开始打印网页上显示的那张很简单的莫尔斯电码对照表。这时他已经冷静下来，将思绪从倒计时上移开，想着关于"科学边界"和申玉菲的事，想到她玩的网络游戏。关于申玉菲，他能肯定的唯一一件事就是她不是爱玩游戏的人，这个说话如电报般精简的女人给他唯一的印象就是冷，她的冷与其他的某些女性不同，不是一张面具，而是从里到外冷透了。

汪淼总是下意识地将她与早已消失的 DOS 操作系统联系在一起，一面空荡荡的黑屏幕，只有一个简单得不能再简单的"c：>"提示符在闪动，你输入什么它就输出什么。一个字都不会多。也不会有变化。现在他知道，"c：>"提示符后面其实是一个无底深渊。

她真会有兴致玩游戏，而且是戴着 V 装具玩儿？她没有孩子，那套 V 装具只能是自己买回去用的，这有些不可思议。

译前提示

本段材料节选自《三体》，是作家刘慈欣创作的科幻小说。《三体》三部曲（又名"地球往事"三部曲）是 2006 年至 2010 年连载、出版的硬科幻小说系列，由《三体》《黑暗森林》《死神永生》三部小说组成，被誉为迄今为止中国当代最杰出的科幻小说，是中国科幻文学的里程碑之作，将中国科幻推向了全世界。2014 年第一部小说的英文版在美国上市，反响热烈，并于 2015 年获得美国科幻奇幻协会"星云奖"提名。2015 年 8 月 23 日，《三体》获第 73 届雨果奖最佳长篇故事奖，这是亚洲人首次获得雨果奖。

由于是科幻小说，节选的篇章中涉及一些专业术语，如"宇宙背景辐射""天体物理"和"莫尔斯电码对照表"。"宇宙背景辐射"可译成 the cosmic microwave background，"天体物理"是 astrophysics，"莫尔斯电码对照表"是 Morse code chart。

另外，本段材料也涉及较多对话，翻译时应采用何种措辞和手法才能表现出对话者的心情？

 参考译文

Three Body: King Wen of Zhou and the Long Night (Excerpt)

Wang dialed Ding Yi's number. Only when Ding picked up did he realize that it was already one in the morning.

"This is Wang Miao. I'm sorry to be calling so late."

"No problem. I can't sleep anyway."

"I have…seen something, and I'd like your help. Do you know if there are any facilities in China that are observing the cosmic microwave background?" Wang had the urge to talk to someone about what was going on, but he thought it best to not let too many people know about the countdown that only he could see.

"The cosmic microwave background? What made you interested in that? I guess you really have run into some problems... Have you been to see Yang Dong's mother yet?"

"Ah—I'm sorry. I forgot."

"No worries. Right now, many scientists have…seen something, like you. Everyone's distracted. But I think it's still best if you go visit her. She's getting on in years, and she won't hire a caretaker. If there's some task around the home that she needs help with, please help her...Oh, right, the cosmic microwave background. You can ask Yang's mother. Before she retired, she was an astrophysicist. She's very familiar with such facilities in China."

"Good! I'll go after work today."

"Then I'll thank you in advance. I really can't face anything that reminds me of Yang Dong again."

After hanging up, Wang sat in front of his computer and printed out the simple Morse code chart. By now he was calm enough to turn his thoughts away from the countdown. He pondered the Frontiers of Science, Shen Yufei, and the computer game she had been playing. The only thing he knew for certain about Shen was that she wasn't the type to enjoy computer games. She spoke like a telegraph and gave him the impression that she was always extremely cold. It wasn't the kind of coldness that some people put on like a mask—hers suffused her all the way through.

Wang subconsciously thought of her as the long-obsolete DOS operating system: a blank, black screen, a bare "c:\>" prompt, a blinking cursor. Whatever you entered, it echoed back. Not one extra letter and not a single change. But now he knew that behind the "c:\>" was a bottomless abyss.

She's actually interested in a game? A game that requires a V-suit? She has no kids, which means she bought the V-suit for herself. The very idea is preposterous.

译文注释

参考译文来自刘宇昆（Ken Liu）。他翻译的《三体》第一部英文版已于2014年11月在美国出版，反响很大。《三体》的第一部和第三部《死神永生》均由他翻译；第二部《黑暗森林》由乔尔·马丁森（Joel Martinsen）翻译。

刘宇昆生于1976年，是美籍华裔科幻作家，他的职业是程序设计员与律师，业余从事科幻小说与诗歌的写作。在接受《新京报》采访时，他提到，科幻小说都会有一些专业术语，有时候只是一小段技术性的描写，但却需要做很多额外的功课。他看了大量的科学论文，也访问了物理学家，复习了一些数学公式；自己实在搞不明白的部分，他也会直接和作家本人交流。相信这样的体验对大家会有一些启示意义。

在翻译汪淼与丁仪的对话时，译者增加了一些语气词，如 oh 和 good，使译文更像是英文的对话。

1. 汪淼产生了一种倾诉的欲望，但旋即觉得幽灵倒计时之事目前还是不要让更多的人知道为好。Wang had the urge to talk to someone about what was going on, but he thought it best to not let too many people know about the countdown that only he could see.

   【注释】一般情况下，"有……的欲望"可以理解成"想要做……"，因此可以翻译成 want to do sth.；have the urge to do sth. 与之相比，显得更为正式。另外，译者进行了增译，译出了"倾诉"的宾语 what was going on。

   "幽灵倒计时"在译文中简单地翻译成 countdown，没有将"幽灵"一词翻译出来。Countdown 指"倒计时"，如新年的倒计时和火箭发射的倒计时都可以用这个词。

   但译文中 he thought it best to not let too many people know... 的表达有语法问题，一般倾向于将 not 放在 to 之前。

2. 现在科学界，很多人都像你说的那样遇到了一些事，心不在焉的，不过你最好还是去看看她，她年纪大了，又不愿雇保姆，要是有什么费力气的事麻烦你帮着干干……Right now, many scientists have... seen something, like you. Everyone's distracted. But I think it's still best if you go visit her. She's getting on in years, and she won't hire a caretaker. If there's some task around the home that she needs help with, please help her...

   【注释】原文是典型的汉语长句，表述的内容较多。对照英文的表达会发现，译者主要采用了断句法，将原句断成了好几个句子。

   原句"现在科学界，很多人都像你说的那样遇到了一些事，心不在焉的"一气呵成，但译成英文时，译者有意识地将它变成了 Right now, many scientists have...seen something, like you. 这一省略号表明了说话人的迟疑，她不确定应该如何表述这一事件。

3. 她退休前是搞天体物理专业的，与国内的这类研究机构很熟。Before she retired, she was an astrophysicist. She's very familiar with such facilities in China.

【注释】 汉语中动词的使用频率很高，英译时经常会把汉语的动词变成英语的名词，如文中的"搞天体物理专业"翻译成 an astrophysicist，没有把动词翻译出来。前文中也提到很多这样的例子，比如"他很会讲故事"可以译成 He is a good story teller.；而"他很会游泳"可以译成 He is good at swimming 或者 He is a good swimmer. 学生在汉译英或英译汉过程中需要有意识地进行转换。

4. 关于申玉菲，他能肯定的唯一一件事就是她不是爱玩游戏的人，这个说话如电报般精简的女人给他唯一的印象就是冷，她的冷与其他的某些女性不同，不是一张面具，而是从里到外冷透了。The only thing he knew for certain about Shen was that she wasn't the type to enjoy computer games. She spoke like a telegraph and gave him the impression that she was always extremely cold. It wasn't the kind of coldness that some people put on like a mask—hers suffused her all the way through.

【注释】 看到"他能肯定的唯一一件事就是……"这样的句型，应当想起 the only thing he knows for certain is that... 这一结构，然后根据具体的语境变换时态。

"而是从里到外冷透了"是翻译这句话的难点所在，翻译时很可能会存在硬译的问题。Hers suffused her all the way through 中 hers 代替的是 her coldness，suffuse 有"充满""弥漫于"的意思。

5. ……一面空荡荡的黑屏幕，只有一个简单得不能再简单的"c：>"提示符在闪动，你输入什么它就输出什么。...a blank, black screen, a bare "c:\>" prompt, a blinking cursor. Whatever you entered, it echoed back.

【注释】 此处的 prompt 是名词，表示"提示符"。Cursor 有"（计算机荧光屏上的）游标、光标"之意，对计算机英语不是很熟悉的学生，在不借助词典的情况下可能无法翻译这些单词。

翻译语篇 2

红 楼 梦（节选）

这里宝玉悲恸了一回，忽然抬头不见了黛玉，便知黛玉看见他躲开了，自己也觉无味，抖抖土起来，下山寻归旧路，往怡红院来。可巧看见林黛玉在前头走，连忙赶上去，说道："你且站住。我知你不理我，我只说一句话，从今后撂开手。"林黛玉回头看见是宝玉，待要不理他，听他说"只说一句话，从此撂开手"，这话里有文章，少不得站住说道："有一句话，请说来。"宝玉笑道："两句话，说了你听不听？"黛玉听说，回头就走。宝玉在身后面叹道:"既有今日,何必当初!"林黛玉听见这话,由不得站住,回头道:"当初怎么样?今日怎么样?"宝玉叹道:"当初姑娘来了,那不是我陪着顽笑?凭我心爱的,姑娘要,就拿去;我爱吃的,听见姑娘也爱吃,连忙干干净净收着等姑娘吃。一桌子吃饭,一床上睡觉。丫头们想不到的,我怕姑娘生气,我替丫头们想到了。我心里想着:姊妹们从小儿长大,亲也罢,热也罢,和气到了儿,才见得比人好。如今谁承望姑娘人大心大,不把我放在眼睛里,倒把外四路的什么宝姐姐凤姐姐的放在心坎儿上,倒把我三日不理四日不见的。我又没个亲兄弟亲姊妹。——虽然有两个,你难道不知道是和我隔母的?我也和你似的独出,只怕同我的心一样。谁知我是白操了这个心,弄的有冤无处诉!"说着不觉滴下眼泪来。

译前提示

本段材料节选自《红楼梦》的"第二十八回 蒋玉菡情赠茜香罗 薛宝钗羞笼红麝串"宝玉诉衷肠的情节。

1. 本段材料中也涉及较多的对话翻译,应该如何措辞才能体现出黛玉和宝玉当时的心情?
2. "外四路的"指血缘关系疏远的亲戚。

参考译文 1

An Excerpt from Chapter 28

Yuhan gives a new friend a scarlet perfumed sash

Baochai bashfully shows her red bracelet scented with musk

When Baoyu recovered sufficiently to look up she had gone, obviously to avoid him. Getting up rather sheepishly, he dusted off his clothes and walked down the hill to make his way back again to Happy Red Court. Catching sight of Daiyu ahead, he overtook her.

"Do stop," he begged. "I know you won't look at me. But let me just say one word. After that we can part company for good."

Daiyu glanced round and would have ignored him, but was curious to hear this "one word," thinking there must be something in it. She came to a halt.

"Out with it."

Baoyu smiled.

"Would you listen if I said two words?" he asked.

At once she walked away.

Baoyu, close behind her, sighed.

"Why are things so different now from in the past?"

Against her will she stopped once more and turned her head.

"What do you mean by 'now' and the 'past'?"

Baoyu heaved another sigh.

"Wasn't I your playmate when you first came?" he demanded. "Anything that pleased me was yours, cousin, for the asking. If I knew you fancied a favorite dish of mine, I put it away in a clean place till you came. We ate at the same table and slept on the same bed. I took care that the maids did nothing to upset you; for I thought cousins growing up together as such good friends should be kinder to each other than anyone else. I never expected you to grow so proud that now you have no use for me while you're so fond of outsiders like Baochai and Xifeng. You ignore me or cut me for three or four days at a time. I've no brothers or sisters of my own—only two by a different mother, as well you know. So I'm an only child like you, and I thought that would make for an affinity between us. But apparently it was no use my hoping for that. There's nobody I can tell how unhappy I am." With that, he broke down again.

参考译文 2

An Excerpt from Chapter 28

A crimson cummerbund becomes a pledge of friendship

and a chaplet of medicine-beads becomes a source of embarrassment

By the time Baoyu's weeping was over, Daiyu was no longer there. He realized that she must have seen him and have gone away in order to avoid him. Feeling suddenly rather foolish, he rose to his feet and brush the earth from his clothes. Then he descended from the rockery and began to retrace his steps in the direction of Green Delights. Quite by coincidence Daiyu was walking along the same path a little way ahead.

"Stop a minute!" he cried, hurrying forward to catch up with her. "I know you are not taking any notice of me, but I only want to ask you one simple question, and then you need never have anything more to do with me."

Daiyu had turned back to see who it was. When she saw that it was Baoyu still, she was going to ignore him again; but hearing him say that he only wanted to ask her one question, she told him that he might do so.

Baoyu could not resist teasing her a little.

"How about two questions? Would you wait for two?"

Daiyu set her face forwards and began walking on again.

Baoyu sighed.

"If it has to be like this now," he said, as if to himself, "it's a pity it was ever like it was in the beginning."

Daiyu's curiosity got the better of her. She stopped walking and turned once more towards him.

"Like what in the beginning?" she asked. "And like what now?"

"Oh, the beginning!" said Baoyu. "In the beginning, when you first came here, I was your faithful companion in all your games. Anything I had, even the thing most dear to me, was yours for the asking. If there was something to eat that I specially liked, I had only to hear that you were fond of it too and I would religiously hoard it away to share with you when you got back, not daring even to touch it until you came. We ate at the same table. We slept in the same bed. I used to think that because we were so close then, there would be something special about our relationship when we grew up—that even if we weren't particularly affectionate, we should at least have more understanding and forbearance for each other than the rest. But how wrong I was! Now that you have grown up, you seem only to have grown more touchy. You don't seem to care about me any more at all. You spend all your time brooding about outsiders like Feng and Chai. I haven't got any real brothers and sisters left here now. There are Huan and Tan, of course; but as you know, they're only my half-brother and half-sister: they aren't my mother's children. I'm on my own, like you. I should have thought we had so much in common—But what's the use? I try and try, but it gets me nowhere; and nobody knows or cares."

At this point—in spite of himself—he burst into tears.

译文注释

两个参考译文均选自冯庆华编著的《实用翻译教程（英汉互译）》一书[10]。参考译文1是杨宪益、戴乃迭译，参考译文2是大卫·霍克斯译。《红楼梦》是中国古典小说的巅峰之作，它能够走向世界在很大程度上依赖于英译本的流传和推广。《红楼梦》最著名、影响最深远的两个英文全译本分别是大卫·霍克斯的译本 *The Story of the Stone* 和中国翻译家杨宪益及夫人戴乃迭的合译本 *A Dream of Red Mansions*。

英国汉学家大卫·霍克斯的重大成就之一就是和自己的女婿翻译了一百二十回的《红楼梦》全译本。这是英语世界第一个《红楼梦》全译本，也是西方汉学史和翻译界的一件大事，为中国文学走向世界做出了重大贡献。

中国著名翻译家、外国文学研究专家、诗人杨宪益与夫人戴乃迭合译了《红楼梦》全本及《儒林外史》全本等多部中国历史名著，在国外皆获得好评，产生了广泛影响。

翻译这一部分时，杨宪益夫妇用了三百多个单词，霍克斯则用了五百多个单词，字数差别较大。杨宪益和戴乃迭的翻译目的是向外国读者介绍中国的文化，让他们能更深入了解中国文化的博大精深。因此，他们的译本更忠实于原作，在翻译时采取了异化的策略和直译的方法，将原

10　冯庆华.1997.实用翻译教程（英汉互译）.上海：上海外语教育出版社，316-319.

文原汁原味地翻译了出来。霍克斯的翻译目的在于与西方读者分享书中的乐趣，满足外国读者的需求，因此他的译本遣词造句更为灵活，不拘泥于原文，更强调译文应符合英文的行文规范和文化习惯，归化的翻译策略和意译的运用较为明显。

1. 蒋玉菡情赠茜香罗 薛宝钗羞笼红麝串

   【注释】杨宪益夫妇的译文是 Yuhan gives a new friend a scarlet perfumed sash/Baochai bashfully shows her red bracelet scented with musk；而霍克斯的译文是 A crimson cummerbund（腰带）becomes a pledge of friendship and a chaplet（花冠）of medicine-beads becomes a source of embarrassment。

   章节名比较难译，需要用尽可能少的字概括原文的含义，又要体现一定的文字之美，是很有挑战性的翻译任务。就表达的内容而言，杨宪益夫妇的译本更加忠实于原文。就文字的地道性而言，两者恐怕不分伯仲。当然，杨宪益夫妇的译文用字更少。

2. 怡红院

   【注释】杨宪益夫妇的译文是 Happy Red Court，而霍克斯的译文是 Green Delights。

   从上面两个例子可以看出，杨宪益夫妇的译文更贴近原文，尽量保留原文的内容，使英文读者有机会了解中国的文化和情调，但这种做法有可能会给英文读者的阅读带来障碍。而霍克斯的译文则更加自由，他或增或减，更多考虑英文读者的感受，以地道的英文来诠释《红楼梦》，但对原作可能不够忠实。

翻译加油站

翻译技巧（六）：语序的调整

汉语和英语中主要成分的语序基本相同，如主语在谓语动词前，宾语在谓语动词之后。但汉语中定语和状语的位置与英语存在着差异。

一、定语的位置

汉语的定语一般由形容词充当，无论单用还是几个连用，一般都放在所修饰的名词之前。而英语中，形容词、定语从句、介词短语、不定式等都可以充当定语，且位置非常灵活。

例 1　一所以搞科研为主的医院

A *research-oriented* hospital（复合形容词作定语，前置于修饰的名词前）

例 2　一个正在门口等的人

A man *who is waiting at the gate*（定语从句，位于修饰的名词后）

例 3　陆地上的鸟

The bird *on the land*（介词短语作定语，位于修饰的名词后）

例 4　他们收下了赠送的礼物。

They accepted the present *offered*.（过去分词作定语，位于修饰的名词后）

例 5　改变物体运动的力与物体本身的质量成正比。

The force *to change the motion of a body* is proportional to the mass *of the body*.（动词不定式和介词短语作定语，位于修饰的名词后）

注意，将汉语译成英语时，修饰由 some, any, every, no 等构成的词，定语应后置。

例 6　他想找一个可靠的人帮助工作。

He wanted to get *someone reliable* to help in his work.

例 7　今天的报纸上有什么重要消息吗？

Is there *anything important* in today's newspaper?

例 8　医生为了救病人，尽到了一切必要的努力。

The doctor did *everything necessary* to save the patient.

Reliable, important 和 necessary 在修饰 someone, anything 或 everything 时，应放在这些词之后。在汉英翻译时，须遵守英语的语法。另外，作表语的形容词作定语时通常后置。

例 9　他是当今最伟大的诗人。

He is the greatest poet *alive*.

例 10　仅这个委员会就有三个女委员。

On this committee *alone* there are three women.

Alive 和 alone 通常都作表语，作定语时应放在修饰的名词之后。而且，以 -ible, -able 结尾的形容词作被 every, the only 或最高级修饰的名词的定语时，常放在名词之后。

例 11　我们一定要用一切可能的办法来帮助他们。

We must help them in every way *possible*.（possible 与 every 一起修饰 way，应后置）

例 12　这是这儿能找到的唯一参考书。

This is the only reference book *available* here.（available 与 the only 一起修饰 book，应后置）

例 13　这是能想得出的最好解决办法。

This is the best solution *imaginable*.（imaginable 与最高级 the best 一起修饰 solution，应后置）

有一些固定的表达也需注意。

例 14　军事法庭

Court Martial

例 15　（联合国）秘书长

Secretary General (of the UN)

例 16　（世界卫生组织）总干事

Director General (of the WHO)

例 17　当选（而尚未就职的）总统

the president elect

在日常的英语学习中，应积累一些特定的固定表达，汉译英表达过程中应遵守这些特例。学习中可以备个笔记本，碰到不熟悉的词时除查词典的释义外，也可将其用法和例句摘抄下来。这样，学生的英语词汇会逐渐丰富起来，并在翻译中灵活运用。

二、状语的位置

英汉两种语言的状语位置存在着相同之处，但也有较大的差异，翻译时要按照英语的行文习惯处理译文。

例 18　他开车非常小心。

He drives *extremely carefully*.

例 19　世界的经济正在飞速发展。

The world economy is developing *rapidly*.

例 20　我是在哈尔滨工作时认识她的。

I made her acquaintance *when I was working in Harbin*.

英语和汉语的状语位置有同有异，翻译时具体问题具体处理，最重要的原则是使译文表达符合英语的语言习惯。

汉语中时间状语一般在地点状语前。译成英语时，地点状语在前，时间状语在后。

例 21　我们得早点到达那里。

We have to be *there early*.

例 22　这部电影是我去年在武汉时看的。

I saw this film *in Wuhan last year*.

例 23　会议将于明天下午在教室召开。

This meeting will be held *in the classroom tomorrow afternoon*.

汉语与英语中地点状语和时间状语出现的顺序不同，汉译英时应遵守英语的语法规则。

如果汉语的方式状语、地点状语和时间状语同时出现，译成英语时，其顺序是方式状语＋地点状语＋时间状语。

例 24　她每天早上在室外高声朗读。

She reads *aloud in the open every morning*.

例 25　王教授此刻正在实验室和他的两个新助手一道工作着。

Professor Wang is working *with his two new assistants in the lab at the moment*.

英语的状语顺序是：方式状语在最前面，地点状语随后，时间状语在最后。只要知道了这一规则，英译时就不会有大问题了。

课后练习

试将下列语篇翻译成英文：

1. 旱是这里的特点。天底下的事就是这般怪：天有阴有晴，月有盈有亏，偏不给你圆圆圆的万事圆满；两岔镇方圆的人守着州河万斛的水，多少年里田地总是旱。夏天里，眼瞧着巫岭云没其顶，太阳仍是个火刺猬，蛰得天红地赤，人看一眼眼也蛰疼；十多里外的别的地方都下得汪汪稀汤了，这里就是瞪白眼，"白雨隔犁沟"，就把两岔镇隔得绝情。

2. 孔乙己是站着喝酒而穿长衫的唯一的人。他身材很高大；青白脸色，皱纹间时常夹些伤痕；一部乱蓬蓬的花白的胡子。穿的虽然是长衫，可是又脏又破，似乎十多年没有补，也没有洗。他对人说话，总是满口之乎者也，教人半懂不懂的。因为他姓孔，别人便从描红纸上的"上大人孔乙己"这半懂不懂的话里，替他取下一个绰号，叫做孔乙己。孔乙己一到店，所有喝酒的人便都看着他笑，有的叫道，"孔乙己，你脸上又添上新伤疤了！"他不回答，对柜里说，"温两碗酒，要一碟茴香豆。"便排出九文大钱。他们又故意的高声嚷道，"你一定又偷了人家的东西了！"孔乙己睁大眼睛说，"你怎么这样凭空污人清白……""什么清白？我前天亲眼见你偷了何家的书，吊着打。"孔乙己便涨红了脸，额上的青筋条条绽出，争辩道，"窃书不能算偷……窃书！……读书人的事，能算偷么？"接连便是难懂的话，什么"君子固穷"，什么"者乎"之类，引得众人都哄笑起来：店内外充满了快活的空气。

第十章
散文翻译

什么是散文？根据《文学翻译读本》[1]（辛红娟，2012），"散文"之名起源于南宋罗大经《鹤林玉露》，用来指称一切句法不整齐的文章。我国古代曾将不押韵、不重对偶的散体文章均称为散文，包括传史书在内，与韵文、骈文对举；又将散文与诗歌对举，泛指不讲究韵律的小说及其他抒情记事之作。随着文学概念的演变和文学体裁的发展，散文的概念也时有变化，在某些历史时期又将小说与其他抒情、记事的文学作品统称为散文，以区别于讲求韵律的诗歌。现代散文是指除小说、诗歌、戏剧等文学体裁之外的其他文学作品。

张培基（1999）在《英译中国现代散文选：汉英对照》[2]中也提到："广义地说，凡是不属于韵文的文章都可称为散文。世界各国人对此有一致的看法。西方人甚至把小说也包括在散文内；我国有些现代叙事性的文章名为散文，但称之为小说也无不可，不便硬加归类。不过，严格说来，我们说的散文应相当于西方的 essay，与诗歌、小说、戏剧并起并坐，文字一般都比较短小精练，如随笔、小品文、杂感、游记、日记、书信、回忆录、通讯报道，等等。

"散文不受韵律、情节、分场分幕的约束，是一种灵活随便、轻松自如的文体。散文作者可无拘无束地直抒胸臆，独抒性灵，因而文如其人（The essay is whatever the author is）。英语中 prose（散文）这个词来源于拉丁文 Proversa oratio，其意思是'坦率的讲话'或'直话直说'（straight forward discourse），也正反映了上述特点。总之，散文最真实，最诚笃，不雕饰，不做作，因而是一种最令人感到亲切的文体。"

一般而言，广义的散文区别于韵文、骈文，它包含所有不押韵、不排偶的散体文章，可概称"大散文"。狭义的散文指除小说、诗歌、戏剧等文学体裁之外的其他文学作品，我们也可称其为"小散文"。按内容和形式的不同特点，散文又可分为杂文、小品、随笔，等等。

---

[1] 辛红娟. 2012. 文学翻译读本. 南京：南京大学出版社，220.
[2] 张培基. 1999. 英译中国现代散文选：汉英对照. 上海：上海外语教育出版社.

无论散文应当如何分类，各类散文都拥有共同的特性。散文重在表情达意，阐明作者的态度和观点，强调词语的形象色彩和感情色彩，特别讲求音韵、节奏、意境的完美，具有较强的可读性和感染力。它的最大特征就是"形散而神不散"。所谓"形散"，主要是指散文的取材广泛，可以不受时间和空间的限制。天上人间，万事万物，只要能引起人们的兴趣，激发人们的感情，都可以成为散文的素材。同时，散文的表现手法不拘一格：可以叙述某一事件的发展，也可以描写某个人物的形象；可以就某一事件发表议论，也可以托物抒情，总之，作者可以根据内容的需要自由调整、随意变化，且文无定式，可长可短，可以意境高远，可以哲理深刻，可以清新脱俗，可以诙谐可爱。而"神不散"主要是指散文的中心思想明确，感情基调贯穿始终。散文所要表达的主题必须明确而集中，无论散文的内容多么宽泛，表现手法多么灵活多变，都需要为更好地表达主题服务。

其次，散文的意境深邃，注重表现作者的生活感受，抒情性强，情感真挚。作者可以借助各种想象与联想，由此及彼，由浅入深，由实而虚，融情于景、寄情于事、寓情于物、托物言志，表达作者的真情实感，实现物我的统一，展现出更深远的思想主题，使读者领会更深的道理。

另外，散文的语言优美凝练，富于文采。所谓优美，就是指散文的语言清新明丽，生动活泼，富于音乐感，行文如涓涓流水，叮咚有声，如娓娓而谈，情真意切。所谓凝练，是说散文的语言简洁质朴，自然流畅，寥寥数语就可以描绘出生动的形象，勾勒出动人的场景，显示出深远的意境。散文力求写景如在眼前，写情沁人心脾。

中国当代白话散文语言的突出特点就是用词考究，句式松散，短句和流水句多，大多运笔成风，不拘一格，行文潇洒自成一体，充分体现了汉语意合的特点。而英语散文大多用词华丽，语言流畅，充满美感，且行文紧凑严谨。中英散文所要传达的神韵都是一致的，而语言习惯的不同却是阻碍传达神韵的最大障碍。能否有效传达这一神韵，直接关系到译文的质量高低。

散文翻译的要点

散文体裁广泛，手法灵活多变，不拘一格。散文翻译过程中，应注意以下内容：

第十章 散文翻译

第一，再现原文的"韵"。

所谓再现原文的"韵"，是指再现原文的声韵和意境等。古人要求散文像花纹一样美丽，线条清晰，色彩斑斓，富有节奏感，读起来朗朗上口；语言简洁，表达力强，生动活泼，富有感染力；文章结构严谨，层次分明，逻辑性强。散文的美可以体现在语音层面和句子层面。语音层面可以体现出音响效果和节奏，虽然节奏和韵律主要体现在诗歌中，但是在散文中有时候也表现得十分突出。句子层面，散文可以通过对照、排比、回环、重复等手段创造文章的节奏美和音韵美。"作品的审美价值往往是通过语言的声响和节奏表现出来的，这在所有的语言中普遍存在。因此，要在译文中再现原文的声响和节奏之妙。一篇好的译文应该读起来朗朗上口，听上去声声入耳"[3]（辛红娟，2012）。

"意境源自中国古典美学，是指通过形象化的、情景交融的艺术描写，把读者引入到一个想象的空间的艺术境界。它讲究味外之味，韵外之致，言有尽而意无穷"[4]（舒舟，何大顺，2008）。散文的精髓就在于其达意传情，译者应当认真品味和揣摩原文所要表述的艺术境界，以译文的形式再现这一意象，在意义、形式、趣味、格调等方面力求与原文等质等量。要做到这一点，译者需要有较多的准备工作。首先，对散文进行充分、细致的解读，其解读不仅包括单个字词的意义、语音、拼写等微妙的细节，也涉及词语的内涵和外延意义、比喻意义和象征意义，以及对句子、语篇的主题意义等的理解。其次，由于散文选材自由，形式开放，对散文的解读还必须考虑到词句以外的意义，如文学背景、社会背景、典故常识、历史地理等。译者要从微观到宏观，再从宏观到微观，反复体会和品味散文词句多方面的意义，从而较好地再现原文的"韵"。

第二，再现原文的"形"。

散文的选材自由宽泛，形式上不拘一格。翻译散文如果完全放弃原作的形式，势必会失去原作之美。然而，由于中英语言文化的差异，原作的形式因素不可能完全照搬进译文。因此，如何在译文中恰如其分地保存原作之形也是散文翻译需要重

---

3 辛红娟.2012.文学翻译读本.南京：南京大学出版社，220-221.
4 舒舟，何大顺.2008.散文意境的传译——基于格式塔意象模型研究.西南农业大学学报（社会科学版），5：106.

视的一大问题。翻译散文时，必须吃透原文总体的风格特征，并在此基础上细心斟酌与推敲用词，努力使译文与原文的整体风格保持一致。

原文的风格不仅是作家和艺术家个人叙事或抒情的一种自由表现形式，也是学者和思想家表达个人思想感情的一种自由方式。对散文风格的准确把握是成功翻译的前提。要翻译出原文的风格，就需要把握各位作家的各自特点，甚至是一位作家不同时期、不同散文的不同特点。抓住其个性化的特点，才能准确传达原文的意义。

尽管散文被认为是与小说、诗歌、戏剧并列的文学体裁，在文学系统中一直占据着重要地位，但散文的汉译和英译都远不如小说和诗歌。"在中文散文英译领域，论译作数量之最，影响之大，当数张培基了"[5]（胡显耀，李力，2009）。他1945年毕业于上海圣约翰大学英文系，曾担任英文《上海自由西报》记者、英文《中国评论周报》特约撰稿者兼英文《中国年鉴》（1944—1945年）副总编、日本东京远东国际军事法庭国际检察局英语翻译。后赴美国印地安纳大学研究英国文学，1949年回国后任北京外文出版社编译等职。张培基的译作涉及现当代几十位中国散文家，包括鲁迅、胡适、朱自清、冰心、巴金、郭沫若、茅盾、老舍、梁实秋、艾青、丁玲、余光中等。另外，他一直为《中国翻译》杂志的《翻译自学之友·汉译英练习》专栏撰稿。他的译文被认为自然流畅并且极具文采，充分体现了译者的翻译理念，令许多读者和翻译爱好者受益匪浅。这些译文后来被收进《英译中国现代散文选：汉英对照》，由上海外语教育出版社出版，不但为中国学者进一步研究翻译理论与技巧提供了丰富的实例文章，而且为外国学者研究中国"五四"以来知识分子的思想发展提供了大量的素材。

另外，在散文翻译领域较有建树的还有刘士聪等人。刘士聪为《中国翻译》和《英语世界》翻译一些小散文，其散文翻译的主要出版物有《英汉·汉英美文翻译与鉴赏》一书。该书汇集了富有"韵味"的汉、英散文34篇，并附有对原文或译文的鉴赏或评价文字，受到了学界的广泛关注。

5　胡显耀，李力. 2009. 高级文学翻译. 北京：外语教学与研究出版社，181.

📝 翻译语篇 1

珍 珠 鸟（节选）

冯骥才

真好！朋友送我一对珍珠鸟。放在一个简易的竹条编成的笼子里，笼内还有一卷干草，那是小鸟舒适又温暖的巢。

有人说，这是一种怕人的鸟。

我把它挂在窗前。那儿还有一盆异常茂盛的法国吊兰。我便用吊兰长长的、串生着小绿叶的垂蔓蒙盖在鸟笼上，它们就像躲进深幽的丛林一样安全；从中传出的笛儿般又细又亮的叫声，也就格外轻松自在了。

阳光从窗外射入，透过这里，吊兰那些无数指甲状的小叶，一半成了黑影，一半被照透，如同碧玉；斑斑驳驳，生意葱茏。小鸟的影子就在这中间隐约闪动，看不完整，有时连笼子也看不出，却见它们可爱的鲜红小嘴儿从绿叶中伸出来。

我很少扒开叶蔓瞧它们，它们便渐渐敢伸出小脑袋瞅瞅我。我们就这样一点点熟悉了。

三个月后，那一团愈发繁茂的绿蔓里边，发出一种尖细又娇嫩的鸣叫。我猜到，是它们，有了雏儿。我呢？决不掀开叶片往里看，连添食加水时也不睁大好奇的眼去惊动它们。过不多久，忽然有一个小脑袋从叶间探出来。更小哟，雏儿！正是这个小家伙！

📖 **译前提示**

本段材料节选自冯骥才《珍珠鸟》的开篇。冯骥才是当代著名作家、文学家、艺术家，创作了大量优秀散文、小说和绘画作品。他的多篇文章入选中小学和大学课本，《珍珠鸟》就是其中之一。《珍珠鸟》生动地描述了珍珠鸟在"我"的细心照料、诚心呵护下由害怕人到亲近人的变化过程。

1. "珍珠鸟"可直译成 Pearl bird。

2. "吊兰"是 bracketplant。

进行语篇翻译时，应注意整个语篇的语体色彩。就这一语篇而言，应选用正式英语还是非正式英语？一般在翻译个人叙事时，应选用非正式英语来表达。另外，这一语篇轻柔婉约，笔触轻盈活脱，翻译时应考虑如何用相应的词汇和结构将这一风格体现出来。

参考译文

A Pair of Pearl Birds (Excerpt)

What a nice pair of Pearl birds my friend gave me! I kept them in a simple cage woven with bamboo strips. Inside the cage I put some dry grass to serve as their nest and keep them warm and comfortable.

It is said that the Pearl birds are easily scared in the presence of man.

I hung the cage over the window next to a pot of exuberant French bracketplant. I put the long trailing vines of the plant with their small green leaves on top of the cage, making the birds feel safe and sound as they did deep in the woods. Their singing, as clear and pleasant as the flute, was an indication that they were very much relaxed and at ease.

When the sunlight streamed through the window, half of the small nail-like leaves of the plant were left in the shadow and the other half illuminated, looking like emeralds, casting greenish specks of light on my desk. The shadows of the birds flashed back and forth among the leaves. You could hardly see their bodies, not even the cage sometimes, but occasionally you could see them putting out their lovely red beaks through the leaves.

As I seldom tried to part the leaves to look at them, gradually they plucked up their courage to put out their small heads to look at me. By and by they became accustomed to my presence.

Three months later some thinner and weaker cries were heard through the more exuberant leaves. I knew what had happened. They must have had a baby bird. However, I was not so curious as to look inside the cage and disturb them, not even when I added food and water for them. A few days later I saw a tiny head thrust out. Oh, it was the tiny baby bird, the one that had been uttering the thin and weak cries.

> **译文注释**

参考译文选自张梦井、杜耀文的《中国名家散文精译》[6]。该书英译了王蒙、刘心武、朱自清、沈从文、茅盾、梁实秋等名家的部分作品。

1. 真好！朋友送我一对珍珠鸟。放在一个简易的竹条编成的笼子里……
   What a nice pair of Pearl birds my friend gave me! I kept them in a simple cage woven with bamboo strips.

   【注释】作者一开篇就用欣喜的语气道出了自己的心声，并以此奠定了全文的轻松基调。因此，翻译该句时首先就应想到要用感叹句。

   如果按照原文的形式，可以翻译成 How nice! My friend gave me a pair of Pearl birds. 而译者把两句话合并，改成了 What a nice pair of Pearl birds my friend gave me! 信息的重点就落在了 a nice pair of Pearl birds 上，与文章的标题更加契合。

   另外，原文中并未指明是谁把鸟儿放在笼子里，译文的表达 I kept them in a simple cage woven with bamboo strips，把施动者直接说成了"我"。这与我们的设想可能有点相悖。一般情况下，朋友送我珍珠鸟时总会有个东西装着，是不是就是这个竹条编成的笼子呢？

2. 我便用吊兰长长的、串生着小绿叶的垂蔓蒙盖在鸟笼上，它们就像躲进深幽的丛林一样安全；从中传出的笛儿般又细又亮的叫声，也就格外轻松自在了。I put the long trailing vines of the plant with their small green leaves on top of the cage, making the birds feel safe and sound as they did deep in the woods. Their singing, as clear and pleasant as the flute, was an indication that they were very much relaxed and at ease.

   【注释】译者将"串生着小绿叶的"这一定语译成了伴随状语 with their small green leaves，是汉译英时常用的翻译手法。

   从句"它们就像躲进深幽的丛林一样安全"用 making 这一现在分词引导，充分发挥了英语长句结构的优点。

   与"串生着小绿叶的"不同的是，定语"笛儿般又细又亮的"译成了插入

---

[6] 张梦井，杜耀文. 1990. 中国名家散文精译. 青岛：青岛出版社，95-96.

语 as clear and pleasant as the flute。因此，译者可以按照语境选择不同的方法翻译相同的句子成分。

3. 阳光从窗外射入，透过这里，吊兰那些无数指甲状的小叶，一半成了黑影，一半被照透，如同碧玉；斑斑驳驳，生意葱茏。When the sunlight streamed through the window, half of the small nail-like leaves of the plant were left in the shadow and the other half illuminated, looking like emeralds, casting greenish specks of light on my desk.

   【注释】译者将"一半被照透，如同碧玉；斑斑驳驳，生意葱茏"翻译成 the other half illuminated, looking like emeralds, casting greenish specks of light on my desk。其中，the other half illuminated 省略了动词 were，emerald 有"翡翠""绿宝石"的意思。

   "斑斑驳驳，生意葱茏"没有直译出来，而是意译成 casting greenish specks of light on my desk。

4. 我呢？决不掀开叶片往里看，连添食加水时也不睁大好奇的眼去惊动它们。However, I was not so curious as to look inside the cage and disturb them, not even when I added food and water for them.

   【注释】译者用 however 一词将该句与上一句连接起来，体现了语篇的衔接意识。另外，译者用 not so...as to 这一结构，很好地处理了原句的内容，译文表达自然而流畅。

翻译语篇 2

落 花 生

我们屋后有半亩隙地。母亲说："让它荒芜着怪可惜，既然你们那么爱吃花生，就辟来做花生园罢。"我们几姊弟和几个小丫头都很喜欢——买种的买种，动土的动土，灌园的灌园；过了不几个月，居然收获了！

妈妈说："今晚我们可以做一个收获节，也请你们爹爹来尝尝我们底新花生，如何？"我们都答应了。母亲把花生做成好几样的食品，还吩咐这节期要在园里底茅亭举行。

那晚上底天色不大好，可是爹爹也到来，实在很难得！爹爹说："你们爱吃花生么？"

第十章 散文翻译

我们都争着答应："爱！"

"谁能把花生底好处说出来？"

姊姊说："花生底气味很美。"

哥哥说："花生可以制油。"

我说："无论何等人都可以用贱价买它来吃；都喜欢吃它。这就是它的好处。"

爹爹说："花生底用处固然很多；但有一样是很可贵的。这小小的豆，不像那好看的苹果、桃子、石榴，把它们底果实悬在枝上，鲜红嫩绿的颜色，令人一望而发生羡慕的心。它只把果子埋在地底，等到成熟，才容人把它挖出来。你们偶然看见一棵花生瑟缩地长在地上，不能立刻辨出它有没有果实，非得等到你接触它才能知道。"

我们都说："是的。"母亲也点点头。爹爹接下去说："所以你们要像花生，因为它是有用的，不是伟大、好看的东西。"我说："那么，人要做有用的人，不要做伟大、体面的人了。"爹爹说："这是我对于你们的希望。"

我们谈到夜阑才散，所有花生食品虽然没有了，然而父亲底话现在还印在我心版上。

译前提示

许地山，名赞堃，字地山，笔名落华生（古时"华"同"花"，所以也叫落花生），是中国现代著名小说家、散文家、"五四"时期新文学运动先驱者之一。

《落花生》是许地山的名作。这篇叙事散文围绕"种花生—收花生—吃花生—议花生"，描述了一家人收获花生的情景，并通过谈论花生的好处，借物喻人，揭示了花生不图虚名、默默奉献的品格，表达了作者不为名利，只求有益于社会的人生理想和价值观。

1. 该文带有"五四"时期的一些语言特征，如"姊姊""爹爹""底"等，其中"底"同"的"。
2. "石榴"是 pomegranate。

参考译文 1

The Peanut

Behind our house there was a patch of land. "It would be a pity to let it go wild," said Mother. "I suggest that since you are all so fond of peanuts you should grow some there."

We children and the little maidservants were all delighted. Some of us bought seeds, some dug up the plot and others watered it. In just a few months we had a harvest.

Mother said, "let's have a harvest festival tonight and invite your father to taste our fresh peanuts."

We all agreed. Mother made a variety of dishes using our peanuts and instructed that the festival should be held in the thatched pavilion in the garden.

The weather was not very good that evening, but even Father put in an appearance, which was a rare event.

"Do you all like peanuts?" asked Father.

"Yes!" We all clamoured to reply.

"Who can tell me what's good about peanuts?"

"They taste good," said older sister.

"They can be made into oil," said older brother.

"Everybody can afford to buy them, whoever they might be, and everyone likes them. That's what's good about peanuts." said I.

Father said, "In fact the peanut has many uses, but the most valuable thing about this little nut is this: it's not like the apple, peach or pomegranate, flaunting their bright, beautiful fruits on their branches for all to see and admire. The peanut lies buried in the soil, waiting until it is ripe before letting people dig it up. If ever you come across a shy peanut plant you cannot immediately tell whether or not it has any nuts. You have to find them to be certain."

We all agreed with this and Mother nodded her head too. Father continued, "So you should all try to be like the peanut, because it is neither grand nor beautiful, but useful."

"Does that mean that people should try to be useful rather than famous or great?" I asked.

"That is what I hope of you all," Father replied.

We talked late into the night before dispersing. Although we ate all the peanuts that evening, Father's words still remain embedded in my heart.

参考译文 2

Peanuts

Behind our house there lay half a *mou* of vacant land. Mother said, "It's a pity to let it lie waste. Since you all like to eat peanuts so very much, why not have them planted here." That exhilarated us children and our servant girls as well, and soon we started buying seeds, ploughing the land and watering the plants. We gathered in a good harvest just after a couple of months!

Mother said, "How about giving a party this evening to celebrate the harvest and inviting your Daddy to have a taste of our newly-harvested peanuts?" We all agreed. Mother made quite a few varieties of goodies out of the peanuts, and told us that the party would be held in the thatched pavilion on the peanut plot.

It looked like rain that evening, yet, to our great joy, Father came nevertheless. "Do you like peanuts?" asked Father.

"Yes, we do!" We vied in giving the answer.

"Which of you could name the good things in peanuts?"

"Peanuts taste good," said my elder sister.

"Peanuts produce edible oil," said my elder brother.

"Peanuts are so cheap," said I, "that anyone can afford to eat them. Peanuts are everyone's favorite. That's why we call peanuts good."

"It's true that peanuts have many uses," said Father, "but they're most beloved in one respect. Unlike nice-looking apples, peaches and pomegranates, which hang their fruit on branches and win people's instant admiration with their brilliant colors, tiny little peanuts bury themselves underground and remain unearthed until they're ripe. When you come upon a peanut plant lying curled up on the ground, you can never immediately tell whether or not it bears any nuts until you touch them."

"That's true," we said in unison. Mother also nodded. "So you must take after peanuts," Father continued, "because they're useful though not great and nice-looking."

"Then you mean one should be useful rather than great and nice-looking," I said.

"That's what I expect of you," father concluded.

We kept chatting until the party broke up late at night. Today, though nothing is left of the goodie made of peanuts, father's words remain engraved in my mind.

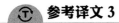
参考译文 3

The Peanut

At the back of our house there was half a *mu* of unused land. "It's a pity to let it lie waste like that," Mother said. "Since you all enioy eating peanuts, let us open it up and make it a peanut garden." At that my brother, sister and I were all delighted and so were the young housemaids. And then some went to buy seeds, some began to dig the ground and others watered it and, in a couple of months, we had a harvest!

"Let us have a party tonight to celebrate," Mother suggested, "and ask Dad to come for a taste of our fresh peanuts. What do you say?" We all agreed, of course. Mother cooked the peanuts in different styles and told us to go to the thatched pavilion in the garden for the celebration.

The weather was not very good that night but, to our great delight, Dad came all the same. "Do you like peanuts?" Dad asked.

"Yes!" We all answered eagerly.

"But who can tell me what the peanut is good for?"

"It is very delicious to eat," my sister took the lead.

"It is good for making oil," my brother followed.

"It is inexpensive," I said with confidence. "Almost everyone can afford it and everyone enjoys eating it. I think this is what it is good for."

"Peanut is good for many things," Dad said, "but there is one thing that is particularly good about it. Unlike apples, peaches and pomegranates that display their fruits up in the air, attracting you with their beautiful colors, peanut buries its seeds in the earth. They do not show themselves until you dig them out when they are ripe and, unless you dig them out, you can't tell whether it bears seeds or not just by its frail stems above ground."

"That's true," we all said and Mother nodded her assent. "So you should try to be like the peanut," Dad went on, "because it is useful, though not great or attractive."

"Do you mean," I asked, "we should learn to be useful but not seek to be great or attractive?"

"Yes." Dad said. "This is what I wish you to be."

We stayed up late that night, eating all the peanuts Mother had cooked for us. But Father's words remained vivid in my memory till this day.

译文注释

译文1和2均选自曾诚的《实用汉英翻译教程》[7]。译文1由Alison Bailey翻译，译文2是张培基翻译的。译文3由刘士聪翻译，选自他的《汉英·英汉美文翻译与鉴赏（中英对照）》[8]。

原文笔调朴实无华、清新自然，没有华丽的辞藻，与原文的内容、格调相映成趣，因而具有强烈的艺术感染力，让人百读不厌。三个译文共同之处较多，基本上都保持了原作的朴素风格，遣词造句通俗简洁，

---

[7] 曾诚.2002.实用汉英翻译教程.北京：外语教学与研究出版社, 91-92.

[8] 刘士聪.2002.汉英·英汉美文翻译与鉴赏（中英对照）.上海：译林出版社, 137-139.

朴实无华，较好地再现了原文的信息，达到了与原文极其相似的功能。

就译文 1 而言，Alison Bailey 用母语翻译这一中国散文，译文的地道性自然毋庸置疑。不过一些中国特有的词汇在翻译时并没有忠实于原文，如将"亩"翻译成 patch（小块土地）。当然，这一译法对英文读者来说可能更好接受。另外，在父亲阐述花生的好处时，提到"你们偶然看见一棵花生瑟缩地长在地上"，Alison Bailey 将该句翻译成 If ever you come across a shy peanut plant，其中的 shy 一词颇为精妙。

译文 2 注重语篇的衔接与连贯，多数句子句对句地译出，但有些句子因英语的语法特点增加了相应的关联词，有一些句子则根据英语的表达习惯而相应调整了语序，使译文一气呵成，如行云流水，毫无斧凿的痕迹。

译文 3 也是可圈可点，如第一段译文清新自然，用词妥帖，读来如行云流水，毫无矫揉造作之感。如原文中"荒芜着"表示一种状态，译作 lie waste 已很好地表达出原意，但译者却在其后加了 like that，使得译文口语色彩更加浓厚，上下句的衔接更加自然。

翻译加油站

翻译技巧（七）：区分主从

汉语的信息重心在许多情况下不体现在形式上，而是体现在内在的逻辑关系上。英语句子很注重信息的主次之分，主要信息放在突出位置，次要信息作为辅助性的描写或叙述手段。因此，汉译英时，应该把汉语的隐性主次关系发掘出来，译成英语的主次表达方式。通常，汉语中表示"结果、行为动作、推论结论、本质、目的"的部分会译成英语的主句或谓语部分；汉语中表示"时间、地点、原因、条件、方式、方法、手段、状态、说明、解释、非本质、修饰、否定"的部分，在英语中则以从句或非谓语动词的形式体现。

一、行为与方式的主从

表示方式和状态的部分应从属于表示行为或动作的谓语部分或表语部分。

例 1　那些厂子，大搞技术革新，充分利用当地资源，生产出大量的、多种多样的药品。

Going in for technological innovation and making full use of local resources, these plants now turn out a wide range of medicine in large quantities.

原文中动词较多，有"大搞""利用"和"生产"，如果译成一个英语句子，就需要找到信息重点，把它处理成句子的谓语动词。"大搞革新"和"利用资源"都可以视作方式，而"生产药品"则是行为，所以应把"生产"翻译成谓语动词，"大搞""利用"译成非谓语。

例 2　游行的人拿着鲜花和彩旗在街道上行进。

The paraders marched in the street, *carrying flowers and banners.*

看完原句，很容易就能得出结论：游行人群的行为动作是"在街道上行进"，状态是"手里拿着鲜花和彩旗"。因此，英译时把"行进"作为谓语动词，"拿着鲜花和彩旗"则作为非谓语结构。

二、手段与目的的主从

表示方法和手段的部分一般从属于表示目的的部分。

例 3　我们用自己动手的方法，达到丰衣足食的目的。

By using our own hands we have attained the objective of "ample food and clothing".

原句结构非常清晰，"自己动手"是方法，"达到丰衣足食"是目的，一目了然。因此，"自己动手"译成非谓语 by using our own hands，而"达到丰衣足食"成为谓语动词 attain the objective of...

例 4　我们可以借助一种专门的仪器观察到电波在传播。

With the help of a special instrument, we can observe the electric waves travelling along.

通过分析可以发现，"借助专门的仪器"是方法和手段，"观察到电波在传播"是目的。因此，译文将"借助专门的仪器"译成介词短语 With the help of a special instrument，而"观察到电波在传播"译成谓语动词 observe the electric waves travelling along。当然，"传播"本身也是动词，译文中处理成现在分词 travelling, observe sth.

doing sth. 表"观察到某物做某事"之意，谓语动词落在"观察"observe 上，而不是"传播"上。

三、原因与结果的主从

表示原因或条件的部分一般应从属于表示结果的部分。

例5 电子表价格便宜，计时准确，在我们生活中使用得越来越广泛。

Electronic watches, *being cheap and accurate*, are finding wider and wider use in our life.

"价格便宜，计时准确"是原因，"使用得越来越广泛"是其结果。因此，译文把原因部分译成 being cheap and accurate，而结果部分作为谓语。

例6 没有农业，人们就不能生存，社会生产就不能继续下去。

Without agriculture, people cannot exist; neither can social production proceed.

原句中，"没有农业"表条件，翻译时应处理成非谓语成分，译文用了介词短语 without agriculture 的表达。"人们不能生存，社会生产就不能继续下去"是没有农业所产生的结果，应当成为主干结构。另外，译文用 neither 一词将前后部分连接起来，行文流畅。

课后练习

◎ **试将下列语篇译成英文：**

1. 一定要让自己持有这样的观念：无论做什么我都能做到得心应手。许多人在接到一份工作时都曾犯过这样的大忌——在潜意识里认为自己一定会失败——这正是他们走向失败的直接原因。比如：有一个人来到一家书店想买一本书，可店员对他说："对不起，我们没有你要买的书"。如果他已经下定决心要买到这本书，那他一定会千方百计地找到它。也许他会再次碰壁，但他绝不会死心。也许他会找到书店经理进行一番协商，并最终买到自己想要的书。

2. 坚强、冷静的人总是会赢得人们的好感和敬意；他就像烈日下一颗浓荫遮地的大树，或是风暴中能够遮风挡雨的巨岩。"谁不爱一颗安静的心，一个温和、平实的生命呢？"无论是狂风暴雨，还是红日当空，无论是天翻地覆，还是生命逆转，一切都等闲视之，因为这样的人永远都是谦和、冷静、沉着的。那种我们称之为坦然自若的平静性格，是修养的最后一课，也是灵魂之花的硕果。它像智慧一样宝贵，价值胜过黄金——是的，胜过足赤真金。

第十一章

诗 歌 翻 译

　　与散文一样，诗歌也是文学四大体裁之一。作为一种重要的文学体裁，诗歌运用富有节奏和韵律的精练语言，以强烈的感情和丰富的想象，高度集中地反映社会生活。根据《辞海》[1]（1979），诗歌"是诗歌文学的一大类别。它高度集中地反应社会生活，饱含着作者丰富的思想和情感，富于想象，语言凝炼而形象性强，具有节奏韵律，一般分行排列。中国诗歌源远流长，优秀作品极为丰富，如《诗经》《楚辞》、汉乐府以及无数诗人的作品。西欧的诗歌由古希腊的荷马、萨福、平达和古罗马的卡图鲁斯、维尔吉、贺拉斯等诗人开始，创作有史诗、颂诗、讽刺诗等。在中国古代，不合乐的称为诗，合乐的称为歌，现在一般统称为诗歌。诗歌按内容的性质，可分为叙事诗和抒情诗；按有无格律，可分为格律诗和自由诗；按是否押韵，又可分为有韵诗和无韵诗"。

　　总之，诗歌的语言高度精练和浓缩，意境悠远，富有节奏感和韵律感，是极具音乐美的产物。它注重结构美和形式美，高度集中地概括和反映社会生活，以灵动的语言表达着人们的喜怒哀乐，用特有的节奏与方式影响着人们的精神世界。诗歌讲究联想，运用象征、比喻、拟人等各种修辞手法，形成了独特的语言艺术。

　　基于诗歌的诸多特性，诗歌是否可译一直是翻译界争论不休的话题。有人说诗歌不能译，因为诗歌经过翻译后，原作的语言美、韵律美和形式美就没有了。美国著名诗人罗伯特·弗罗斯特（Robert Frost）就说过：Poetry is what gets lost in translation. 但多年来大量外国诗歌已被译成中文。不少诗歌经过译者的不断尝试，译文质量已达到很高的水平，这说明诗歌还是可译的。

　　"翻译难，又以诗歌翻译为最难！"[2] 要使译文做到信、达、雅，音韵节律形神兼备或堪与原诗媲美，让普通读者和翻译行家都认可，的确非常不易。我国诗歌翻译家江枫也说过："诗，恰恰应该是翻译过后除了表面信息还留下了美和言外之意的

1　《辞海》编辑委员会. 1979. 辞海（上）. 上海：上海辞书出版社，887.
2　罗选民. 2012. 衍译：诗歌翻译的涅槃. 中国翻译，2：60.

那种东西。留下得越多越是好诗；经不起翻译的就连散文都不是，怎么会是诗，更不会是好诗。"

"不同语言的特质、文化的差异和审美功能决定了诗歌翻译确实非常困难，具有一定程度的不可译性。但人类文化的共通性，人类经验的相似性，语言认识新事物和新环境的功能，使得诗歌翻译在某种程度上又是可行的……不可译性和可译性是二元对立的，在一定的条件下可以相互转化。诗歌作为一种独特的文学体裁而具有一些特质，如音乐性、外在表现形式、鲜明的风格等。翻译过程中，这些因素的难以把握使其韵味不易被保留，从而加大翻译难度，造成诗歌似乎不可译的表象。但是，通过译者的主观能动，以其深厚的母语文化功底、高超的文学造诣，以及对译入语语言及文化的深刻了解、掌握与运用，在翻译中进行再创造，以传达诗歌的精髓与精妙，译者能够成功'播散异邦的种子'（苏珊·巴斯奈特语）"[3]（辛红娟，2012）。

限于篇幅的关系，本章主要探讨有韵诗，特别是唐诗的英译问题。唐诗在中国文化中占有极为重要的地位，是中国文化中最为瑰丽的文化遗产。"中国的古典诗歌发展到唐代，达到了光辉灿烂的顶点。唐代是中国诗史上的黄金时代。从清康熙年间编纂的《全唐诗》来看，作家两千二百多人，作品四万八千多首，成为诗歌史上的一代钜观。后经历代相继补逸，唐诗已超过五万多首"[4]（张步云，1990）。

英译唐诗在中西文化交流史上占有非常重要的位置，是整个中国文化外传中最为丰硕的成果，它以其独特的魅力赢得了世界的普遍认可，并且对西方许多诗人的创作乃至对整个译入语文化都产生了重大影响，尤其以在美国产生的影响最为巨大。

根据《文学翻译新视野》[5]（李冰梅，2011），英国对中国古诗的翻译远远早于美国。19世纪英国人译中国诗之多，可能超出其他欧洲国家的总和。19世纪末20世纪初是中国古诗英译的短暂繁荣时期，直到"二战"以后才再次复苏。中国古诗的最早英译者是英国的威廉·琼斯爵士（Sir William Jone），而现在能找到的最早的中国古诗英译本是英国人彼得·佩林（Peter Perring）所译的《花瓣：中国求爱诗》（*The Flower Leaf: Chinese Courtship in Verse*）。

---

3 辛红娟.2012.文学翻译读本.南京：南京大学出版社，165.
4 张步云.1990.唐代诗歌.合肥：安徽教育出版社，1.
5 李冰梅.2011.文学翻译新视野.北京：北京大学出版社.

另外,翟理斯在中国古诗英译史上写下了浓重的一笔。他比较注重作品的文学性,1883年编译了《中国文学瑰宝》(Gems of Chinese Literature)两卷本。1901年《中国文学史》的出版为翟理斯赢得了很高的声誉。《中国文学史》是第一部以"史"的方式编写的中国文学史,全书正文440页中有46页介绍了唐诗,并译介了孟浩然、王维、李白、杜甫、白居易、韩愈等人的诗篇。翟理斯采取了直译押韵的诗体形式进行英译,目的是使英文尽量传达出唐诗的风貌。

继翟理斯之后,英国另一位极为重要的汉学家是阿瑟·韦利(Arthur Waley),他为中国古典诗歌的翻译也做出了巨大贡献。韦利精通中国文化,具有文学、思想、巫术、绘画、历史等各方面的知识。"1953年由于其对中国古诗翻译的重大贡献而获得女王诗歌勋章,他的汉学成就之后英国尚没有别的学者能超过他。韦利冲破诗歌韵律的束缚,采用了自由诗体的形式,试验性地创造了一种'跳跃节奏',以英诗的重读与汉诗的汉字相对应,多采用直译的方式,力求译文准确无误,再现原诗风貌。"[6](李冰梅,2011)

与英国不同,美国在20世纪之前对于中国诗歌并没有太大的热情。1912年由哈丽特·蒙罗(H. H. Munro)、庞德(Ezra Pound)等人创办的《诗刊》发起了新诗运动。他们以打破传统诗风,开创诗歌新局面为己任,大量吸收外来因素。于是中国诗歌就这样开始进入这些新诗人的视野,并迅速形成一股向中国古诗学习的高潮。中国古诗的含蓄克制、简洁丰富而强烈的意象等,与他们当时极力反对的直接抒情、为抒情而抒情的造作的诗歌主张不谋而合,于是出现了美国翻译中国古诗的第一次浪潮。庞德、艾米·洛威尔(A. Lowell)、艾思柯(Florence Ayscough)、宾纳(W. Bynner)和弗莱彻(W. J. Bainbridge-Fletcher)均是这一时期杰出的翻译家。他们的翻译虽然并不完全局限于唐诗,但无疑对唐诗的译介最多。就美国而言,中国诗歌的影响在1922年达到高潮后开始逐渐消退。但到了20世纪50年代末,伴随着美国社会的各种思潮和运动,美国掀起了第二次"中国热",这次高潮虽然不如第一次那样轰轰烈烈,但却要持久得多,且对中国诗的翻译和借鉴的范围更广更深,李白、王维、白居易、杜甫、元稹、寒山等诸多唐代诗人都深受喜爱。许多美国诗人各选一位中国古人为师,如雷克斯罗斯(Kenneth Rexroth)以杜甫为师,史奈德(Gary

---

6 李冰梅.2011.文学翻译新视野.北京:北京大学出版社,95.

Snyder）以寒山为师，他们不仅翻译中国诗人的作品，而且在自己的创作中也经常化用或直接借用一些中国古诗名句，诗歌风格也深受影响。这一时期的主要译者除了雷克斯罗斯、史奈德外，还有阿瑟·库柏（Arthur Cooper）、洪业（William Hung）等。

总体而言，中国唐诗的英译大致呈现出两种倾向：一种是所谓的"创意英译"[7]（钟玲，2003）。这些译诗优美流畅，注重译诗自身的美，带有强烈的创造性，许多译诗已被选入重要的美国诗歌创作选集中加以经典化；而另一方面，刘若愚、洪业、柳无忌、杨宪益、许渊冲等学者的译作则强调忠实地再现原文。

诗歌英译的要点

诗歌作为一种文学体裁，语言凝练浓缩，形式工整，富于韵律和节奏，形象表达作者的丰富情感，集中反映社会生活并具有一定的节奏和韵律。许多名家都提出过自己的译诗观点，王佐良和郭沫若等都认为应当"以诗译诗"。江枫认为，诗是艺术性最强的语言艺术，没有形式便没有艺术美。作为艺术品的诗，绝不可能脱离其艺术形式而存在。诗之成其为诗，并不在于说了些什么，而在于是怎样说的。所以，译诗应该力求形似而后神似。

庞德虽然翻译了大量的中国唐诗，但实际上他不太懂中文，往往根据日译本转译而来。在诗歌翻译时，他努力寻求与原作诗人的心灵契合，强调诗歌语言的能量与细节来再现原作诗人的诗性体验与诗性情感。庞德往往将其诗学革新的观念融入其翻译实践中，并由此产生了"创意翻译法"。他认为，翻译诗歌时：一要抛弃维多利亚时期那种矫揉造作、生僻古涩的翻译措辞；二是优秀的诗歌译作可以看作是具有自身独立意义的新诗作品；三是每篇译作都有必要看成是一定程度对原作的评鉴。

另外，国内诗歌英译集大成者恐怕当属许渊冲。许渊冲是一位多产的杰出诗歌翻译实践家和理论家，在古诗英译方面做出了极大贡献。他从事文学翻译长达六十余年，译作涵盖中、英、法等语种。他的诗歌翻译主要集中在中国古诗的英译，形成了韵体译诗的方法与理论，被誉为"诗译英法唯一人"。他的译文忠实原文，韵律丰富，节奏感强，并基于多年的翻译实践，提出了"三美论"。"三美论"认为，诗歌翻译要有节奏，押韵，顺口，好听，做到音美；还要在诗句长短和对称等方面

---

[7] 钟玲．2003．美国诗与中国梦．桂林：广西师范大学出版社，34．

做到大体整齐以实现形美；翻译可以不求意似，但必须要传达原文深层次的意美。在重要性上，意美最重要，音美和形美依次次之，"也就是说，要在传达原文'意美'的前提下，尽可能传达原文的'音美'；还要在传达原文'意美'和'音美'的前提下，尽可能传达原文的'形美'；努力做到三美齐备。如果三者不能得兼，那么，可以不要求'形似'和'音似'，但要尽可能传达原文的'意美'和'音美'"[8]（许渊冲，1983）。

翻译语篇 1

黄鹤楼送孟浩然之广陵

李白

故人西辞黄鹤楼，

烟花三月下扬州。

孤帆远影碧空尽，

唯见长江天际流。

译前提示

《黄鹤楼送孟浩然之广陵》是中国文学史上著名的离别诗之一。李白寓离情于写景之中，描绘了一幅意境开阔、风流倜傥的诗人送别画。

1. 原诗是典型的七言绝句，充分体现了李白七言绝句的艺术特色。它用字凝练，句式整齐，格律严整，与一般的英语诗歌存在着较大的差别。这一形式上和用词上的差别对翻译有何影响？
2. "楼""州"和"流"是这一绝句的韵脚，在翻译时如何将这一押韵绝句传达出来也是翻译该诗的最大难点之一。
3. "长江"是指长江还是指"长长的江"？

8　许渊冲.1983.再谈"意美、音美、形美".外语学刊，4: 68.

参考译文 1

Seeing Meng Haoran Off to Kuangling

My old friend, going west, bids farewell at Yellow Crane Terrace,

Among misty blossoms of the third month, goes down to Yang-chou.

His lone sail's far shadow vanishes into the azure void.

Now, only the Long River flowing to the sky's end.

参考译文 2

Farewell

—On seeing Meng Haojan off from Brown
Crane Tower as he took his departure for Kuangling

And so, dear friend, at Brown Crane Tower you,

Bidding the west adieu,

'Mid April mists and blossoms go,

Till in the vast blue—green

Your lonely sail's far shade no more is seen,

Only on the sky's verge the River's flow.

参考译文 3

Seeing Meng Haoran Off at Yellow Crane Tower

My friend has left the west where towers Yellow Crane

For River Town while willow—down and flowers reign.

His lessening sail is lost in the boundless azure sky,

Where I see but the endless River rolling by.

译文注释

以上三个译本均选自许渊冲的《中诗英韵探胜》[9]。前两个译文的翻译时间基本接近：译有 *Meng Hao-Jan*（《孟浩然》）的 Paul Kroll 于 1975 年翻译本诗，而醉心于中国古代文学的 John A. Turner 于 1976 年翻译了本诗。许渊冲的译文稍晚一些，译于 1987 年，翻译过程中可能对前两个译文进行过一定的参考。

1. 《黄鹤楼送孟浩然之广陵》讲究格律，它的音乐美体现在节奏和韵律两个方面。节奏上，该诗由四个诗行组成，每行三顿，例如"故人/西辞/黄鹤楼"；从韵律上来讲，原诗采用了 aaba 式的尾韵。

2. Paul Kroll 喜欢用自由体翻译诗歌，他的译文把原诗中离别的场景大致地翻译了出来。译文中句法几乎完全仿照原诗，许多词语也是对汉语的逐字翻译，如"三月"译为 the third month，"碧空"译为 the azure void。同时，该译文采用了原文的诗行断句和节奏，但没有复制原诗的音韵。另外，"广陵""扬州"借用了原语的读音，但是"烟花"的"烟"却译成带有西方特征的 misty。

3. John A. Turner 的译文则是押韵的，采用了 aabccb 的尾韵。但句式长短不一，添加了副标题，并打破了原诗四个诗行的形式。他将"黄鹤楼"的"黄"译成了 brown，异于一般译者的选择。但 Turner 的译文对原诗气势的传达比 Kroll 的译文好一些。

4. 许渊冲在翻译诗歌时，主张音形意美。为了再现原诗的音乐美，他采用了英语格律诗的形式，以"步"代"顿"，即以英语的"音步"代替汉语的"顿"，以再现原诗的节奏；同时，许渊冲的译文对原诗的韵式也进行了一定的模拟。另外，许渊冲的译文句式整齐，分为四个诗行，每一诗行基本上符合抑扬格七音步的节奏，韵式为英语格律诗中常见的两行转韵 aabb 式。

---

[9] 许渊冲. 2010. 中诗英韵探胜. 2 版. 北京：北京大学出版社.

翻译语篇 2

青青河畔草

青青河畔草，郁郁园中柳。

盈盈楼上女，皎皎当窗牖。

娥娥红粉妆，纤纤出素手。

昔为倡家女，今为荡子妇，

荡子行不归，空床难独守。

译前提示

本诗选自《古诗十九首》。《古诗十九首》是在汉代汉族民歌基础上发展起来的五言诗，内容多写离愁别恨和彷徨失意，思想消极，情调低沉。但它的艺术成就却很高，长于抒情，善用事物来烘托，寓情于景，情景交融。《古诗十九首》习惯上以句首标题，依次为：《行行重行行》《青青河畔草》《青青陵上柏》《今日良宴会》《西北有高楼》《涉江采芙蓉》《明月皎夜光》《冉冉孤生竹》《庭中有奇树》《迢迢牵牛星》《回车驾言迈》《东城高且长》《驱车上东门》《去者日以疏》《生年不满百》《凛凛岁云暮》《孟冬寒气至》《客从远方来》《明月何皎皎》。

本诗写的是一位歌舞女子思念在外游荡的丈夫，难以忍受一个人的寂寞。诗人在自然率真的描摹中，显示了从良倡家女的个性，也通过她使读者了解在游宦成风而希望渺茫的汉末，中下层妇女的悲剧命运。

1. 皎皎：本义指月光白亮，这里形容在春光照耀下楼上女子明艳多彩。
2. 窗牖：窗的一种，用木条横直制成。
3. 娥娥：形容容貌的美好。红粉妆：指艳丽的妆饰。
4. 倡家女：古代凡是以歌唱为业的艺人叫做"倡"，"倡家女"指歌伎。
5. 荡子：指长期漫游四方不归乡土的人，与"游子"意思相近。

参考译文 1

And within, the mistress, in the mid most of her youth,

White, white face, hesitates, passing the door,

Slender, she puts forth a slender hand.

And she was a courtesan in the old days,

And she has married a sot,

Who now goes drunkenly out,

And leaves her too much alone.

参考译文 2

Green, green riverside grass she sees;

Lush, lush the garden's willow trees.

Fair, fair, she waits in painted bower,

Bright, bright like a window-framed flower.

In rosy, rosy dress she stands;

She puts forth slender, slender hands.

A singing girl in early life,

Now she is a desexed wife.

Her husband's gone far, far away.

How to keep lonely bed each day!

译文注释

第 1 个译文由庞德翻译，第 2 个译文由许渊冲翻译。以上译文均选自许渊冲的《汉魏六朝诗汉英对照》[10]。

10　许渊冲. 2009. 汉魏六朝诗汉英对照. 北京：中国对外翻译出版公司，82.

第十一章 诗歌翻译

1. 庞德是美国著名的意象派诗人,他翻译中国古诗的初衷就是要为意象派诗歌运动寻找新的动力,因此他的译诗往往是从内容、形式到整体风格的全方位改造与再创作,更接近于仿译。

   庞德的译文仅仅保留了原诗哀伤的意境,对于句意、形式等并不讲究忠实于原诗。以"盈盈楼上女,皎皎当窗牖。娥娥红粉妆,纤纤出素手。"为例。这四句主要描摹了女子凭窗远眺的情景,似一幅静态的图画。庞德将之译成:

   And within, the mistress, in the midmost of her youth,

   White, white face, hesitates, passing the door,

   Slender, she puts forth a slender hand.

   译文仅保留了原诗孤寂冷清的意境氛围,对原诗所述情景却进行了彻底的重构。他变原诗的"当窗牖"为"犹豫着,穿过房门"(hesitates, passing the door),少妇由凭窗远眺变为深闺徘徊,原诗中的静态意象转化成了动态意象。他也没有翻译"娥娥红粉妆"一句,原诗四句被译为三句,韵律、句长等也都与原诗截然不同。

   又如"昔为倡家女,今为荡子妇。荡子行不归,空床难独守。",庞德译为:

   And she was a courtesan in the old days,

   And she has married a sot,

   Who now goes drunkenly out,

   And leaves her too much alone.

   庞德把"荡子"翻译为 a sot(酒鬼),因而也顺理成章地把末句译为 Who now goes drunkenly out, and leaves her too much alone.

   与前四句一样,庞德充分发挥其想象,重构原诗所述情景,但译文与诗句的原意有较大的差距,这可能与他本人不懂中文有一定的关系。

2. 许渊冲采用以叠字译叠字的策略,但他的译文也并非完全忠实于诗歌的原意,最突出的是"娥娥红粉妆"一句。他将此句译为 In rosy, rosy dress she stands. "娥娥"本是形容女子姣好的容貌,此处修饰女子略施粉黛的容颜。而许渊冲则以"rosy, rosy(玫瑰红的)"译"娥娥",写女子身穿玫瑰红的衣裳。这恐怕也是出于音韵翻译的考虑,但译文与原文意义偏差较大。

   另外,末句"荡子行不归,空床难独守"讲述该女子在无果的等待中不禁感慨造化弄人,她"昔为倡家女",期待着幸福的婚姻生活,然而

"今为荡子妇",只能独自忍受寂寞孤单的夜晚。许渊冲将末句译为 Her husband's gone far, far away. How to keep lonely bed each day! 该译文虽未紧贴字面意义,如将"行不归"译为 has gone far, far away,只译了"远行"而未译"不归";将"空床难独守"译为感叹句 How to keep lonely bed each day! 但原句的主要意义与情感风格在译文中得以保留,同时在格律上以四音步译五言三顿,且 away 和 day 押韵,韵脚与"归"发音近似,所以说许渊冲对于此句的创造性翻译是成功的。

翻译加油站

翻译技巧(八):长句的翻译

汉语中有很多长句,翻译成英语时主要有以下四种方法:顺译法、断句法、换序法和合句法。

一、顺译法

顺译法,就是按照原文的顺序进行翻译。这种方法多用于单一主语的长句,但要分清句中的信息重心。

例1 当他们活着一天,总要尽量多工作、多学习,不肯虚度年华,不让时间白白地浪费掉。

As long as they are living, they always work and study as hard as possible, unwilling to dream their life away, let alone waste even a single moment of their lives.

例2 其中有一半是近 5 年才来到温哥华地区的,这使温哥华成为亚洲以外最大的中国人聚居地。

Half of them have come to Vancouver area the past five years only, making it the largest Chinese settlement outside Asia.

上述两个例子均按照原文的顺序进行翻译,未做断句处理。在决定句子主谓时,应将句子的信息中心体现出来,如第一句的重点应是"尽量多工作、多学习,不肯虚度年华",而第二句则是"有一半是近 5 年才来到温哥华地区的"。"区分主从"的技巧可参见上一章"散文翻译"中翻译加油站的内容。

二、断句法

断句法，也叫分译法，是指对原文进行层次划分，分别译成两个或两个以上的句子。它适用于以下情况：

第一，句子较长，内容较复杂。

例 3　如今没奈何，把你雇在间壁人家放牛，// 每月可以得他几钱银子，你又有现成饭吃，// 只在明日就要去了。

There is no way out but to set you to work looking after our neighbor's buffalo. You will make a little money every month, and you will get your meals there too. You are to start tomorrow.

原文就一句话，但包含的信息较多，分析后会发现主要包含三大内容：第一，没办法，只能让你去给邻居放牛；第二，这样做有两大好处，既可以赚钱又有饭吃；第三，明天你就要开始去放牛了。因此，翻译成英文时可以将原句断成三句话来表达。

例 4　接着，他继续设想，// 鸡又生鸡，// 用鸡卖钱，// 钱买母牛，// 母牛繁殖，卖牛得钱，// 用钱放债，// 这么一连串的发财计划，当然也不能算是生产的计划。

He went on indulging in wishful thinking. Chickens would breed more chickens. Selling them would bring him money. With this he could buy cows. The cows would breed too and selling oxen would make more money for him. With the money, he could become a money lender. Such a succession of steps for getting rich, of course, had nothing at all to do with production.

原句选自马南邨《燕山夜话》中《一个鸡蛋的家当》一文。该文提到明朝的一个人因捡到一颗鸡蛋，继而对积累家当进行了一系列假想，但这样的假想并不能视作生产计划。本句是典型的长句，信息非常复杂。译文将它分成了七个短句，很好地再现了积累家当的一系列步骤的设想。

上述例子均为长句，信息含量大，特别是第二个例子的信息量非常大。翻译时，可以适当断句，使表达更为清晰。

第二，汉语的总分复句。

例 5　王冕天性聪明，// 年纪不满二十岁，就把那天文、地理、经史上的大学问，无一不贯通。

Wang Mian had genius. While still in his teens, he mastered the whole field of astronomy, geography, the classics and history.

例6　但他性情不同，// 既不求官爵，又不交纳朋友，// 终日闭门读书。

He was, however, eccentric. He did not look for an official post, and did not even have any friends. All day he studied behind closed doors.

例7　灾难深重的中华民族，一百年来，其优秀人物奋斗牺牲，摸索救国救民的真理，// 是可歌可泣的。

For a hundred years, the finest sons and daughters of the disaster-ridden Chinese nation fought and sacrificed their lives, in quest of the truth that would save the country and the people. This is really moving.

例5和例6都是总分关系，例7是分总关系。翻译时，可以将总说的句子单独成句，使译文的逻辑关系更清晰。

第三，为了表达原文的强调语势。

例8　我们的民族将再也不是一个被人侮辱的民族了，// 我们已经站起来了。

Ours will no longer be a nation subject to insult and humiliation. We have stood up.

例9　这首歌并不曾继续多久，// 就和笛声共同消失在黑暗里了。

The singing did not last very long. Soon, together with the sound of the flute, it faded away in the darkness.

例8强调"我们已经站起来了"，所以这部分在译文中单独成句。例9强调了"这首歌不曾继续多久"，译文也做了断句处理。

三、换序法

翻译过程中，译者有时按照译文读者的思维习惯，对原文的语序加以调整，使译文表达正确无误，通俗易懂，这种方法叫做换序法。

例10　我认为好就好在很多人都很关心电视的影响，而且对我们不喜欢的东西也有能力加以改变。

What is good, *I suppose*, is that many people are concerned about TV's influence and that we have the power to change what we do not like.

例 11　这三个县经历了那场中国 70 年代第四次极为严重的遍及数省的自然灾害。

The three counties underwent the fourth most serious natural disaster that plagued several provinces *in China in the 1970s*.

例 10 的译文将原句的主谓成分"我认为"处理成插入语 I suppose，放在译文主语 what is good 之后，使句子的重心更加明确。例 11 的译文则把"中国 70 年代"放在句尾，将"第四次自然灾害"提前，从而突出了这三个县经历了第四次自然灾害的事实。

四、合句法

汉译英时，有可能会把两个或两个以上的句子翻译成一个英文的句子，这一方法叫做合句法或合译法。

例 12　中国和澳大利亚昨天签订了一项保护协定。协定的目的是既保护澳大利亚各公司在华的利益，也鼓励中国在澳大利亚进一步的投资。

China and Australia yesterday signed an investment protection agreement as much designed to encourage further Chinese investment in Australia as to protect Australian companies in China.

原文有两句话，译文通过 as much...as 的结构把这两句话合成了一句，句子结构紧凑，信息又没有遗漏。

例 13　旧历新年快来了。这是一年中的第一件大事。除了那些负债过多的人以外，大家都热烈地欢迎这个佳节的到来。

The traditional New Year was approaching, the first big event of the year, and everyone, except those who owed heavy debts—which traditionally had to be paid off before the year—was enthusiastically looking forward to it.

原文有三句话，围绕"新年"这一话题展开。译文将这三句话合在一起翻译，一气呵成。同时，还增译了中国过年前要还债的习俗，帮助英文读者更好地理解这一内容。

课后练习

∞ 试将下列诗歌翻译成英文：

1.
登鹳雀楼
王之涣

白日依山尽，黄河入海流。

欲穷千里目，更上一层楼。

2.
静 夜 思
李白

床前明月光，疑是地上霜。

举头望明月，低头思故乡。

3.
乡 愁
余光中

小时候
乡愁是一枚小小的邮票
我在这头
母亲在那头

长大后乡愁是一张窄窄的船票
我在这头
新娘在那头

后来啊

乡愁是一方矮矮的坟墓

我在外头

母亲在里头

而现在

乡愁是一湾浅浅的海峡

我在这头

大陆在那头

第十二章

专八汉译英

英语专业八级考试（TEM 8，Test for English Majors—Band 8），全称为全国高校英语专业八级考试，1991年起由教育部实行，高等学校外语专业教学指导委员会主办，参加对象是英语及相关专业的大四学生。考试及格者由高等院校外语专业教学指导委员会颁发成绩单。成绩分三级：60～69分是合格；70～79分是良好；80分及以上是优秀。考试合格后颁发的证书终身有效。从2003年起，考试不合格能够补考一次，补考合格后只颁发合格证书。

高校外语专业教学测试办公室下发给各校的《关于英语专业八级考试（TEM 8）题型调整的说明》中提到，从2016年起将对TEM 8考试的试卷结构和测试题型做局部调整。新专八的题型包括：听力理解（讲座和对话）、阅读理解（选择题和简答题）、语言知识、翻译及写作。

《关于英语专业八级考试（TEM 8）题型调整的说明》对汉译英部分的相关规定如下：

1. 测试要求

能运用汉译英的理论和技巧，翻译我国报纸杂志上的文章和一般的文学作品。速度为每小时250至300个汉字。译文要求忠实原意，语言通顺、流畅。

2. 测试形式

本部分为做答题，将一段150个汉字组成的段落译成英语。考试时间是25分钟。

因此，新专八仅对汉译英做考察，对英译汉不做要求。旧专八对汉译英项目的要求是"应试者运用汉译英的理论和技巧，翻译我国报刊杂志上的论述文和国情介绍，以及一般文学作品的节录。速度为每小时约250至300个汉字。译文必须忠实原意，语言通顺"。从中我们可以发现，汉译英的内容稍有变动，文学作品依然是考试内容之一，但我国报纸杂志上的论述文和国情介绍已延伸至报纸杂志上的所有文章。因此，考试涉及的内容更加宽泛，考试的要求也相应提高了。

汉译英满分为 10 分。阅卷教师根据考生的译文忠实性和语言的适切性打分，译文的忠实性占 7 分，语言的适切性占 3 分。汉译英的优秀标准包括：首先，须正确翻译词语，能突破原文的表层含义，实现指称、语体、搭配等多方面的对等；同时，应避免原文的冗长信息，补充汉语句子间的隐形逻辑关系，译文表达应符合英语的信息架构，没有语言失误，或仅有轻微失误，如介词、名词、代词和冠词等的误用。

专八汉译英的要点

纵观 2001 年以来汉译英的题型、体裁和题材，不难发现，除描写文一般不予考虑外，其他体裁都有可能涉及。从旅行札记生活随笔、景点介绍到人生哲理，从一般应用文到较高雅的文学作品，几乎都囊括其中，但主要集中在记叙、论说、应用、散文等体裁。当然，2015 年考的关于茶花展的介绍属实用翻译，其他年份均属文学翻译试题，因此本教材将专八汉译英归入到下篇非实用翻译中。

另外，专八考试每年选题都有微小变化，字数虽有不同变化，但还是根据难易程度控制在 150～190 个字左右。要注意的是，2016 年新专八中，汉译英试题的原文字数降到了 110 个字，时间也从原来的 30 分钟缩短为 20 分钟。所以，新专八虽对翻译速度的要求有所降低，但考生还是要把握好时间，在有限的时间内尽量使译文达到新专八的要求，即"忠实原意，语言通顺、流畅"。

考生在汉译英过程中，可以遵循以下步骤：

第一，抓紧时间通读原文，尽量透彻理解原文。这一过程中可对原文的信息重点进行标注并同时思考译文的句式等内容。

第二，根据原文所表达的意思、语气以及上下文的语境选择恰当的句子结构和表达手段，忠实表达原文。

第三，校对译文，检查译文在理解和表达上的问题，并修改错译和漏译部分。

第四，润色译文，在译文中运用地道的语言流畅地表达原文。

汉译英考试中，考生必须在考试时间内读透短文，用地道的英语表达原文的内容。因此，考生不仅要了解汉英两种语言的不同特点，还要懂得一定的翻译理论和翻译技巧，并在给定的时间内，不借助任何词典和参考书，仅凭自己的知识储备完成一定体裁或风格的翻译试题。

从这一意义上说，汉译英的准备工作应当尽早开始，比如从开始学习汉英翻译课起，每周能坚持两三百字的翻译练习。在完成翻译练习后，能够对照参考译文进行参照学习，把其中的好词佳句摘抄下来，并在今后的翻译练习中加以运用。

当然，没有一定量的英语阅读而只做汉英翻译练习也是毫无意义的。只有在充分的输入（即英语阅读）前提下，考生的输出（即译文）才可能做到流畅通顺，地道自然，否则只是机械地操练，可提高余地不大。

另外，在一段时间的自我练习后（如一个学期或一年后），考生也可以拿前几年的专八真题进行训练，在规定时间内（如30分钟或20分钟），不借助词典的帮助完成翻译任务。记住，很重要的一点是将自己的译文与参考译文进行对比和分析，并从中汲取好的表达方式。

不过，翻译能力的提高也不是一朝一夕的事情。好的译文来源于日常的学习和积累；只有平时就做有心人，才可能在专八考试中取得理想的成绩。

翻译语篇 1

泊珍到偏远小镇的育幼院把生在那里养到 1 岁的孩子接回来。但泊珍看他第一眼，仿似一声雷劈头而来。令她晕头胀脑，这 1 岁的孩子脸型长得如此熟悉，她心里的第一道声音是，不能带回去！

痛苦纠聚心中，眉心发烫发热，胸口郁闷难展，胃里一股气冲喉而上。院长说这孩子发育迟缓时，她更是心头无绪。她在孩子所待的房里来回踱步，这房里还有其他小孩。整个房间只有一扇窗，窗外树影婆娑。就让孩子留下来吧，这里有善心的神父和修女，这里将来会扩充为有医疗作用的看护中心，这是留住孩子最好的地方。这孩子是她的秘密，她将秘密留在这树林掩映的建筑里。

她将秘密留在心头。

第十二章 专八汉译英

译前提示

本段材料中的画线部分是2012年专八的汉译英真题。考试内容节选自台湾小说家蔡素芬的长篇小说《烛光盛宴》。蔡素芬曾以《盐田儿女》感动了无数台湾读者，《烛光盛宴》是她2009年的新作。该小说着眼于"两岸历史与爱情"，由大陆小姐泊珍、台湾女子菊子以及故事代述者的现代女性"我"，三种身份、三段时空交错浓缩了台湾近六十年的历史，也交织出三个女子命运的经纬。

参考译文

With pains gathering in her heart, she felt something burning hot between her eyebrows. Her chest was brimmed with sorrow and depression which was about to run out of her throat in any moment. She felt even more lost when the director said that the child had suffered from developmental retardation. She paced up and down in the room where her child had lived along with other children. The room had only one window, out of which the tree shadows were dancing. Leave the child here. There are kind-hearted priests and nuns here. The place will be developed into a nursery center with medical care. This is the best place for the child. The child was her secret, and she would keep this secret in the building shaded by trees.

译文注释

2012年的考题难点应该在第一句话，其他的内容难度适中。

1. 痛苦纠聚心中，眉心发烫发热，胸口郁闷难展，胃里一股气冲喉而上。With pains gathering in her heart, she felt something burning hot between her eyebrows. Her chest was brimmed with depression and sorrow which was about to run out of her throat in any moment.

   【注释】这句话描写了人物的情感活动，如"痛苦""郁闷"，同时伴随着痛苦和郁闷所引发的生理反应，如"眉心发烫发热""胃里一股气冲喉而上"。翻译本句时考生可能会觉得比较困难，因为这是此次考试的难点所在。

"痛苦"可以用 pain，而"郁闷"可以用 gloom。但如果把"一股"翻译成 a gust of，这股气流感觉过于强劲，a flow of 更为合适一些。"气"如果翻译成 atmosphere 是不合适的。

参考译文中没有直译"胃里一股气冲喉而上"，而是用意译的手法来处理这一部分。

2. 院长说这孩子发育迟缓时，她更是心头无绪。She felt even more lost when the director said that the child had suffered from developmental retardation.

   【注释】"发育迟缓"可以译成 developmental retardation，这个词很可能是不少考生的拦路虎。因此，在日常学习中需要积累一些固定的表达，这样在考试时才能成竹在胸。

   另外，专八考试中也会出现一些四字格，如"心头无绪"等。考试过程中，如果一时想不起该词的贴切表达，就从已掌握的词汇中选择较为合适的词来表达。切勿花太多时间在个别字词上，以免不能按时做完。

3. 这孩子是她的秘密，她将秘密留在这树林掩映的建筑里。The child was her secret, and she would keep this secret in the building shaded by trees.

   【注释】本句中"秘密"重复了两次，是为了强调而采用的修辞性重复，所以在译文中最好重复"秘密"一词，以体现原文的修辞效果。因此，如把这句话译成 This child would be her secret, which she would keep in the building shaded by the trees. 稍欠妥当，secret 一词不应用 which 来替代。

翻译语篇 2

生活就像一杯红酒，热爱生活的人会从其中品出无穷无尽的美妙。将它握在手中仔细观察，它的暗红色中有血的感觉，那正是生命的痕迹。抿一口留在口中回味，它的甘甜中有一丝苦涩，如人生一般复杂迷离。喝一口下肚，余香沁人心脾，让人终身受益。红酒越陈越美味，生活越丰富越美好。当人生走向晚年，就如一瓶待开封的好酒，其色彩是沉静的，味道中充满慷慨与智慧。

译前提示

本段材料是 2013 年专八的汉译英真题。它从一杯红酒入手阐述深刻的生活哲理，语言较为精练，翻译时要注意选词的正确性。

第十二章 专八汉译英

参考译文

Life is like a glass of red wine; and those who love life can savour the endless wonder from it. Holding the glass for a careful observation of the wine, you will see blood in its dark redness, which is the very sign of life. Taking a sip in your mouth, you will taste a trace of bitterness and astringence in its sweetness, which suggests the complicatedness and mystique of life. Drinking a mouthful, you will be fully refreshed by its lingering aroma and benefited in your lifelong time. The older the wine, the mellower it is. And the richer the life, the happier we feel. Life in its later years is like a bottle of premium wine to be opened, of which the colour is placid, and the flavor is filled with generosity and wisdom.

译文注释

本篇材料翻译时很容易选词错误，一定要注意正确的选词。

1. 生活就像一杯红酒，热爱生活的人会从其中品出无穷无尽的美妙。Life is like a glass of red wine; and those who love life can savour the endless wonder from it.

   【注释】"一杯红酒"的"杯"应用 glass 或 goblet (高脚玻璃杯) 来表达，a cup of 一般跟咖啡和茶，a mug of（通常指周边垂直的有柄瓷杯或金属杯，容积较大）一般跟啤酒或牛奶。

   此处的"酒"应当翻译成 wine，不能翻译成 beer、alcohol 或 whisky 等词。

2. 抿一口留在口中回味，它的甘甜中有一丝苦涩，如人生一般复杂迷离。Taking a sip in your mouth, you will taste a trace of bitterness and astringence in its sweetness, which suggests the complicatedness and mystique of life.

   【注释】"抿一口"如直译成 drink a mouth，意思就完全不对了；如果翻译成 drink a gulp 也不合适，因为 gulp 表示"一大口"的意思。最贴切的表达是 take a sip。

3. 当人生走向晚年，就如一瓶待开封的好酒，其色彩是沉静的，味道中充满慷慨与智慧。Life in its later years is like a bottle of premium wine to be opened, of which the colour is placid, and the flavor is filled with generosity and wisdom.

【注释】"晚年"有较多译法，如 in one's old age，in one's later years，in one's decling years 和 in one's remaining years 等。In one's old age 和 in one's later years 属中性表达，而 in one's decling years 和 in one's remaining years 的语义较为消极，不建议在此使用。

"开酒瓶"的动词可以用 open、uncork 和 unseal，这里的"瓶"绝对不能翻译成 vase，"好酒"可以翻译成 premium wine。

翻译语篇 3

流逝，表现了南国人对时间最早的感觉。"子在川上曰：逝者如斯夫。"他们发现无论是潺潺小溪，还是浩荡大河，都一去不复返，流逝之际青年变成了老翁而绿草转眼就枯黄，很自然有错阴的紧迫感。流逝也许是缓慢的，但无论如何缓慢，对流逝的恐惧使人们必须用"流逝"这个词来时时警戒后人，必须急匆匆地行动，给这个词灌注一种紧张感。（2016年汉译英真题）

参考译文

They realised that both the babbling brook and the mighty river would flow on, and that their waters would never return. They found that as time passed by, young men would become old and the green grass would turn yellow and wither in almost the blink of an eye. A sense of urgency naturally arose over the elusiveness of time. No matter how slowly time flowed, the very fear of its transiency compelled people to use the word "passage" to warn the coming generations of the necessity of taking prompt action; thus instilling the word with a sense of tension.[1]

翻译语篇 4

茶花（camellia）的自然花期在12月至翌年4月，以红色系为主，另有黄色系和白色系等，花色艳丽。本届花展充分展示了茶花的品种资源和科研水平，是近三年

1　由新东方的唐静老师翻译。

来本市规模最大的一届茶花展。为了使广大植物爱好者有更多与茶花亲密接触的机会，本届茶花展的布展范围延伸至整个园区，为赏花游客带来便利。

此次茶花展历时2个月，展期内200多个茶花品种将陆续亮相。（2015年汉译英真题）

参考译文

Camellia's flowering period starts from December and ends in the next April, and the colors of the flowers are bright and showy with red in majority, yellow, white and other colors in minority. The Camellia Show is the city's largest one in recent three years, which fully displays various species of camellia as well as human's scientific research of it. In order to provide the plant-lovers with more opportunities of closely appreciating the beauty of camellia, the Camellia Show is extended to the whole garden so that it can bring more convenience to the visitors.

The Camellia Show lasts two months, in which more than 200 various camellias will be presented successively.

翻译语篇 5

朋友关系的存续是以相互尊重为前提的，容不得半点强求、干涉和控制。朋友之间，情趣相投、脾气对味则合、则交；反之，则离、则绝。朋友之间再熟悉，再亲密，也不能随便过头，不恭不敬。不然，默契和平衡将被打破，友好关系将不复存在。每个人都希望拥有自己的私密空间，朋友之间过于随便，就容易侵入这片禁区，从而引起冲突，造成隔阂。待友不敬，或许只是一件小事，却可能已埋下了破坏性的种子。维持朋友亲密关系的最好办法是往来有节，互不干涉。（2010年汉译英真题）

参考译文

Friendship is likely to be established and continued between those people who have common interest and temper, without which, they would easily split and even break off their friendship. We should not be too casual to our friends without the due respects no matter how familiar or close we are. Otherwise, mutual understanding and balance would be lost and the friendships gone. Everyone hopes to have his personal private world. When the friends are too casual with each other, this forbidden territory might be easily intruded, resulting in conflicts and estrangements between them. The lacking of respects to friends, which seems to be not important, might be a seed of destruction to friendship. The best way to keep a close friendship is to be reciprocally respectful and courteous to each other without mutual interference.

翻译语篇 6

我想不起来哪一个熟人没有手机。今天没有手机的人是奇怪的，这种人才需要解释。我们的所有社会关系都储存在手机的电话本里，可以随时调出使用。古代只有巫师才能拥有这种法宝。

手机刷新了人与人的关系。会议室门口通常贴着一条通告：请与会者关闭手机。可是会议室里的手机铃声仍然响成一片。我们都是普通人，并没有多少重要的事情。尽管如此，我们也不会轻易关掉手机。打开手机象征我们与这个世界的联系。手机反映出我们的"社交饥渴症"。最为常见的是，一个人走着走着突然停下来，眼睛盯着手机屏幕发短信。他不在乎停在马路中央还是厕所旁边。（2009年汉译英真题）

参考译文

Mobile phones have renewed the interpersonal relationships. There is usually a note on the door of a conference room, which reads "Please turn off your mobile phone during the meeting." However, the meetingroom invariably echoes with the mobile rings. Although we are all ordinary people with few matters of great urgency, however, we are reluctant to turn off the mobile phone unless absolute necessary. Turning on the mobile phone is the symbol of our contact with the world. Mobile phone reflects our hunger for social communication, as can often be seen in a phone user who comes to a sudden halt on his way to edit text messages with eyes glued to his phone, regardless of whether he is in the middle of the road or beside a public toilet.

翻译语篇 7

都市寸土千金，地价炒得越来越高，今后将更高。拥有一个小小花园的希望，对寻常之辈不啻是一种奢望，一种梦想。

我想，其实谁都有一个小小花园，这便是我们的内心世界。人的智力需要开发，人的内心世界也是需要开发的。人和动物的区别，除了众所周知的诸多方面，恐怕还在于人有内心世界，心不过是人的一个重要脏器，而内心世界是一种景观，它是由外部世界不断地作用于内心渐渐形成的。每个人都无比关注自己及至亲至爱之人心脏的健损，以至于稍有微疾便惶惶不可终日。但并非每个人都关注自己及至亲至爱之人的内心世界的明暗。（2008年汉译英真题）

参考译文

I think everyone has, in fact, a small garden at the bottom of his heart, that is, his inner world. Just as there is a need for human beings to develop their intelligence, so is the case with their inner world. Apart from the well-known various aspects, man also differentiates from animals in that he has an inner world. Heart is no more than an important organ, but the inner world is somewhat a landscape, which gradually takes its shape under constant influences from the external world. Everyone is so much concerned about the physical condition of his own heart or those of his beloved that even a minor disease would throw him into constant anxiety. However, not everyone cares about the weather condition of the inner world of his or his beloved ones.

翻译语篇 8

暮色中，河湾里落满云霞，与天际的颜色混合一起，分不清哪是流云哪是水湾。

也就在这一幅绚烂的图画旁边，在河湾之畔，一群羊正在低头觅食。它们几乎没有一个顾得上抬起头来，看一眼这美丽的黄昏。也许它们要抓紧时间，在即将回家的最后一刻再次咀嚼。这是黄河滩上的一幕。牧羊人不见了，他不知在何处歇息。只有这些美生灵自由自在地享受着这个黄昏。这儿水草肥美，让它们长得肥滚滚的，像些胖娃娃。如果走近了，会发现它们那可爱的神情，洁白的牙齿，那丰富而单纯的表情。如果稍稍长久一点端详这张张面庞，还会生出无限的怜悯。（2007年汉译英真题）

参考译文

It was beside this splendid picture that a flock of sheep were lowering their heads and grazing on the river bank. Hardly any of them spared time to raise their heads and take a glance at the beautiful dusk. It seemed that they were seizing the day to snatch one more feed before heading home. This is a scene on the shore of the Yellow River bank, in which the shepherd who was taking a rest was nowhere to be seen, leaving these lovely creatures leisurely enjoying themselves in the dusk. The water and grass here were so ample and luxuriant that the sheep were nurtured very fat. When approaching near, you would have a close look of their white teeth and their rich yet innocent facial expression.

翻译语篇 9

中国民族自古以来从不把人看作高于一切，在哲学文艺方面的表现都反映出人在自然界中与万物占有比例较为恰当的地位，而非绝对统治万物的主宰。因此我们的苦闷基本上比西方人为少为小：因为苦闷的强弱原是随欲望与野心的大小而转移的。农业社会的人比工业社会的人享受差得多，因此欲望也小得多。何况中国古代素来以不息于物不为物役为最主要的人生哲学。（2006年汉译英真题）

参考译文

The Chinese nation has never believed in human supremacy. And the notion finds full expression in the philosophy, literature and art that humans coexist with other species in nature with a proportionally proper rather than an absolutely dominant position. Therefore, we generally suffer less depression than Westerners, as the degree of the suffering varies with that of our desire and ambition. People in the agricultural society have much less enjoyment than those in the industrial society, and hence less desire. Moreover, the main Chinese ancient philosophy of life is always to be free from the encumbrance or enslavement of the outside world.

翻译语篇 10

一个人的生命究竟有多大意义,这有什么标准可以衡量吗?提出一个绝对的标准当然很困难;但是,大体上看一个人对待生命的态度是否严肃认真,看他对待工作、生活的态度如何,也就不难对这个人的存在意义做出适当的估计了。

古来一切有成就的人,都很严肃地对待自己的生命,当他活着一天,总要尽量多工作、多学习,不肯虚度年华,不让时间白白浪费掉。我国历代的劳动人民以及大政治家、大思想家等等都莫不如此。(2005年汉译英真题)

参考译文

What is the significance of life? Is there any criterion for its measurement? Difficult as it is to advance an absolute one, it will not be so to judge the very meaning of one's existence generally from whether he is serious about life and what his attitudes are towards work and life.

Throughout the ages, all people of accomplishment take their lives seriously. As long as they are alive, they would rather devote themselves to more work and study than let a single minute slip by in vain. And the same is true of the common labourers as well as the great statesmen and thinkers in our country.

翻译语篇 11

在人际关系问题上我们不要太浪漫主义。人是很有趣的,往往在接触一个人时首先看到的都是他或她的优点。这一点颇像是在餐馆里用餐的经验。开始吃头盘或冷碟的时候,印象很好。吃头两个主菜时,也是赞不绝口。愈吃愈趋于冷静,吃完了这顿筵席,缺点就都找出来了。于是转喜为怒,转赞美为责备挑剔,转首肯为摇头。这是因为,第一,开始吃的时候你正处于饥饿状态,而饿了吃糠甜如蜜,饱了吃蜜也不甜。第二,你初到一个餐馆,开始举筷时有新鲜感,新盖的茅房三天香,这也可以叫做"陌生化效应"。(2004年汉译英真题)

参考译文

We should not be too romantic in interpersonal relations. Human beings are interesting in that they tend to first see good in a new acquaintance. This is like dining in a restaurant. You will be not only favorably impressed with the first dish or cold dishes, but also profuse in praise of the first two dishes. However, the more you have, the more sober you become until the dinner ends up with all the flaws exposed. Consequently, your joy would give way to anger; your praises to criticism or even fault-finding; and your nodding in agreement to shaking the head. What accounts for all this is, in the first place, you are hungry when you start to eat. As the saying goes, "Hunger is the best sauce", and vice versa.

翻译语篇 12

得病以前,我受父母宠爱,在家中横行霸道,一旦隔离,拘禁在花园山坡上一幢小房子里,我顿感打入冷宫,十分郁郁不得志起来。一个春天的傍晚,园中百花怒放,父母在园中设宴,一时宾客云集,笑语四溢。我在山坡的小屋里,悄悄掀起窗帘,窥见园中大千世界,一片繁华,自己的哥姐,堂表弟兄,也穿插其间,个个喜气洋洋。一霎时,一阵被人摒弃,为世所遗的悲愤兜上心头,禁不住痛哭起来。(2003年汉译英真题)

参考译文

Before I was taken ill, I had been a spoiled child of my parents, getting things my way in the family. Once isolated and confined to a small house on the slope of the garden, I suddenly felt that I was neglected and became very depressed. One spring evening, my parents held a party in the garden where all sorts of flowers were in full bloom. For a time, many guests gathered there, cheering and laughing. In the small house on the slope, I secretly drew the curtain apart, only to be met by the bustling and exciting scene in the garden. I saw my brothers, sisters and cousins among the adults, all in jubilation. All at once, overwhelmed by the forlorn feel of being abandoned, I could not help bursting into tears.

翻译语篇 13

大自然对人的恩赐，无论贫富，一律平等。所以人们对于大自然，全都一直并深深地依赖着。尤其在乡间，上千年来人们一直以不变的方式生活着。种植庄稼和葡萄，酿酒和饮酒，喂牛和挤奶，除草和栽花；在周末去教堂祈祷和做礼拜，在节日到广场拉琴、跳舞和唱歌；往日的田园依旧是今日的温馨家园。这样，每个地方都有自己的传说，风俗也就衍传了下来。（2002年汉译英真题）

参考译文

All people are blessed by nature, rich and poor alike. That accounts for their deep-rooted attachment to her, especially in the country where their ways of life have been kept intact for thousands of years. They grow crops and grapes, brew the wine that they drink, raise cows for milk, and weed their gardens for the cultivation of flowers. On weekends they go to church, and on holidays they enjoy playing music while singing and dancing in open squares. Thus their olden homelands remain as sweet as ever, each with a unique folklore from which its customs have derived.

翻译语篇 14

乔羽的歌大家都熟悉。但他另外两大爱好却鲜为人知,那就是钓鱼和喝酒。

晚年的乔羽喜爱垂钓,他说:"有水有鱼的地方大都是有好环境的,好环境便会给人好心情。我认为最好的钓鱼场所不是舒适的、给你准备好饿鱼的垂钓园,而是那极其有吸引力的大自然野外天成的场所。"钓鱼是一项能够陶冶性情的运动,有益于身心健康。乔羽说:"钓鱼可分三个阶段:第一阶段是吃鱼;第二阶段是吃鱼和情趣兼而有之;第三阶段主要是钓趣,面对一池碧水,将忧心烦恼全都抛在一边,使自己的身心得到充分休息。"(2001年汉译英真题)

参考译文

In his later life, Qiao Yu took to fishing/angling in his old age. He said: "Where there is fish and water, there is good environment, and good environment fills one's heart with joy (makes one feel delighted; delights everyone; gives delight to everyone). I think the best place for fishing is not a comfortable man-made fish-pond where hungry fish are ready (provided) for you, but an enchanting place in the wild where everything is natural." Fishing/Angling is a game that can help improve one's temperament/character. It is good for mental and physical health. Qiao Yu said: "Fishing falls into three stages. The first stage is just for eating fish. The second stage is for eating fish and for enjoying the pleasure of fishing as well. (The second stage is for enjoying the pleasure of fishing as well as eating fish.) The third stage is mainly for the pleasure of fishing facing a pool of green water, one casts/throws aside all anxieties and worries and enjoys /takes a good rest, both mental and physical."

课后练习

☯ 试将下列画线部分译成英文:

1. 现代社会无论价值观的持有还是生活方式的选择都充满了矛盾。而最让现代人感到尴尬的是,面对重重矛盾,许多时候你别无选择。<u>匆忙与休</u>

闲是截然不同的两种生活方式。但在现实生活中，人们却在这两种生活方式间频繁穿梭，有时也说不清自己到底是"休闲着"还是"忙碌着"。譬如说，当我们正在旅游胜地享受假期，却忽然接到老板的电话，告知我们客户或工作方面出了麻烦——现代便捷先进工具在此刻显示出了它狰狞、阴郁的面容——搞得人一下子兴趣全无。接下来的休闲只能徒有其表，因为心里已是火烧火燎了。（2011年汉译英真题）

2. 当我在小学毕了业的时候，亲友一致地愿意我去学手艺，好帮助母亲。我晓得我应当去找饭吃，以减轻母亲的勤劳困苦。可是，我也愿意升学。我偷偷地考入了师范学校——制服，饭食，书籍，宿处，都由学校供给。只有这样，我才敢对母亲说升学的话。入学，要交十元的保证金。这是一笔巨款！母亲作了半个月的难，把这巨款筹到，而后含泪把我送出门去。她不辞劳苦，只要儿子有出息。当我由师范毕业，而被派为小学校校长，母亲与我都一夜不曾合眼。我只说了句："以后，您可以歇一歇了！"她的回答只有一串串的眼泪。（2014年汉译英真题）

参考答案

上　篇

∞ 第一章　翻译的标准

1. Well, the years have passed, and I'm not a little girl anymore. Mom is in her mid-seventies, and those hands I once thought to be so rough are still doing things for me and my family. She's been our doctor, reaching into a medicine cabinet for the remedy to calm a young girl's stomach or soothe the boy's scraped knee. She cooks the best fried chicken in the world...gets stains out of blue jeans like I never could...

2. I had never enjoyed flying kites. What's more, I detested it because I regarded it as the play of kids with little promise. My younger brother, however, was crazy about kites. He was about ten years old then, weak and thin, frequently troubled with sickness. Since he couldn't afford it or was not allowed to play it by me, he would stand there with his small mouth open in a gape, looking into the sky, sometimes for hours running.

∞ 第二章　翻译的过程

1. I have been planting morning glories for three to four years now. As morning glories cannot be planted on cement floors, I plant them in many clay pots. As there is no place to get new earth to add in, the earth in the pots is used repeatedly year after year.

2. When it comes to the Tsinghua people, I would cherish sweet memories of my dear teachers. The first coming into my mind would be Mr. Yu Pingbo and Mr. Yu Guanying, two amiable and rigorous professors who taught me Chinese reading and writing respectively in my first year. In his writing course, Mr. Yu Guanying strictly pointed out my mistake of taking creepers for redbuds, but at the same time he encouraged me to write more for him to correct. When Professor He Lin taught History of Western Philosophy for sophomores, he

did not frown at me after reading my English book report which was nearly one hundred pages. Instead, he praised me in class. It was under his guidance that I read many English versions which were translated from the works of the ancient Greek philosophers, in a joyful mood as if I had discovered a new world.

✿ 第三章 汉英语言差异

London has many beautiful parks and gardens, but Kew Gardens is the most beautiful of all. It's only twenty minutes by bus from the middle of London and it's open every day. All through the year you can see lots of flowers, because Kew gets its plants—100,000 different ones—from many countries. The plants that like hot weather live in glasshouses which we call greenhouses. The biggest is the Palm House. It's nearly 150 years old. The idea of the Palm House is clever. A lot of light can get in to the plants. Inside you can climb a stair twenty meters to the top. It's exciting to look down on palm trees, oranges and bananas.

✿ 第四章 中西文化差异

1. "Cool carl" is a group of fashion icons quietly emerging from the current "clan" context. Just as the name suggests, those people possess the quality of being both "cool" and thrifty as a "carl". It is a kind of "stinginess" which is the latest trend and with a positive meaning because what the "cool carl" advocates is "saving glorious; waste shameful". "Cool carl" is not necessarily poor or miserly but the kind of people with relatively high academic degrees and salaries. Their ways of penny pinching cannot be interpreted as meanness but as thrift.

2. By the next morning, however, the soap was being honored by being used. Getting up later than usual, he saw his wife leaning over the wash-stand rubbing her neck, with bubbles like those emitted by great crabs heaped up over both her ears. The difference between these and the small white bubbles produced by honey locust pods was like that between heaven and earth.

中 篇

✍ 第五章 商务广告的翻译

1. If information is power, then inspiration must be the power of our potential, the power that moves us from the systematic to the spontaneous. At Compaq we believe technology is no longer simply a tool for information. It is a tool for inspiration. With the touch of a button, we no longer fire-up just our computers, but our imagination. We're moving beyond the limitations of Information Technology to a new technology. Welcome to the new IT. Inspiration Technology from Compaq.

2. Tsingtao Brewery Company Limited has invested a lot to import the newest equipment and the world class management technology. What's more, with the advanced operation methods it adopts, this company produces beer of high quality. After it is put into the market, most consumers warmly welcome it for its fresh feel, soft taste and high quality.

   Excellent materials, advanced equipment, tight quality management and strict staff training are the basis of brewing the beer. Tsingtao Brewery Company Limited can meet these demands sufficiently, so it can produce better beer than other companies.

   Cheers, China!

✍ 第六章 企业介绍的翻译

1. As a jointly-ventured comprehensive economic entity, our company is the first domestic enterprise which specializes in producing different kinds of gifts and souvenirs. Our company is large in scale and strong in technical force. The machines and raw materials are imported, while products are designed and produced by local forces.

2. Haier is the world's 4th largest white goods manufacturer and the most valuable brand in China. With 29 manufacturing plants, 8 comprehensive R&D centers, 19 overseas trading companies all over the world and more than 50,000 global employees, Haier has developed into a giant multinational

company. In 2008, Haier gained global revenue of RMB119 billion.

第七章 旅游文本的翻译

1. One of the most famous monuments in the world, the Statue of Liberty was presented to the United States of America in the 19th century by the people of France. The great statue, which was designed by the sculptor August Bartholdy, took ten years to complete. This great monument has been a symbol of liberty for the millions of people who have passed through New York Harbor to make their home in America.

2. Once a small village, Hong Kong has evolved into one of the world's largest metropolises in just one century. Being the living fusion of East and West, Hong Kong serves as a gateway into Chinese mainland and Asia's leading financial center, enjoys a lot of cultural and geographical advantages, and is prestigiously named the "Pearl of the Orient", "Gourmet Paradise" and "Shopping Paradise".

Small as this place is, Hong Kong has created a number of world records, including the famous Tsingma Bridge and Big Buddha. Apart from being the paradise for shopping and dining, the city treasures its cultural heritage and you can find traces of the old Hong Kong in many spots as well as a lot of popular tourist attractions.

第八章 科技文本的翻译

1. Care of Your Microwave Oven

a. Turn the oven off and remove the power plug from the wall socket before cleaning.

b. Keep the inside of the oven clean. When food splatters or spilled liquids adhere to oven walls, wipe with a damp cloth. Mild detergent may be used if the oven gets very dirty. The use of harsh detergent or abrasives is not recommended.

c. The outside oven surfaces should be cleaned with a damp cloth. To prevent damage to the operating parts inside the oven, water should not be allowed to seep into the ventilation openings.

d. Do not allow the Control Panel to become wet. Clean with a soft, damp cloth. Do not use detergents, abrasives or spray of cleaners on the Control Panel. When cleaning the Control Panel, leave oven door open to prevent oven from accidentally turning on.

2. Of all the sciences, biology has the greatest relevance to the understanding of man. It was slightly more than a century ago, in 1859, that Darwin set forth the revolutionary idea, which this book encompasses—that man, together with every other living thing, is a product of a process of evolutionary development. Man has not only evolved, but is still evolving. Human evolution is not all in the past. It is also an actuality and a concern for the future. The problem of possible genetic damage to human populations from radiation exposures, including those resulting from the fallout from testing of atomic weapons, has quite properly claimed much popular attention in recent years.

下 篇

第九章 小说的翻译

1. Drought characterized the place. How strange are the ways of the world: there are cloudy skies and there are bright skies, there are full moons and there are crescent moons, but total satisfaction is an elusive dream. The people in the area around Crossroads Township conserved every drop of water in the Zhou River, yet for years there hadn't been enough for the fields. In the summer you could see the peaks of the Shaman Mountain Range disappear in the clouds while here the sun beat down mercilessly, turning the fields into hot embers and stinging the people's eyes. Ten li away the rain fell in buckets while the local residents could only glare in anger. "Raindrops fill the ditches of nearby furrows" was the despairing cry of Crossroads Township.

2. Kong Yiji was the only long-gowned customer who used to drink his wine standing. A big, pallid man whose wrinkled face often bore scars, he had a large unkempt and grizzled beard. And although he wore a long grown, it was

dirty and tattered. It had not by the look of it been washed or mended for ten years or more. He used so many archaisms in his speech that half of it was barely intelligible. And as his surname was Kong, he was given the nickname Kong Yiji from kong, yi, ji, the first three characters in the old fashioned children's copybook. Whenever he came in, everyone there would look at him and chuckle. And someone was sure to call out:

"Kong Yiji! What are those fresh scars on your face?"

Ignoring this, he would lay nine coppers on the bar and order two bowls of heated wine with a dish of aniseed peas. Then someone else would bawl:

"You must have been stealing again!"

"Why sully a man's good name for no reason at all?" Kong Yiji would ask, raising his eyebrows.

"Good name? Why, the day before yesterday you were trussed up and beaten for stealing books from the Ho family. I saw you!"

At that Kong Yiji would flush, the veins on his forehead standing out as he protested, "Taking books can't be counted as stealing…Taking books…for a scholar…can't be counted as stealing." Then followed such quotations from the classics as "A gentlemen keeps his integrity even in poverty," together with a spate of archaisms which soon had everybody roaring with laughter, enlivening the whole tavern.

∽ 第十章 散文的翻译

1. Feel that you can accomplish anything you undertake. When undertaking a task, a lot of people feel that they are going to fail, which is the direct cause of their failure. Here is an illustration. A man goes to a store for a book. The shop assistant says, "Sorry, we do not have the book you want." But the man that is determined to get the book inquires where he can get it. Again receiving an unsatisfactory answer, the determined buyer consults the manager and finally gets the book he wants.

2. The strong, calm man is always loved and revered. He is like a shade-giving tree in the sun, or a sheltering rock in a storm. "Who does not love a tranquil

heart, a sweet-tempered, balanced life?" It does not matter whether it rains or shines, or what changes come to those possessing the blessings, for they are always sweet, serene, and calm. That exquisite poise of character, which we call serenity, is the last lesson of culture and the fruitage of soul. It is precious as wisdom, more to be desired than gold—year, than even fine gold.

第十一章 诗歌的翻译

1.
On the Stork Tower

The sun beyond the mountains glows;

The Yellow River seawards flows.

You can enjoy a grander sight

By climbing to a greater height.

2. 译文 1

Before my bed

There is bright moonlight

So that it seems

Like frost on the ground;

Lifting my head

I watch the bright moon,

Lowering my head

I dream that I'm home.

（Arthur Cooper 译）

译文 2

Before my bed the moon gleams bright,

And frosts the floor with a hoary light.

My eyes to the fair moon overhead roam—

Head bent, I'm lost in dreams of home.

（马红军译）

3.   **Nostalgia**

When I was a child,

Nostalgia seemed a small stamp:

"Here am I

And there...my mother."

Then I was a grown-up,

Nostalgia became a traveling ticket:

"Here am I

And there...my bride."

During the later years,

Nostalgia turned to be a graveyard:

"Here am I

And yonder...my mother."

And now at present,

Nostalgia looms large to be a channel:

"Here am I

And yonder...my Continent!"

第十二章 专八汉译英

1. Being hasty and at leisure are two quite distinct lifestyles. But in the real world, people have to frequently shuttle between these two lifestyles, sometimes not sure whether they are "at ease" or "in a rush". For example, we are enjoying our holidays in the resort while suddenly we receive phone calls from the boss who tells us there are some troubles with our customers and work—so at this moment the modern, convenient and advanced device

shows its ferocious and gloomy features—and we lose all the appetite for the upcoming vacation. The subsequent leisure is the mere showy since we are in a restless and anxious state of mind.

2. After I had graduated from the primary school, relatives and friends all suggested that I should not further my study but learn a trade to help my mother. Although I knew I ought to seek a livelihood to relieve mother of hard work and distress, I still aspired to further my study. So I secretly took an entrance examination of a normal school since it provided free uniforms, books, room and board. Only with that did I have the courage to tell mother that I wanted to go on study. However, the admission to the school needed a security deposit of ten yuan. What a large sum of money for my family! However, mother managed to raise the money after two weeks' tough efforts and saw me off in tears. She would spare no efforts for me as long as I could have a bright future. When I graduated from the normal school and was appointed as the headmaster of a small school, mother and I spent a sleepless night. At that time I said to her, "Now you can have a rest." But she said nothing in reply, only with tears streaming down her face.

参考文献

巴尔扎克.1951.高老头.傅雷,译.上海:平明出版社.

包惠南.2001.文化语境与语言翻译.北京:中国对外翻译出版公司.

陈　刚.2004.旅游翻译与涉外导游.北京:中国对外翻译出版公司.

陈宏薇.2009.高级汉英翻译.北京:外语教学与研究出版社.

陈小慰.2006.新编实用翻译教程.北京:经济科学出版社.

丹尼斯·史密斯.2001.母亲的微笑//《读者文摘》亚洲有限公司.《读者文摘》读本丛书（一）中英对照.广州:广东世界图书出版公司.

邓炎昌,刘润清.1989.语言与文化:英汉语言文化对比.北京:外语教学与研究出版社.

丁大刚.2008.旅游英语的语言特点与翻译.上海:上海交通大学出版社.

方梦之.2002.翻译新论与实践.青岛:青岛出版社.

冯庆华.1997.实用翻译教程(英汉互译).上海:上海外语教育出版社.

《辞海》编辑委员会.1980.《辞海》经济分册.2版.上海:上海辞书出版社.

赫胥黎.1933.天演论.严复,译.上海:商务印书馆.

胡显耀,李力.2009.高级文学翻译.北京:外语教学与研究出版社.

黄粉保.2000.论小说人物语言个性的翻译.中国翻译,2:44-46.

黄国文.1988.语篇分析概要.长沙:湖南教育出版社.

黄鸣奋.1997.英语世界中国古典文学之传播.上海:学林出版社.

黄忠廉.2000.翻译本质论.武汉:华中师范大学出版社.

金颖若,楚湘黔.2006.花溪旅游指南.贵阳:贵州人民出版社.

劳伦斯·韦努蒂.2004.译者的隐身:一部翻译史.上海:上海外语教育出版社.

老舍. 2001. 二马. Julie Jimmerson，译. 北京：外文出版社.

李冰梅. 2011. 文学翻译新视野. 北京：北京大学出版社.

李运兴. 2000. 翻译中的文化成分 // 罗选民. 英汉文化对比与跨文化交际. 沈阳：辽宁人民出版社.

连淑能. 1993. 英汉对比研究. 北京：高等教育出版社.

林语堂. 2002. 吾国与吾民. 黄嘉德，译. 西安：陕西师范大学出版社.

刘靖之. 1981. 翻译论集. 北京：生活·读书·新知三联书店.

刘宓庆. 1998. 文体与翻译（增订版）. 北京：中国对外翻译出版公司.

刘士聪. 2002. 汉英·英汉美文翻译与鉴赏（中英对照）. 上海：译林出版社.

鲁 迅. 2000. 彷徨. 杨宪益，戴乃迭，译. 北京：外文出版社.

罗新璋. 1983. 我国自成体系的翻译理论（续）. 翻译通讯，4：10.

罗选民. 2012. 衍译：诗歌翻译的涅槃. 中国翻译，2：60-66.

罗左毅. 2012. 英汉实用翻译教程. 南京：南京大学出版社.

马会娟. 1999. 对奈达的等效翻译理论的再思考. 外语学刊，3：74.

潘文国. 2010. 汉英语言对比概论. 北京：商务印书馆.

彭 萍. 2010. 实用旅游英语翻译（英汉双向）. 北京：对外经济贸易大学出版社.

莎士比亚. 2001. 汉姆莱特. 朱生豪，译. 北京：中国国际广播出版社.

舒舟，何大顺. 2008. 散文意境的传译——基于格式塔意象模型研究. 西南农业大学学报（社会科学版），5：106-109.

司显柱，曾剑平，等. 2006. 汉译英教程. 上海：东华大学出版社.

泰 勒. 1988. 原始文化. 2版. 蔡江浓，译. 杭州：浙江人民出版社.

王东风. 1998. 语篇连贯与翻译初探. 外语与外语教学，6：39-42.

王治奎. 2005. 大学汉英翻译教程. 4版. 济南：山东大学出版社.

韦琴红. 2006. 英汉科技文本的语篇特征对比分析. 杭州电子科技大学学报（社会科学版），2：30-34.

参考文献

魏　羽，高宝萍 . 2010. 汉英科技翻译教程 . 西安：西北工业大学出版社 .

翁显良 . 1982. 见全牛又不见全牛——谈文学翻译（上）. 翻译通讯，3：35-38.

吴敬梓 . 1996. 儒林外史（上册）. 杨宪益，戴乃迭，译 . 长沙：湖南出版社 .

伍　锋，何庆机 . 2008. 应用文体翻译：理论与实践 . 杭州：浙江大学出版社 .

辛红娟 . 2012. 文学翻译读本 . 南京：南京大学出版社 .

辛　凌，王婷 . 2009. 大学英语实用翻译教程 . 重庆：重庆大学出版社 .

许渊冲 . 1983. 再谈"意美、音美、形美". 外语学刊，4：68-75.

许渊冲 . 2009. 汉魏六朝诗汉英对照 . 北京：中国对外翻译出版公司 .

许渊冲 . 2010. 中诗英韵探胜 . 2 版 . 北京：北京大学出版社 .

严俊仁 . 2004. 汉英科技翻译 . 北京：国防工业出版社 .

杨自俭，李瑞华 . 1990. 英汉对比研究论文集 . 上海：上海外语教育出版社 .

杨自俭 . 2000. 关于中西文化对比研究的几点认识（代序）——英汉文化对比与跨文化交际学术研讨会开幕词 // 罗选民 . 英汉文化对比与跨文化交际 . 沈阳：辽宁人民出版社 .

印晓红，杨瑛 . 2010. 商务口译入门 . 上海：上海交通大学出版社 .

曾　诚 . 2002. 实用汉英翻译教程 . 北京：外语教学与研究出版社 .

张步云 . 1990. 唐代诗歌 . 合肥：安徽教育出版社 .

张美芳 . 1999. 从语境分析看动态对等论的局限性 . 上海科技翻译，4：10-13.

张梦井，杜耀文 . 1990. 中国名家散文精译 . 青岛：青岛出版社 .

张培基 . 1999. 英译中国现代散文选：汉英对照 . 上海：上海外语教育出版社 .

张　艳 . 2013. 陌生的葛浩文与熟悉的葛浩文——葛浩文小说翻译艺术究指 . 广东外语外贸大学学报，4：79-82.

钟　玲 . 2003. 美国诗与中国梦 . 桂林：广西师范大学出版社 .

张保红 . 2010. 文学翻译 . 北京：外语教学与研究出版社 .

Beaugrande, R. & Dressler, W. (1981). *Introduction to Text Linguistics*. London: Routledge.

Bell, Roger T. (1991). *Translation and Translating: Theory and Practice.* Longman: London and New York.

Halliday, M. A. K. & Hasan, Ruqaiya (2001). *Cohesion in English.* Beijing: Foreign Language Teaching and Research Press.

Holmes, James S. (1988). *Translated!: Papers on Literary Translation and Translation Studies.* Amsterdam: Rodopi.

Lin Yutang. (2000). *My Country and My People.* Beijing: Foreign Language Teaching and Research Press.

Lovell, Julia. (2009). *The Real Story of Ah-Q and Other Tales of China: The Complete Fiction of Lu Xun.* London: Penguin.

Nida, Eugene A. & Taber, Charles T. (1969). *The Theory and Practice of Translation.* Leiden: E. J. Brill.

Venuti, Lawrance. (1995). *The Translator's Invisibility: A History of Translation.* London and New York: Routledge.